Note on the Author

Catherine Arnold read English at Cambridge University and holds a further degree in psychology. A journalist, academic and historian, Catherine's previous books include the novel *Lost Time* and the acclaimed *Necropolis: London and Its Dead*, and *Bedlam: London and Its Mad*, also available from Simon & Schuster.

Praise for *City of Sin: London and Its Vices*

'Welcome to the world of rakes, pimps and the debauched aristocracy. *City of Sin* provides a romp through London's history at a cracking pace, covering every disreputable person we know' *Julie Peakman, Books Quarterly*

'she leads us briskly and entertainingly through her theme – "vice" here translating mainly as "sex". To pack 2,000 years of this stuff into 400 pages is a challenge, but Arnold achieves it admirably' *Sarah Bakewell, Independent*

'. . . hugely entertaining . . . *City of Sin* is full of useful bawdy information . . . Arnold is never judgemental, and is a delightful travelling companion through the centuries of the city of sin, pointing out the sites, and leaving us to understand the despair and the hypocrisy, as well as the pleasure, that inevitably seems to surround sex' *Jeanette Winterson, The Times*

'. . . there's plenty to get stuck into here Arnold arranges her formidable research lucidly, showing us how to abused sex slaves of the Roman era were supplanted by medieval and Tudor whores, Victorian streetwalkers and 20th-century call girls' *Evening Standard*

'It is the third in a trilogy of lively London histories by Catharine Arnold, the others being on death and madness. In each, she leads us briskly through her theme – "vice" here translating mainly as "sex". To pack 2000 years of the stuff into less than 400 pages is a challenge, but Arnold achieves it admirably' *Independent*

'She has gathered a wealth of artistic and literary references, some of which are reproduced as illustrations, adding to the impression that the reader has opened a cabinet of curiosities: often titillating, sometimes shocking, frequently entertaining . . . the book is a lively affirmation of sexual desire in all its varieties' *Stephanie Merritt, New Review, Observer*

CITY OF SIN

London and Its Vices

CATHARINE ARNOLD

SIMON &
SCHUSTER

London · New York · Sydney · Toronto

A CBS COMPANY

First published in Great Britain by Simon & Schuster UK Ltd, 2010
This edition first published in paperback by Simon & Schuster UK Ltd, 2011
A CBS COMPANY

1 3 5 7 9 10 8 6 4 2

Simon & Schuster UK Ltd
1st Floor
222 Gray's Inn Road
London WC1X 8HB

www.simonandschuster.co.uk

Simon & Schuster Australia
Sydney

A CIP catalogue record for this book is available
from the British Library.

ISBN: 978-1-84739-372-2

Typeset by M Rules
Printed in the UK by CPI Cox & Wyman, Reading, Berkshire RG1 8EX

This book is dedicated to my husband, Mark Adams,
and to my great friend Ronald Frame. Thank you
for your love, understanding and patience.

Contents

Acknowledgements

I would like to thank the following for their invaluable help: Cambridge University Library; the Hallward Library; the University of Nottingham; Dr Simon Lee Price; Susan Johnson of Prostitute Outreach Workers; my editor Kerri Sharp; and last but not least my agent, Charlie Viney. Many thanks to you all.

Introduction

When it comes to sex, London has always had a bit of a reputation. One scrap of manuscript, dating from 1058, shows a young woman of Southwark, seated on a clapped-out mule, her hair falling over her shoulders. She is exciting the attention of travellers on the highways by means of her indiscreet clothing, and holding a little gilt rod in her hand, to indicate her profession. This is the first picture of a prostitute actively soliciting on the streets of London, and it gives some indication of the state of affairs even then. Of course, this early version of the permissive society had its critics. One Richard of Devizes, a monk, condemned the capital in 1180. 'I do not at all like that city,' he wrote

all sorts of men crowd together there from every country under the heavens. Each race brings its own vices and its own customs to the city. No one lives in it without falling into some sort of crimes. Every quarter of it abounds in great obscenities ... Whatever evil or malicious thing that can be found in any part of the world, you will find in that one city. Do not associate with the crowds of pimps; do not mingle with the throngs in the eating-houses; avoid the dice and gambling, the theatre and the tavern. You will meet with more braggarts there than in all France; the number of parasites is infinite . . . jesters, smooth-skinned lads, Moors, flatterers, pretty boys, effeminates, pederasts, singing and dancing girls, quacks, belly-dancers, sorceresses, extortioners, night-wanderers, magicians, mimes, beggars, buffoons: all this tribe fill all the houses. Therefore, if you do not want to dwell with evil-doers, do not live in London.

From smooth-skinned lads and pretty boys to dancing girls and beggars, these are the very characters I set out to conjure back to life in these pages; from the Roman slave girls left shivering on the docks at Bankside to their Victorian counterparts cruising Piccadilly and the Ratcliffe Highway; from the pampered page boys of the Elizabethan court to the telegraph boys blackmailing their rich homosexual lovers in the Cleveland Street scandal; from *grandes horizontales* Anne Boleyn and Nell Gwyn to party girls Christine Keeler and Mandy Rice-Davies and the notorious Cynthia Payne; and from rakish aristocrats such as the Earl of Rochester, author of some of the most obscene poetry ever written, to persecuted homosexual pioneers Oscar Wilde and Radclyffe Hall. The thread which links this chequered history of a motley crew is one which links us all: sex. And it was ever thus. London is driven by desire, requited and unrequited. From time immemorial, commerce, industry, art and sport have all run on sex and the sometimes elusive promise of fulfilment. Paris is the city of Love but London is the city of Lust, a peculiar combination of our Anglo-Saxon ribaldry and British reticence; only a Scotsman (Lord Alfred Douglas) could have devised the description of 'the love that dare not speak its name' for homosexuality (it would have been shouted from the rooftops in other nations); only a British audience would have taken the repressed self-denial of *Brief Encounter* to its collective bosom; and only Britain could have produced that most bawdy of bawds, Cynthia Payne, or Mandy Rice-Davies, creator of an inspired put-down when an elderly aristocrat denied having met her, let alone availed himself of her services: 'Well, he would say that, wouldn't he?'

While Henry VIII's knights jousted for the favours of a court lady, today's Premiership footballers are held up as supreme specimens of the athletic male body, competing for the attentions of their beautiful celebrity female counterparts; while Victorian crowds once gathered in Hyde Park to watch top courtesans such as 'Skittles' Walters, mistress of the Prince of Wales, clad in a tightly cut riding habit, put her horse through its paces, so a century later tabloid readers dropped their marmalade reading about the exploits of Christine Keeler and Lord Boothby (not, I hasten to add, with each other). Philip Larkin might have observed that 'Sexual intercourse began in 1963 (which was rather late for me),' but London had been swinging long before the 'Chatterley' ban was lifted – right back to Roman times.

My journey begins in Roman London, and follows the fate of the slave girls trafficked to service the soldiers who descended on 'Londinium' for rest and relaxation. What was life like for these creatures, huddled on the docks in chains? And how did Londinium become the Las Vegas of the Roman Empire, with its bath houses, theatres, circuses and brothels? What were the scenes on feast days and holy days, when scores of Londoners thronged the streets in raucous festivities, parading alongside models of giant phalluses, while orgies took place in full public view?

Such images of decadence were eventually removed when the Romans left for good, and London temporarily disintegrated into a string of villages along the banks of the Thames. But prostitution was back in business under the Normans, with the Conqueror himself, William, making a decent income from the properties he rented out to bawds. This was with the connivance of the Church: St Mary Overie, a nunnery in Southwark, became a celebrated brothel, presided over by the Bishop of Winchester.

Prostitution flourished in medieval London, centred on the maze of streets around Cock's Lane, Maiden Lane and the intriguingly named 'Gropecunt Lane'. Many women plied their trade in these narrow streets, such as the memorable Alice Strumpette and the delightful Clarice la Claterballock.

Henry VIII issued an edict to close the stews in 1546, in a desperate attempt to halt the progress of syphilis, but even the king was powerless to stop London's sex trade, which prospered as the newly opened theatres set up business on the Bankside and patrons of the Globe and the Rose flocked to brothels with names such as Ye Boar's Hedde or The Cardinal's Cap.

Out in the streets, Tudor London was described by one visitor as 'a paradise for women, a prison for servants, and a hell for horses', where young women enjoyed considerable freedom, parading around in tight-fitting gowns with deep cleavages, some even displaying their nipples, tipped with rouge for the purpose. Such freedom came at a price, however: women faced brutal punishment if arrested for prostitution, whipped at the cart's arse before being imprisoned in Bridewell, the terrifying house of correction. Not that this was enough to deter them; an ambitious whore who could stay the course and keep her head even while giving head, as the song goes, stood to make a fortune. One such was Donna Hollandia, redoubtable madam of Holland's Leaguer, the best brothel in London. But while copulation thrived in the laissez-faire days of James I, London's sex trade suffered under Oliver Cromwell's Commonwealth. Theatres were closed, maypoles axed and adulterers even faced the death penalty. It is scarcely surprising that the restoration of the monarch in 1660 met with unconfined joy, and London, under the licentious Charles II, erupted into one giant party.

Charles II's reign saw the return of the theatres and, for the first time, the rise of the actress, personified by Nell Gwyn, who blazed a career path from orange girl to mistress of the king. Nell is one of the *grandes horizontales,* bad girls made good, whose lives are celebrated in this book. Others, now forgotten, also feature, such as Priss Fotheringham, a Scottish jailbird whose astonishing *pièce de résistance* meant she died a wealthy woman. And there is an account of a certain 'Mr Hammond' who operated 'Prick Office' over by Smithfield Market.

As London developed, the sex trade moved Up West, first to Covent Garden, 'The Garden of Venus', where whores cruised the coffee houses and, according to one author, there were enough depraved women to form a colony. The fortunes of two representative characters illustrate this dramatic period in the history of sex: Hogarth's Moll Hackabout, a dreadful warning to young women, and Fanny Hill, Cleland's cheerful libertine, who breathlessly narrates her sexual odyssey with women as well as men. There is also a detour to examine the wilder shores of love: not merely the 'molly houses' or homosexual brothels which operated under threat of death, but the cross-dressers, the fans of flagellation, the lesbians and even one case of auto-erotic asphyxiation. This chapter would not be complete without a visit to the Hellfire Club; nor could this book have omitted to mention the notorious rake, roué and future Chancellor of the Exchequer, Francis Dashwood – even though the majority of sins were committed outside London.

While the popular image of the Victorian era is of a tight-lipped, buttoned-up, repressive society, the fact is that, in the shadowy underworld of nineteenth-century London, prostitution, in all its forms, had become one of the most successful industries in this entrepreneurial culture. As London's sex trade moved further West, into the Haymarket and Piccadilly, prostitutes of all types, male and female, high class and low, were drawn like moths to the statue of Eros and the bright lights of the West End. Here you could glimpse the elite corps of kept women posing in the supper clubs and scouting for new aristocratic lovers, the pale and lovely shopgirls turning a trick to keep themselves in bonnets while wasting away with tuberculosis; and the desperate park women, disfigured by disease, paid by their sisters to keep out of sight and go away.

The reign of Queen Victoria was the golden age of prostitution, with over 50,000 prostitutes working the streets of London in the 1850s. Drawing on interviews by the social reformers Henry Mayhew and Dr William Acton, I describe the fate of a representative handful of girls, lured to London by the promise of fame and fortune, ranging from the kept women who lived in solitary splendour in St John's Wood to the underpaid seamstresses and milliners who were driven into prostitution to supplement their meagre wages and for whom survival was a matter of 'offer up your body or die'. And we'll meet the notorious 'Walter', author of the explicit sexual memoir *My Secret Life*, one of the most bleakly honest accounts of male sexuality ever published. Other forms of sexuality were evident, too, such as the remarkable duo of Boulton and Park, a pair of transvestites who liked nothing better than to drag up and parade along Burlington Arcade pretending to be 'laydies', and the writer Oscar Wilde, the sexual martyr who ended up in jail, not merely for being homosexual but for believing that he could outwit the British judiciary. I pay a visit to Holywell Street, now lost beneath Kingsway, but once the home of the Victorian pornography industry, patronized alike by depraved old roués and pleasurably shocked young ladies who pressed their faces to the windows the better to see the wares inside. And, more disturbingly, I describe the tragic consequences of the Criminal Law Amendment Act 1885, which, while protecting the innocent by raising the age of consent to sixteen, drove prostitutes off the streets but made them far more vulnerable, putting them at the mercy of killers such as Jack the Ripper.

Two world wars, which brought with them the prospect of imminent death, added a new dynamic to London's sexuality in the twentieth century, as thousands of military personnel descended on the city. While impending oblivion caused hitherto respectable types to seek out strange bedfellows, prostitutes such as Marthe Watts did their bit for the war effort: this redoubtable lady celebrated VE Night by taking home forty-nine clients. *Pace* Philip Larkin, sexual intercourse began long before 1963, but Swinging London certainly got off to a good start with high-society scandals as that celebrated decade began, such as the Profumo Affair and the salacious revelations about Margaret, Duchess of Argyll's mysterious 'headless' lover; then there were sexual intrigues such as Tory peer Lord Boothby's alleged affair with the infamous villain Ronnie Kray.

Finally, I ask if human nature has changed so very much at all over the centuries, or are the latest stars in London's sexual firmament, such as 'Belle de Jour', just the latest incarnations of some familiar old characters.

This is not, of course, the first book to investigate the sex life of London, and I would like to acknowledge inspiration in the form of E. J. Burford's entertaining and scholarly accounts, including *Bawds and Lodgings* and *The Orrible Synne*. On a slightly different note, I am also indebted to Nickie Roberts, whose revisionist *Whores in History* examines prostitution from the working girls' point of view and puts up a spirited defence of the prostitute's calling. I would also recommend Fergus Linnane's entertaining *London the Wicked City*; Ronald Pearsall's *The Worm in the Bud*, an absorbing study of sex in the Victorian era; and Matt Houlbrook's *Queer London, Perils and Pleasures in the Sexual Metropolis 1918–1957*, a masterful guide to homosexual London. Last but certainly not least there is Dan Cruikshank's recent *The Secret History of Georgian London*, a splendidly illustrated account of a lively period in London's sexual history.

My own interest in the compelling history of London and sex developed years ago, thanks to a liberal censorship policy in my parents' house, which meant I read anything I could get my teenage hands on, suitable or unsuitable alike, from *Nana* to *Nova* (a short-lived but cutting-edge glossy magazine). Books ranged from Steven Marcus's classic study of pornography, *The Other Victorians*, to Sir Richard Burton's translation of *The Arabian Nights*. Curiously, the only thing I read which really shocked me was the *Schoolkids* issue of *Oz* magazine, provided courtesy of our student neighbours. Despite all that exposure to high-class 'erotica', I found the cartoons quite disturbing.

My fascination with the sex trade increased when I first moved to London and the daily journey to and from my office took me through Soho. Every evening, I walked from New Oxford Street down through Berwick Street Market to catch the 14 bus to Fulham, past Raymond's Revue Bar and the fleshpots of the sex industry, intrigued by the tawdry neon and the flickering bead curtains, and the red telephone boxes stuffed with cards advertising every possible form and deviation of recreational sex. At night, I saw another aspect of London's sex life, in the sophisticated bars of Knightsbridge and Chelsea, where attractive young women were always in demand, as escorts, companions, confidantes. It was a fascinating world for a writer, and as a good listener I was always popular with the jaded businessmen who wanted a date for dinner and a sympathetic ear. And so, although I cannot flatter myself that I share all the experiences of the 'smooth-skinned lads, Moors, flatterers, pretty boys, effeminates, pederasts, singing and dancing girls, quacks, belly-dancers and sorceresses' that you are going to read about, I do feel amply qualified to offer you an introduction to London, city of sin.

1

LUPANARIA

'Quo loco recta vin ad lupanur, amicus?'
('Which way to the brothel, mate?')

Southwark, Londinium, AD 80

Bruised, half-naked and in chains, the slave girls shivered on the docks, beneath the lashing rain and grey skies of Albion. Garments in rags, hair in rats' tails, they faced a future of pain, exploitation and early death. Two thousand years before such matters were the stuff of international concern and television documentaries, these young women were London's first sex slaves, brought in to service the Roman military in low-grade brothels or *lupanaria*.

This chapter tells how these women were brought to London to work in such horrific conditions, and why there were other women, also working in the sex trade, who were empowered and in control. We will also take a look at the age-old connection between sex and power, as demonstrated by the excesses of the Roman emperors, and why the flourishing underworld of brothels and bath houses disappeared along with the Roman rulers.

The wretched human freight which fetched up on our shores was corralled in a 'Romeland' or dockyard at Queenhithe, across the River Thames from Bankside. In this compound the unfortunate creatures were prepared for auction like cattle in a market, paraded before an audience of brothel keepers who were positively encouraged to handle the merchandise before purchase, and examine and fondle every part of their bodies.[1] Despite the depredations of a rough voyage, these were some of the most beautiful women in the world, sold into slavery from every part of the Roman Empire. Flame-haired Gauls with porcelain skin; ebony princesses seized in North Africa; sultry Sicilians ripped from the lemon groves; proud Jewish girls from the recently defeated Palestine, the cloudless skies and Mediterranean heat of their native country now only a distant memory.

The Roman troops that these pitiful women would service had been in the country since AD 43, when the Emperor Claudius had dispatched three legions of the Army of the Rhine and a contingent of the Praetorian Guard to seize the dark and murky island of Britannia for the greater glory of the Roman Empire.[2] Although the Britons had a reputation for being war-mad savages, this was not a particularly bloody campaign. King Cymbeline, who died in AD 43, had welcomed Roman traders and craftsmen to Britain, and there had been plenty of traffic in the opposite direction, with British noblemen enjoying the delights of Rome, and, somewhat less fortunately, British slaves exported to the Eternal City. Many members of the aristocracy, in debt to Roman usurers, saw the so-called invasion as the only way to fulfil their financial obligations.[3]

The Roman army, led by General Aulus Plautius, marched up from the coast until it arrived at a wide, estuarial river: the Tamesis, or Thames.[4] It was here, while waiting for a standoff with the Britons, that the Roman engineers built pontoon bridges across the river, and it was here that they established their bridgehead, consisting of a small military settlement in the form of a fort, with an earthwork guarding the entrance to the bridge.

The Roman settlement on the Tamesis was of considerable size, consisting of a cohort (one tenth of a legion) constituting between 600 and 1000 men, along with their support systems and camp-followers, who provided food and sex, making the total establishment around 2000 people.[5] Camp-followers led a rough and ready life, almost as unhappy as that of the slaves, following their men from one campaign to another but without the benefit of legal recognition, since Roman soldiers were not permitted to marry until the second century AD.

It was here, at the bridgehead, that the brothels, or *lupanaria*, were constructed, an essential resource providing release from sexual tension. For any soldier enquiring '*quo loco recta via ad lupanar, amicus?*' ('which way to the *lupanaria*, mate?')[6] a signpost at the turn-off from the highway would have indicated the way: however illiterate the soldiers and sailors disembarking from the warships nearby, there was one international symbol for a brothel: the palm of a hand. *Lupanaria* derives from *lupa*, the she-wolf who suckled

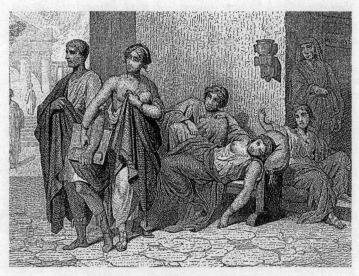

Scene from a Roman brothel or lupanar.

the infants Romulus and Remus, the mythical founders of Rome. According to Livy, the she-wolf was a symbol for the famous whore Acca Laurentia; whores were associated with she-wolves on the grounds that they advertised their services with high-pitched, wolf-like cries and gave their bodies to all comers.[7] *Lupa* was also suggestive in another sense: with the she-wolf's propensity to lick her cubs came the implication that *lupae* were proficient in oral sex.

Open for business twenty-four hours a day, every day of the week, these brothels were primitive, functional places, with a no-frills approach to sexual satisfaction. Built of timber, with thatched roofs and brightly painted plaster interiors, they stood on clay foundations. Inside, the houses were divided into cells, each with its narrow wooden bunk and straw mattress. There were no refreshments, entertainments or preliminaries. Each man took his pleasure quickly, making way for the next. Eventually, these flimsy constructions were replaced with brick tenements, but they were rudimentary places, catering for the lowest common denominator, 'the poor bloody infantry'. The women themselves had no rights: they were the absolute property of their *leno* (pimp) or *lena* (madam); they received no payment for their services and were treated with utter contempt; they had no more value than a fish. The name, *puta,* or 'common whore', derives from *puteus,* a well or a tank. Every single one of them faced the ultimate humiliation of a life on her back, submitting to whatever sexual indignity was forced upon her.[8] It was a fate reflected upon by the dramatist Plautus. In his play *Pseudolus,* a jealous lover threatens his two mistresses that if they are found to be unfaithful, they will be carried away to a brothel and worked so hard they will die of exhaustion.[9] Under these conditions, it was scarcely surprising that the majority of women were claimed by death before the age of thirty.[10]

The *lupanaria* attracted other forms of vice. The land beyond the fort consisted of a dank, marshy strip, known as the *pomerium*, or no-man's land, deliberately left clear so that approaching enemies could be spotted from a distance. As the years passed, this region, which went by the name of Southwark, etablished itself as a den of iniquity. Taverns opened, where barmaids and waitresses competed for business with the unhappy denizens of the *lupanaria*. These girls were known as *assellae* because they traded their sexual services in return for the *as,* the smallest denomination of coin, as befitted their lowly nature.[11] As well as the sex industry, every other immoral activity moved in: gaming houses, cockpits and bear-baiting rings sprang up, attracting low-life of every description: thieves, cut-purses, con artists, runaway slaves and fugitives from justice, safe from prosecution outside the city limits. In its capacity as a *pomerium*, Southwark tolerated illegal or restricted activities. It was the Las Vegas of Londinium.

And, like Las Vegas, Southwark was a centre of sexual activity, where the popular sex gods Isis, Apollo and Hermes were worshipped in magnificent temples and celebrated in wild, wine-fuelled processions culminating in frenzied public orgies. During the mid twentieth century, archaeologists discovered the remains of a substantial Roman temple to the south of Southwark Cathedral, with stone foundations and tessellated floors. A jug inscribed with the legend 'LONDINI AD FANUM ISIDIS' ('In London, at the Temple of Isis') had been found nearby in 1912. This pottery jug would have been used during acts of worship and on the specific 'days of drinking' when devotees performed their religious duties at the temple,[12] including carrying the gigantic model phalluses in the procession. Isis, the principal goddess of Egypt, was a women's deity; the wife of Osiris and mother of Horus, she was a fertility goddess, the universal mother and the queen of the dead. She took the form of a beautiful dark-haired woman in a tight-fitting dress, and women were her most constant devotees, from empresses to the lowest *puta*. The Temples of Isis were also well known as 'houses of assignation', where women conducting secret affairs could rendezvous with their lovers or ask the advice of the priestesses on all aspects of love, and where bored wives could pick up a willing toyboy.

There was also a temple to Harpocrates, a bringer of good luck,

13

renowned for his sexual prowess and usually depicted as a man with a penis two or three times taller than the rest of him. Harpocrates' picture was often to be found on the walls and ceilings of Roman brothels, to welcome the client and spur him on to maximum prowess. Figures with one vast penis, or multiple penises, were popular among the Romans. There were lamps consisting of male figures, with the oil or wick held in the erect penis; this item was designed to protect lovers from the evil demons lurking in the dark, and help them redouble their efforts in their amorous pursuits. Penises with wings were another popular conceit; and there were even phalluses engraved on the handles of workmen's tools.[13]

Hermes was the women's favourite male god and 'Herms', or fertility figures, were a common sight in the streets of early Londinium. These statues, sited at major intersections, consisted of upright squared pillars, six foot high, with a bust of Hermes on top and a large, erect penis, complete with testicles, on one side of the pillar. Passing women would touch or even fondle the stone penis, praying for the god's intervention to make them more desirable, to arouse passion in a lover or to help them become pregnant.[14]

The annual procession devoted to Hermes consisted of priests and laymen carrying massive phalluses, followed by young girls carrying baskets of fruit and flowers while chanting a hymn to Priapus, the god of fertility. According to the Roman poet Catullus, women hung garlands on the god's enormous penis to indicate how many lovers they had entertained the previous night. Quite often, the garlands of a single woman were sufficient to cover the penis from root to tip.[15] In Bacchanalian scenes, crowds of drunken women danced naked, followed by scores of enthusiastic young men, events coming to an inevitable conclusion when they copulated in full public view while enthusiastic spectators cheered them on.

Another popular god in Londinium was Attys, usually portrayed with his tunic pulled up to expose his enormous penis and testicles and a pendulous belly, indicating that he was not only a god of lechery but of gluttony too.[16] Meanwhile, according to Juvenal, the all-female devotees of the goddess Bona Dea became so crazed with lust that they were prepared to rape any passing male or even drag donkeys from their stables, although Juvenal also claims that the occasions included 'more than a suggestion of Lesbian practices'.[17]

Meanwhile, on the north bank of the Thames, Londinium was emerging. The wealthy economic migrants flooded in: governors, civil servants, administrators, merchants and professionals from all corners of the Roman Empire, bringing with them their retinue of family, servants, slaves. By AD 61, just as it was about to be burned to the ground by the vengeful Queen Boudicca, Londinium had become the epitome of Roman civilization, described by Tacitus as 'a place not signified by the name of colonia but crowded with merchants and provisions'.[18]

Londinium recovered from Boudicca's onslaught and rose again, like a phoenix from its own ashes. Three hundred years later the city was awarded the accolade *Augusta* (the Worshipful). With its palaces and temples, baths and theatres, shops, offices and villas, Londinium had become a byword for civic pride within the empire. These outstanding municipal achievements could only be matched, of course, by an equally magnificent sex industry, celebrated for the number and quality of its *lupanaria* and *thermiae* (bath houses, frequented by both men and women). Then there were the numerous *meretrices* (prostitutes, from *merere*, to earn), and *prostibulae* – the independent prostitutes who worked for themselves instead of handing their earnings over to a pimp or a madam. While the most wretched girls worked in the soul-destroying conditions already described in the military brothels, the high-class bordellos offered the greatest luxury, refreshment and entertainment. All tastes were catered for here: willing partners, male as well as female, were on hand to provide every form of sexual pleasure.

The Romans brought with them their outrageous attitude towards sex. The most pleasure-loving society on earth, this was also the cruellest: a culture in which human beings were pitted against wild animals in public circuses in the name of sport, and men possessed the power of life or death over their slaves, and even their own wives. A recurring theme of this book will be the link between voracious sexual appetite and immense power, and the extraordinary inability of the ruling class to adhere to the strict moral guidelines which they issue to their subjects.

We have only to look at the sex lives of the Roman emperors to gain some insight into the colossal double standards that operated. One reason for this, of course, was the Roman belief that their rulers were 'divine' and as such given total dispensation from any moral constraint. Like the gods above, they were entitled to do as they wished. As the Victorian historian of prostitution William Sanger commented, it was difficult to discover a single character in the long list of Roman rulers who was not 'stained by the grossest habits'.[19] These are but a few examples: Julius Caesar, 'the bald adulterer', was also known as 'husband of all men's wives', as it was commonly accepted that any man in the empire would step aside and allow himself to be cuckolded. Augustus, who introduced legislation to enforce marriage and fidelity among his subjects, was a well-known adulterer who, as an older man, sent out his friends to procure women for him, having them stripped and inspected like slave girls. As for the Emperor Tiberius, according to the historian Suetonius, one of his retirement activities on the isle of Capri consisted of training up small boys, referred to as his 'little fishes', to swim between his thighs and nibble on his 'secret parts like unweaned babes being put to the nipple of a breaste . . .'[20]

The emperor Caligula (12 BC–AD 41), who succeeded Tiberius, committed incest with his sisters, set up a brothel in the imperial palace, and most famously attempted to make his favourite horse, Incitatus, a member of the Senate. The nature of Caligula's relationship with the horse has not been recorded.

Lest we be lulled into a false sense of security and think it was only the men who behaved badly, let us take a look at some of the Roman Empire's most notorious women: according to Seneca (4 BC–AD 65), Augustus' daughter Julia had dozens of lovers. Julia roamed the streets at night looking for sex, and finding it in the Forum, the very place where her hypocritical father had laid down his laws against adultery. Meanwhile, the Empress Messalina, wife of Claudius (immortalized by Robert Graves in *I, Claudius*), was the most ill-famed woman in the imperial family, selling herself in the public street like a professional whore. Still unsatisfied when the brothels closed for the night, she had to be thrown out. Messalina's most famous exploit was to hire a prostitute famous for her stamina and challenge her to a sex contest, to see who could accommodate the greatest number of men in a single night. Messalina won.[21]

Understandably, given role models such as these, sexual excess was socially acceptable. Inevitably, brothels played an essential part in public life. Young Romans were encouraged to take their pleasure with prostitutes rather than seduce and violate other men's wives and daughters, a sentiment that originated in Ancient Greece when the statesman and philosopher Solon established the first state-run brothels, or *pornai*, in Athens in 600 BC, using the revenue to finance military campaigns. Cato the Elder (234–149 BC) regarded brothels as an essential public service. 'Blessed be they who are virtuous, who when they feel their virile members swollen with lust, visit a brothel rather than grind at some husband's private mill!'[22] Encountering a young acquaintance leaving a brothel in Rome one afternoon, Cato greeted him with the words, 'well done, my boy!', although when he saw the youth leaving the brothel again later that same day, he did add, 'when I said "well done!" I didn't mean that you should make the whorehouse your home!'[23]

Freedom of sexual expression was, of course, available only to men. While brothels were regarded as a healthy outlet for the male appetite, a formidable double standard dictated that patrician wives and daughters must be paragons of chastity, beyond reproach. The age of marriage was twelve years old for a girl, affairs were forbidden (though they inevitably occurred as frequently as in any other culture) and widows were not permitted to remarry.

The wretched young women left shivering on the docks of Queenhithe at the start of this chapter were forced into a life of sexual slavery; they possessed no autonomy. But some women made a conscious decision to enter the oldest profession. And, in Londinium, prostitution was controlled with as much zealous bureaucracy as every other aspect of Roman life. A woman who wished to become a prostitute (rather than being forced into it) had to go before a public official known as the *aedile*, who was responsible for public health and sanitation. Londinium's *aedile* was based at the Cripplegate Fort, or near the crossroads now known as Addle Street and Wood Street.[24] The aspiring whore then had to complete an application stating her name, date of birth, status and the name under which she wished to trade. Status was considered significant as, at one stage, extremely high-born women were seeking permission to become prostitutes, and the role of the *aedile* was to dissuade them.

However, if a woman persisted, she was granted a licence, or *Licentia Stupro* (licence to carry out a shameful practice), which set out her charges. If she worked in a brothel, this list would be displayed outside her cubicle, like a menu. Being licensed also ensured that she got paid. If the client refused to pay, she was legally entitled to sue him.[25] In return for the professional protection afforded by licensing, the prostitute was required to pay a fee, the *Lenonium Vectigal*, originally introduced by Caligula. One paragraph of this law stated that the prostitute must pay a portion of her daily earnings to the state. The tax was adjusted annually, via a census of the prostitutes. This law applied to male prostitutes as well and provided a massive income to the government, distributed according to the current emperor's ethical scruples or political needs.[26]

Thus prostitution in Roman London was a business like any other. We know this from the existence of *spintriae*, or brothel tokens, which clearly indicated the services a whore was willing to provide, on a sliding scale of prices. Like the pornographic artwork recovered from the ruins of Pompeii, *spintriae* were for many years locked away in museums for fear of offending delicate sensibilities, and only went on public display towards the end of the twentieth century. But they provide a fascinating guide to the generous selection of sexual positions on offer. Fellatio, for instance, was cheaper than vaginal intercourse, while the deeply penetrative positions, such as 'doggy style' (sex from behind) were more expensive as they put the prostitute at greater risk of vaginal soreness, meaning that she could service fewer clients.[27]

Another legal requirement was that prostitutes undergo regular inspection for venereal disease or *morbus indecens aie cunnientis* – otherwise known as 'the filthy disease of the cunt'. This occupational hazard of the prostitute and the military man, which has blighted the history of sexuality ever since, first appeared in Rome in 183 BC when General Manlius' troops returned victorious from Asia Minor, accompanied by thousands of Syrian girls, who were sold at the slave market and launched an epidemic of venereal disease, characterized by a sore known as the *ulcus turpe*, or 'shameful ulcer', which was probably a form of syphilis. As a result, the army introduced draconian rules in 150 BC about frequent bathing and washing the genitals.[28] But these measures were insufficient to prevent the spread of the disease. The historian Pliny the Elder (AD 23–79), anxious to exonerate the Romans from the spread of the disease, blamed it on the 'dirty Egyptians'. The euphemism *ficus*, or 'figs', was used to describe the nodules characteristic of syphilis, as in a poem by Martial, dating from AD 100, where a young man asks Priapus whether a girl is playing hard to get because she is 'full of figs'. The condition is mentioned by Ovid and Catullus, and over 200 years later, another writer, D. Magus Ansonius, describes a wretched citizen unsuccessfully trying to get rid of the putrid ulcers on his penis by repeated washing.[29]

The registered prostitute faced other legal requirements. For instance, she was permitted to wear the *toga*, the sleeveless tunic worn by Roman men but not the *stola*, the long elegant tunic worn by Roman matrons. She was expected to wear a distinctive floral fabric which distinguished her from 'respectable' women and she was not permitted to wear purple, the colour associated with *imperium*, or power. But these regulations were frequently broken, and many prostitutes defiantly dressed in diaphanous silk gowns which 'seemed invented to exhibit more conspicuously what they were intended to hide'[30] and lightened their hair with henna or lemon juice.

Like the other trades of Londinium, the brothels flourished magnificently. With the garrisons full to overflowing with military men, trade was brisk in the *lupanaria*, while the brothels were always busy. These marble palaces witnessed scenes of depravity not just inside but outside too. To the edification of passers-by, prostitutes and their clients copulated freely underneath the arches, or *fornices*, an activity subsequently described as 'fornication'. Debased by the Teutons to *vokken*, this was the origin of the modern 'fucking'.[31]

Whores were everywhere, hanging around the race courses to tempt the lucky punters or console the losers; they were on hand at the circuses, to provide additional excitement, and there to add to the spectacle at the public games. Public gardens were popular, too, with the whores lying in wait for their punters, and frolicking among the statues and temples.[32] Even grocery stores were not immune, with the girls soliciting in the butchers', and bakers' shops offering space for prostitutes to ply their trade 'round the back', after tempting their clients with saucy *colyphia*, little bread rolls shaped like penises (from *colyphium*, the gladiators' term for penis).[33]

There has long been an association between sex and death, and some women, known as *bustuariae*, even worked the cemeteries which lined the roads out of Londinium, using gravestones to advertise their services. A prostitute would chalk up her speciality and prices on a particular tombstone, enabling prospective clients to liaise with her in the graveyard after sunset. The tomb operated as her bed and, when not engaged with a client, she doubled at burials as a professional mourner.[34]

Alongside the experienced prostitutes, another type of woman was exploited in the form of the virgin. Whenever a pimp acquired a fresh virgin (usually a slave girl), he would leave a laurel wreath on the front door, together with a lamp and a posted description of the young girl's attributes. She was then put up for auction, and the 'lucky man' was crowned with the laurel wreath when he succeeded in taking her virginity.[35]

But it was in the bath houses that the most scandalous behaviour took place. Bath houses, or *thermiae*, were magnificent establishments, more like our modern spas or expensive leisure clubs. Although they were designed for getting clean, many other activities legitimate and otherwise took place in these awesome buildings. Intended for social, if not sexual, intercourse, they featured art galleries, gift shops, reading rooms and restaurants, and also served as hotels, offering a bed for the night to travellers and guests.

Women were charged more than men to enter the bath houses, since it was assumed that they could easily earn back the entrance fee from eager clients. A number of leather 'bikinis', dating from the first century AD and now on display at the Museum of London, may well have been the uniform of the local prostitutes.[36] Whores and their clients soon infiltrated the bath houses, to such an extent that special areas were incorporated into the design to accommodate them, with private spaces for massage and 'extras' provided by skilled *fellatrices* – male as well as female. This was indeed the birth of the massage parlour.[37] Inevitably, such establishments attracted less salubrious neighbours. Outside the baths sprang up the *pervigiles popinae*, or all-night bars, which became the focus for antisocial behaviour culminating in street fights, stabbings and even murders. This must have been the scene witnessed by regulars at the Roman baths excavated at Cheapside and Huggin Hill, near Queenhithe, the latter dating from the second century AD and constructed from the best Purbeck marble, imported from Dorset, and fed by a natural spring.

The walls of the baths featured graffiti, similar to those found in Pompeii, and the baths, like the brothels, catered for all tastes. Plutarch mentions that the *palaestrae*, or exercise yards, of the bath houses were much frequented by homosexuals.[38] The bath houses were, like today's private leisure clubs, the province of the rich. The poor simply could not afford the fees, in the form of 'oil money', the cleansing procedure performed by the *sordidus unctor*, or attendant, which had to be undergone before one was admitted to the water. This process consisted of having olive oil rubbed all over one's body, which was then scraped off with a blunt blade, removing the oil and the dirt from the skin. Although in one instance Emperor Septimus Severus issued instructions in Rome that oil money was to be distributed free to the citizens, and it is possible that a similar system operated in Londinium to bribe the British populace into taking a bath.

There is no evidence of organized prostitution in Britain before the Romans, but human nature alone suggests that every settlement must have had its share of good-time girls. What does emerge is that Celtic women seemed to have had a far greater degree of sexual equality than their Roman counterparts, as this exchange from AD 151 between the Empress Julia Domna and the wife of the Caledonian chieftain Argentocoxus indicates. Julia, who had something of a reputation as a flirt, was the consort of Emperor Septimus Severus, who spent some time in Britain. Apparently she teased Argentocoxus' wife about the Scottish habit of sharing their women. The chieftainess retorted: 'We have intercourse openly with the best of our men; while you allow yourselves to be seduced in private by anyone including the worst of men!'[39]

The Britons did not treat their women as possessions or inferiors, but as equals. The Roman historian Strabo observed that the women 'fought alongside their menfolk, and as bravely'.[40] The Romans could not have produced a Boudicca, for they would never have taken orders from a woman. Sadly, however, the British resistance was eventually broken, and these brave, free-spirited women reduced to slavery and the brothels.

We began this chapter by reflecting on the unhappy fate of the slaves deposited at Queenhithe. This was just the start. During the 400 years of Roman occupation, Londinium became a dockside city, with ocean-going merchant ships and warships arriving in town, bearing their parties of sailors anxious for shore leave. This was another explanation for the development of brothels. According to ancient superstition, women, whores or otherwise, were not permitted on board ship: they were regarded as unlucky and any unfortunate woman who found herself on board would have been thrown overboard to drown.

Business flourished until AD 409 when the legions were recalled to Rome by Emperor Honorius, and the Britons were left to the tender mercies of the raiding Saxons. Thousands of Britons chose to leave their homeland with the Romans, and those who remained spent the next forty years unsuccessfully attempting to stem the Saxon tide. Eventually, in 457, the Roman-British forces were overwhelmed at the battle of Crayford, and Southwark and then Londinium fell to the Saxons.

Following the departure of the Romans, the loss of an affluent leisured class had led to the collapse of the sex trade, at least in the form in which it had previously operated. As Londinium ceased to function like a Roman city and disintegrated into a series of settlements along the banks of the Thames, the bath houses and the pleasure domes and their urbane professional clients became things of the past; and the whores were forced to change their modus operandi.

Little is known of what became of the prostitutes of this period. It is known, however, that brothels as such did not exist in Northern Europe. Instead, each Saxon village had its local prostitute, who lived slightly apart from the main settlement. The word 'whore' derives from *hore* or *hure* or *hore-cwen*, a filthy woman, and by association *hore-hus* is a whorehouse or brothel.[41]

The solitary whore's clientele consisted of local older men, horny youngsters, husbands and the occasional stranger. She could usually expect to live in peace and provide a service to the community, although penalties, when the elders chose to impose them, were severe: the Visigoths ruled that whores must be publicly whipped and their noses split open, whilst one early Aryan form of Christianity practised among the German tribes saw promiscuous girls and women put to death.[42] If this seems grim, it is worth recalling that conditions for 'respectable' women were little better: regarded as the property of their husbands and fathers, they were traded like horses and sold into wedlock for financial or political gain (*wed* means payment or pledge, later symbolized by a ring).

Ironically, despite the deeply misogynistic attitudes of the Church, it was the arrival of Christianity on these shores which provided a boost for women, and whores in particular. In one respect, the Augustinian form of Christianity as practised in London offered salvation for women; no longer merely seen as chattels to be bought and sold, they achieved a certain status. A great deal of the early converts to Christianity were women, and particularly prostitutes, who were impressed by the fact that the original 'scarlet woman' of the Christian story, Mary Magdalene, played such an important role in Christ's life. In her capacity as a reformed prostitute who became one of his greatest followers, Magdalene was an impressive role model.

By 670 Christianity had been imposed throughout the land, and by 850 the Bishop of Winchester (later known as St Swithin) had established the nunnery of St Mary Overie. This establishment was founded on the same spot as the Roman garrison where the first of London's prostitutes had serviced the Roman army. Built in Southwark, it would become one of the most notorious brothels in London, and the 'nuns' who dwelt there would become known as 'the Winchester Geese'. From servicing their colonial masters, the prostitutes of London were now, to all intents and purposes, owned by the Church.

2

'GET THEE TO A NUNNERY!'

Sex, Church and State in medieval London

After a period of relative inactivity, prostitution in medieval London flourished once again, as it would continue to do over the following centuries, despite the depredations of the Norman Conquest, the Crusades and the Black Death, and despite the best efforts of Church and state to control it.

The booming sex trade indicated that Londoners were alive and kicking, whatever the horrors and upheavals that confronted them. And the allure of London's ladies of the night sometimes proved so strong that their appeal was enough to prevent an attempted coup. When Earl Godwin, who had raised an army against King Edward the Confessor, was anchored off Bankside in 1052, it was noted that his band of loyal supporters diminished the longer it stayed, because they could not resist sneaking off to visit the ladies of the Bankside.[1]

Meanwhile, conditions in the sex trade had improved for the girls at the top of their profession. Overseas clients presented them with new clothes and jewellery, instructed them in manners and foreign tongues; the premises were built of stone, instead of mud and thatch. The girls enjoyed better working conditions than their predecessors in Roman times. Much of this was courtesy of the Church, which received a rich income stream from the properties it leased out to pimps and bawds. In addition to St Mary Overie, the Bishop of Winchester owned other properties in Chancery Lane and Fetter Lane.[2] England's royal family also dabbled in this form of investment: William the Conqueror derived an income from a series of brothels in Rouen, a fact which would not have occasioned comment during his lifetime.[3]

Whilst a modern reader may struggle to reconcile the Church's attitude towards prostitution with its avowed injunction to chastity, the ecclesiastical authorities had no such reservations. Despite the official line about celibacy, the Church turned a blind eye. Taking to heart the comment of Saint Augustine that 'Suppress prostitution, and capricious lusts will overthrow society,'[4] the Church operated on the principle that prostitution fell into the category of 'necessary evils'. St Thomas Aquinas himself compared prostitution 'like unto a cesspool in the palace; take away the cesspool and the palace becomes an unclean evil-smelling place'.[5] The Church then displayed a further level of hypocrisy by excommunicating any prostitutes who plied their trade while taking a share of the profits.

The Church was a calling to which resorted many who were incapable of making a living any other way, and there is a rich seam of anecdotal literature concerning the failings of the priesthood. Despite their frequent injunctions to others to turn away from sin, the men of God proved incapable of controlling their own sexual urges and their sexual excesses were legendary. The Dutch humanist Erasmus (1466–1536) complained that there were many monasteries where there was no discipline and which were worse than brothels, where a monk might be drunk all day long, go with a prostitute openly, waste the Church's money on vicious pleasures and be a quack and a charlatan, and yet still be considered an excellent brother and fit for promotion to the role of abbot.[6] Many of the great cathedrals featured sculptures lampooning the sexual antics of the clergy. According to the Victorian historian of prostitution, Sanger, 'in one place a monk was represented in carnal connection with a female devotee. In others were seen an abbot engaged with nuns, a naked nun worried by monkeys, youthful penitents undergoing flagellation at the hands of their confessor, and lady abbesses offering hospitality to well-proportioned strangers!'[7]

This outrageous behaviour went all the way to the top. At the Vatican, prostitutes lived in apartments owned by the Church and openly plied their trade. Pope Alexander VI, father of the infamous Cesare Borgia, was fond of holding family gatherings at the papal palace. On one occasion, fifty whores were hired to dance with servants and guests alike:

> At first they wore their dresses, then they stripped themselves completely naked. The meal over, the lighted candles, which were on the table, were set on the floor, and chestnuts were scattered for the naked courtesans to pick up, crawling about on their hands and knees between the candlesticks. The Pope, the Duke [Cesare Borgia] and his sister Lucrezia all watched. Finally, a collection of silk cloaks, hose, brooches and other things were displayed, and were promised to those who had connection with the greatest number of prostitutes. This was done in public. The onlookers, who were the judges, awarded prizes to those who were reckoned to be the winners.[8]

From this and other accounts it can safely be deduced that the ancient Roman tradition of sexual excess had taken root and was thriving within the medieval Vatican. Given these examples, it is scarcely surprising that the populace had low expectations of their clergy. One writer, Guerard, related an anecdote from around 1065, concerning a kindly abbot who had rescued a young servant girl from the lewd attentions of a monk and offered her a bed for the night at his abbey. He was astonished to wake up the next morning and find the girl in his own bed. She had assumed that he had rescued her from the monk only because he wanted her for himself.[9]

Even the Crusades presented an occasion for sin. This series of holy wars fought between Christians and Muslims in Palestine, which began in 1097, saw thousands of women accompany the armies to the Holy Land, some as camp-followers attached to one particular man, some as cooks, cleaners and nurses, and many as prostitutes. Some women specialized in servicing the pilgrims bound for Jerusalem, while female pilgrims supported themselves by selling their favours along the way; some even abandoned a life of piety in favour of the oldest profession. English nuns were particularly prone to this change of career.[10]

Ecclesiastical mischief remained a standing joke throughout the medieval period. Back in London, the poet Geoffrey Chaucer exploited the yawning chasm between public piety and private misbehaviour to great comic effect in his *Canterbury Tales* verse sequence (*c.* 1386). These recognizable comic types reflect the popular perception of churchmen as a venal set, and it seems only appropriate that they set off on their pilgrimage from the Tabard Tavern in Southwark, already well established as a centre of low life.

Chaucer's motley crew includes several stereotypes, among them a debonair monk, a pleasure-loving friar and a couple of depraved Church executives. The Monk, for instance, far from being buried away in a cloister or doing good works, is depicted as a burly, athletic man with a bald, shining head, grey, protuberant eyes and something of the thug about him.[11] His main passion is hunting, animals and women, as his golden pin in the shape of a love knot indicates, and he is too busy chasing the birds, of the feathered and unfeathered variety, to drive himself mad studying theology.

The Friar, whom we meet next, is equally sophisticated: no hair shirts for him. Instead, he is a talented musician, a harpist and singer with a lisping voice, and better acquainted with the taverns of the towns he visits than the beggars and lepers who should be his natural constituents.[12] The Summoner and the Pardoner, meanwhile, constitute a repellent couple. The Summoner's job was to cite delinquents who appeared before the ecclesiastical court. Summoners had a reputation for corruption and abuse, even by the standards of the medieval Church, and this one is presented as a particularly vile specimen. His face is disfigured by leprosy, with scabby eyebrows and patchy beard, he is as lecherous as a sparrow (these birds were considered particularly lewd) and loose in his morals, willing to lend other men his concubines for up to a year without complaint, while he privately went after a 'finch' of his own, to use yet another analogy of birds and women.

Although the Summoner is nothing if not an equal opportunities lecher, Chaucer also insinuates that he fancies the Pardoner, whose task is to sell papal indulgences, many of which are fake. The Pardoner is effeminate, with long, lank yellow hair and no beard. 'I trow he were a gelding, or a mare,' Chaucer speculates, and mentions his high, sweet voice and talents as a singer, suggesting that he has been castrated, making him all the more attractive to the Summoner, who sings along with him, supplying the bassline or 'burden'. At this point Chaucer takes the opportunity to make a really filthy double entendre as he watches the two of them together. The Summoner, according to Chaucer, looks at the Pardoner and 'bears to him a stiff burden'.[13]

Convents, which should have operated as a sanctuary offering women a life of contemplation and prayer, were equally depraved. As the role of nunneries was chiefly charitable, rather than devotional, many of the inmates clung to the sophisticated manners they had learned out in the world, and no great effort was made to control their sexuality.

Chaucer's nun is a good example. Madame Eglentyne, or the Prioress, models herself on the sophisticated French court (although her French is strictly East End, as spoken at Stratford at Bowe, and she is characterized by her soft red lips, beautiful clothes and the observation that she is certainly not underdeveloped.[14]

There is a mysterious man in her life, signified by the little gold brooch she wears, decorated with a crowned 'A' and inscribed with the Latin motto '*Amor vincit onmnia* – Love conquers all'. She has fancy table manners, keeps pet dogs and affects a ladylike sensibility, crying at the sight of a mouse in a trap and eating and drinking with great delicacy. Madame Eglentyne emerges as extremely refined when compared with real-life counterparts such as the Mother Superior at Amesbury, Wiltshire, during the twelfth century, who was so lewd that her nuns were quick to follow her example. The doors stood open day and night, and the building was more like a brothel than a convent.[15]

From time to time, the Church attempted to put its house in order and demanded that its clergy remain celibate. Hitherto, this requirement of clerical life had not been strictly enforced and priests had openly married or kept mistresses known as *focarii*, or 'hearth girls'. As the Church attempted to enforce celibacy, former wives and lovers were left with no choice but to enter the convents and swell the ranks of the depraved nuns, or to become wandering whores.[16]

The Bankside brothels became known in colloquial terms as 'the stews', since they were located near the ponds which provided London's supply of fresh fish. In 1161 King Henry II imposed his 'Ordinance for the governance of the stews' which in effect guaranteed the Bishop of Winchester's right to exploit the brothels of Southwark for the next 400 years: as a result, many of London's most attractive churches were actually built on the proceeds of prostitution. But Henry's ordinance had other implications for London's working girls. At a time when many European cities were attempting to banish prostitution, this ordinance represented an attempt to control the sex trade by creating an official red-light district in Southwark, the area that had been associated with prostitution 'time out of mind'. Henry wanted to abolish the role of the madam and replace her with a male brothel keeper or 'stewholder'. As Roberts says, this ordinance was both 'prohibitive and protective',[17] as it laid down the rights of whores to follow their chosen profession but also curtailed their freedom of movement. The historian John Stow listed some of these rules:

NO STEWHOLDER or his wife to prevent any single woman from going and coming freely at all times she wishes to.

NO STEWHOLDER to keep any woman to board; she must be allowed to board elsewhere at her leisure.

NO STEWHOLDER to charge her for her room more than fourteen pence a week.

NO STEWHOLDER to keep his doors open on the religious Holy days: the Bailiff to ensure that they were removed from the parish.

NO WOMAN to be detained against her will if she wished to give up whoring: nor must the stewholder receive any married woman nor a nun.

NO WOMAN to take money to lie with any man, but she had to lay with him all night: and no man was to be enticed into the stewhouse; nor could any man be held for non-payment of his debt – he had to be taken to the Lord of the Manor's prison.[18]

The whores were allowed to sit still in their doorway, but they were banned from importuning, and were not permitted to advertise themselves with gestures or calls, or to seize men by the gown or harness. Swearing, grimacing and throwing stones at passers-by were also discouraged, and the penalty for such activities consisted of three days and nights in jail and a fine of six shillings and eight-pence. The whores also had to leave the brothel during parliamentary sittings and Privy Council meetings, presumably so that politicians were compelled to attend them rather than seek consolation in the arms of loose women.

Further rules stated that the bailiff was to visit the house once a week and ensure that the whores were healthy and that none of them wanted to leave. And the 'stewholder' himself had to abide by certain rules: for instance, he was forbidden to keep a boat, to prevent him from rowing potential clients across the river.[19] In an effort to curtail prostitution, citizens were banned from rowing across the Thames to Bankside after sundown, but this measure was ineffectual; resourceful men found a means of getting across, and other brothels inevitably sprang up on the north bank of the river. When King John was instrumental in building the new stone London Bridge in 1209, the law became impossible to enforce and the bridge became a royal road to the whorehouse.

Compared with French brothels and houses of ill fame elsewhere in the capital, the Bankside stews were dull, functional places. No entertainments were permitted, and it was forbidden to serve any 'breed, ale, flesh or fyssh' while 'coles, wod or candel nor anie othere vitaill [necessity]' were banned.[20] Even the reference to the client staying all night had a practical function, to cut down on promiscuity and contain disease.

According to Stow's *Survey of London*, there were originally about eighteen of these brothels. The exteriors were painted white, so that they were clearly visible across the river, and they had similar names to taverns: Ye Boar's Hedde; The Castle; The Cross Keyes; The Cardinal's Cap (accompanied by a suggestive illustration of a scarlet skullcap reminiscent of a foreskin) and, rather more poetically, The Half Moon; The Unicorn and The Blue Maid.[21] That these institutions appeared similar to taverns was entirely intentional. Many places of entertainment operated in the shadowy half-world where legitimate inns also doubled as brothels, and many of the girls who worked in the taverns seized the opportunity for extra remuneration by entertaining their patrons. There was also plenty of scope for enterprising amateurs, married women who, feeling neglected by their husbands, repaired to 'houses of assignation' where they could satisfy their own appetites with willing paramours or turn a coin with a wealthy client looking for an upmarket girl.

While the taverns provided entertainment in the form of food and drink, the whorehouses effectively solved the problem of where to billet the large numbers of unattached men descending on London in search of work; they were the perfect municipal solution to overcrowding. One contemporary engraving of a medieval brothel shows us the kind of welcome a young man could expect: a handsome young noble is being attended by two young whores, watched by his jester, who looks horrified by the proceedings while slyly peeping through his fingers. The bed looks rather hard, but there are adequate refreshments. The girls appear somewhat coy, but the second is draped in a banner encouraging enticement to sin, designed to overcome the power of the cross worn around the young nobleman's neck, while the first girl is administering manual stimulation.[22] These brothels also supplied the 'daughters of the city' or civic whores who were rolled out to greet distinguished visitors, draped in suitably diaphanous raiment, although there is no evidence that the City of London followed the continental practice of actually hiring the whores for their guests.

Despite all attempts by the authorities to restrict the sex trade to Bankside, prostitution inevitably flourished in other areas of London, spreading gradually to encompass West Smithfield, particularly Cock's Lane, outside Newgate. Records have revealed a maze of alleys in Moorgate and Cripplegate (near our contemporary Coleman Street and Guildhall) full of brothels. There was no mystery as to the trade that was conducted in these small streets, as one name indicates. The first mention of it appears in 1276, when a property belonging to Henri de Edelmonton was apparently located in the memorable thoroughfare of Gropecunt Lane.[23] The Anglo-Saxon name indicates the most abject, desperate form of prostitution, with clapped-out, prematurely aged prostitutes catering for a desperate clientele who were charged a tiny sum in exchange for the opportunity to put their hands up their skirts.

Maiden Lane was nearby, along with Love Lane, full of 'wanton maidens' according to the historian John Stow.[24] Gropecunt Lanes were not restricted to England. In Paris, the Rue Trousse Puteyne literally meant 'the slut's slit'. Back in England, Gropecunt Lane eventually became the more respectable 'Grape Street' and eventually 'Grub Street', the home of the literary hack (reminding all those who live by the pen that there is more than one way to prostitute oneself). Codpiece Lane became Coppice Lane, but there was nothing that could be done about Sluts' Hole, which was transformed into Sluts' Well before disappearing for ever into the Tenter Ground in 1700.[25]

The stews also represented another development in London's sex trade: the return of the bath house. Bathing and washing had not been popular pursuits in early medieval London. Indeed, the Danish invasion back in 870 AD must have come as a relief for many women, amateur and professional, since Danish soldiers, unlike the Saxons, were famous for their good looks and high standards of personal hygiene. According to the medieval historian John of Wallingford (died 1214), the Danes represented a serious threat to jealous husbands and local lads. Not only did they comb their hair every day and take a bath on Saturdays, but they changed their clothes regularly. It was scarcely surprising that they were particularly successful in seducing married women, and even persuading the daughters of the nobility to become their concubines.[26]

Most Londoners of the period were careless of personal hygiene and did not regard cleanliness as being next to godliness. In some cases, indeed, the reverse was true. Consider this account of Thomas à Becket, murdered on the orders of Henry II in Canterbury Cathedral in December 1170. When his faithful acolytes went to recover the body, they peeled off layer after layer of garments to reveal a stinking hair shirt, hopping with fleas. Dirt and squalor ruled supreme. King John took a bath every three weeks and King Henry III would bravely 'repair to the wardrobe at Westminster where he was wont to wash his head', a decidedly hazardous procedure.

On rare occasions, for those higher up the social scale, wooden tubs were used as baths. In the summer months, some Londoners would bathe in the Thames, but this was scarcely a practice which could be adopted all year round. There were few lavatories, as such: brimming chamber-pots were emptied into the street and the contents carried off down the gutters into the nearest river or stream. In 1306 Ebbgate Street, near the river, just south of Thames Street, was choked with shit *quarum putredo cadit super capitas hominum transeuntium* – falling on the heads of passers-by.[27] There were public latrines, or 'necessary houses', over running streams, with the human by-products then passing into the water supply and hence into the food chain. A cleansing team dispatched to Newgate gaol in 1283 consisted of *thirteen* workmen and took five days to clean the latrine, or *cloacum*. They were well recompensed for their labours though, receiving 6d a day, three times more than unskilled workers at the time. Particularly noisome streets were referred to as Pissing Lane, Stynkyng Alley or even Shiteburnlane.

But public bathing became fashionable once more when returning Crusaders brought with them their taste for the Turkish bath, or 'hammam'. Public bath houses opened in France, Germany and eventually London. The enterprising owner would blow a horn to announce opening time, and locals would strip and walk to the bath house, stark naked during the summer months. Soon a taste for optional extras developed, and, just as in Roman London, 'the stews' became synonymous with brothels. Cleanliness also became desirable to the sex worker (and her client). Although few remedies were known, there was a recognition that venereal disease flourished in insanitary conditions, and being able to offer a clean whore and washing facilities were incentives.

The attitude of the authorities towards prostitution and licentious behaviour in London fluctuated according to who was in power. Despite the fact that the Church and the crown derived a considerable income from prostitution, their stance vacillated between tolerance and strict punishment according to the personal views of the reigning monarch. For instance, Richard I took a

*A medieval 'stew' or bath house. Note that hospitality
extended to dining facilities in the tub.*

decidedly liberal view of prostitution, no doubt because he had great
recourse to brothels himself, to such an extent that he was actually
arrested in a brothel in Paris. When Richard's brother, King John,
succeeded him in 1199, he took no action against the stews. John's
son, King Henry III, grew up to be one of the most avaricious and
close-fisted monarchs in history, notorious for his high taxes, but for
some unaccountable reason the brothels escaped his attention.

But the mood changed significantly when Edward I came to
power in 1272. A moral crusader (as well as a king levying taxes to
pay for his part in the Crusades), Edward set about a clean-up campaign. In 1285 he ruled that 'no courtesans nor common brothel
keepers shall reside within the walls of the City, under pain of
imprisonment'.[28] Edward's rationale was that the presence of prostitutes or 'women of evil life' attracted criminals and murderers,
and that any common prostitute found within the city walls was to
be imprisoned for forty days and reminded of the fact that she
belonged beyond the city limits, in Southwark. As well as taking a

firm line on prostitution, Edward I drove out the remaining Jews who had not already left England after the massacre unintentionally initiated by Richard I when he banned the Jews from his coronation on the grounds that he was a 'Crusader'. This thoughtless gesture led to anti-Semitic riots, although Richard later punished the protagonists. Despite the fact that the royal family had relied on the Jews for their financial and medical acumen, they had long suffered exclusion and persecution. The Jews, and the 'Turks' or Muslims, were even excluded from visiting brothels. In 1290, Edward stated that: 'those who have dealings with Jews and Jewesses and those who commit bestiality and sodomy are to be burned alive after legal proof that they were taken in the act and publicly convicted'.[29] This was especially hypocritical on Edward's part, as subsequent records reveal that, not only did the king derive an income from the stews of Southwark, but he had also issued a licence to run a brothel to Isaac of Southwark, one of the richest Jews in England.[30]

The pleasure-loving Edward II was content to let the brothels flourish, although his own tastes ran to boys. He was murdered, horribly, at Berkeley Castle in Gloucestershire, when a red-hot poker was rammed up his anus until it reached the intestines – a ghastly 'punishment' for weak governance and for his homosexuality. Edward's greatest achievement was to found the Lock Hospital in Southwark in 1321. Originally intended for lepers ('locks' refers to the 'locks', or rags, that patients used to cover their lesions), it took on a new role centuries later in 1747, as the Lock Hospital on Hyde Park Corner, specializing in venereal disease, and generations of afflicted Londoners had cause to be grateful to its founder.[31]

When Edward's son, Edward III, succeeded in 1327, he took an enlightened attitude to the brothels. In 1345 he reviewed the legislation of 1161 on the stews of Southwark recommending that the prostitutes wore a distinguishing mark in the form of a red rosette. A similar system operated in Avignon, France, while in Switzerland harlots wore a little red cap. Unfortunately, when it came to lewd and immoral behaviour, one law operated for the rich and another for the poor. Edward III's Plantagenet court was characterized by immorality, with the royalty and aristocracy free to indulge their sexual proclivities to the full. There was even a brief fashion for female 'topless jousting' with scantily clad young women appearing at tournaments 'dressed in a lascivious, scurrilous and lubricious fashion, with their breasts and bellies exposed',[32] according to one contemporary writer, while another described 'ladies wearing foxtails sewed withinne to hide their arse'.[33]

While such frolics were tolerated with amusement in court circles, immorality lower down the social scale was dealt with more harshly. As one contemporary nobleman expressed it, 'those that were rich were hangid by the purse, and those that were poor were hangid by the necke!'[34] The street whores, or 'nightwalkers', received the most draconian penalties, such as the 'cucking' and 'ducking' stools.

A 'cucking stool' sounds inoffensive enough, but its origins are truly disgusting. According to Tacitus, in Germany, cowards, sluggards, debauchees and prostitutes were suffocated in mires and bogs by this method, along with 'pests' and useless members of society.[35] 'Cucking' derives from the old Icelandic '*kuka*'; like the Latin '*caca*' it means shit. Although it sounds like a joke to us now it was anything but. The unfortunate victim was fastened into a chair outside his or her own house and then wheeled to the location, where the chair was attached to a fulcrum and suspended over a deep pit of excrement into which they were lowered and where they would choke to death. The tradition lasted into Norman times, when it was used as a punishment for bakers and brewers who adulterated their products, and for 'bawds' (madams) and 'scalds', noisy and aggressive women who fought in the street.

The milder-sounding 'ducking' or gagging stool, where the miserable villain was dipped only in water, was not really preferable: although in theory the miscreant was dipped only two or three times to the point of suffocation, many mistakes were made, ending with the occupant of the chair being drowned, either by accident or intentionally.[36]

Then there was the 'thew', a special type of pillory like an upright crucifix, into which the victim's head and wrists were locked. For an hour or two, this could be tolerated as a punishment by ridicule. But it developed into an instrument of torture, with victims being locked in the apparatus for days. While friends and relations might feed the victim, others would pelt him with bricks, stones, rotten vegetables and dung. The victims would inevitably defecate where they stood, fully clothed, to their infinite humiliation. Compared with this, the stocks, where only the legs were locked up, was comparatively tame.

At the very least, prostitutes did not escape being whipped at the cart's arse, paraded through the streets and imprisoned in Newgate gaol, while their pimps received comparatively light sentences. One such was William de Dalton, imprisoned in 1338 for keeping a house of assignation in the city. Within two months, his influential friends had obtained his release, allowing him to set up shop else-where.[37] In the same year, Robert de Stratford, a cordwainer who belonged to a powerful guild (a tradesmen's organization), was charged with living off the immoral earnings of Alice Donbelly and Alice Tredewedowe and others. He agreed to be tried by jury, and was fined six shillings and eightpence, a comparatively small amount. His guild was no doubt influential in saving him from the humiliation and embarrassment of the common pimp's punish-ment: being whipped at the cart's arse and put in the stocks.[38]

Criminal prosecution seemed to have little effect on the flour-ishing trade. More brothel districts sprang up north-west of the city, including Moorgate, Cripplegate, Holborn, Shoe Lane, Fleet Street and Chancery Lane. In January 1340, one Gilbert le Strengmakere, along with Margery de Wantynge, Isabella Actone, Joseph Sewy and his concubine Salerna Livynge were charged with keeping dis-orderly houses and harbouring prostitutes and men of ill fame.[39] The same charge sheet features two sisters, Agnes and Juliana, who were apprehended running a house of ill repute in Holborn, and Agnes, widow of Robert-at-Hale, for letting a house in Shoe Lane to 'a woman of bad character'.[40]

One intriguing aspect of these documents is that many of the prostitutes have unusual names: for every Agnes or Alice, there was a Juliana or a Salerna. It was the custom for whores to use assumed names, partly to protect their identities and partly to make them appear more exotic. 'Ionette' was in fact 'Janet', from the stews of Southwark, while the exotic-sounding Petronella doubtless began life with a more sober moniker. Petronella was a favourite name with prostitutes for centuries.

Surnames were also adaptable. At this period, many people did not possess a specific surname, so the authorities would invent one. Some anonymous clerk of the charge sheet has given us the memorable Alice Strumpette (in order to distinguish her from other, law-abiding, Alices) and the delightful Clarice la Claterballock, whose speciality consisted of clattering her clients' 'ballocks' , conjuring up a vivid mental image of her particular technique.[41]

These records also remind us of the darker side of the criminal underworld and go some way to explaining why the authorities were so keen to crack down on prostitution. At Christmas 1339 an unpleasant incident occurred at the home of Ellen de Evesham, who kept a disorderly house just off Fleet Street. That week, 'certain foreigners from her house attacked a man who was passing along the highway with a light, bound and beat him up, and carried him to the said Ellen's house while she was present, with a lighted candle in her hand.'[42] As well as this form of violence (which appears to have been an abduction or punishment for a client who had reneged on his payment), other aspects of the dark side of the trade emerge. Prostitutes have been mistreated by their pimps and madams from time immemorial; what is perhaps less well known is that such households contain other victims of abuse. How else to explain the curious story of one John Bunny, whose case came up in 1366? Bunny had been sold, with his master's estate, to Joan Hunt, who kept a brothel on the far side of London Bridge. Joan had set him to hard work, treated him badly and starved him, and, through this hard labour, Bunny had developed physical injuries, probably a hernia. When Bunny complained, Joan's lover, Bernard, physically assaulted him. When Bunny fell ill, she turned him out on the streets to starve. It is not known what punishment Joan received for her harsh treatment, but, mercifully, the story has a happy ending. The judge was so appalled by Bunny's condition that he set him free.[43]

Another grim aspect of prostitution comes to light with an account from 1438, when a woman called Margaret was charged with: 'Procuring a young girl named Isabel Lane for certain Lombards and men unknown; which Isabel was deflowered against her will in Margaret's house and elsewhere, for certayne sums of money which Margaret collected, and then afterwards took the girl over to the common stews on the banks of the Thames in Surrey against her will for immoral purposes with a certain gentleman on four occasions against her will'.[44]

Margaret was a real hard case. In the same indictment she was also charged with taking a girl named Joan Wakelyn to a house in the parish of St Katherine Coleman as agreed with 'a certain important Lombard' who paid Joan 12d. For her 'wicked and unlawful behaviour', Joan had to give Margaret 4d from her earnings. And in turn Joan pimped Margaret, taking her, at dark, to the home of a 'very prodigal Venetian'. The report concludes that 'both women for a long time taking no thought for the safety of their souls had carried on this base and detestable manner of life . . .'[45]

Another explanation for the authorities clamping down on prostitution and other forms of lawlessness was the fear of imminent revolt. Among the disenchanted masses, political dissent was on the rise. Brothels, taverns and even church crypts proved handy meeting places for the disillusioned peasantry; largely illiterate, they could at least foment opinion, share their views and make plans for revolt, aided and abetted by organizers such as John Ball, the worker priest who preached equality for all men with the slogan 'When Adam dalf and Eve span, Wo was thane a gentilman?'[46] Unlike the prostitutes, whose ultimate goal was to earn a crust and eventually retire, these were potential revolutionaries, many of them former soldiers who had served in the Hundred Years War and remembered the horrors of the conflict, as described by Geoffrey Chaucer, 'the thousand carrion corpses lying in the bushes with their throats slit, the towns burnt to the ground with nothing left standing'.[47] They had arms in their cottages and they knew how to use them. They were violent agitators, who represented a real danger to the king.

But, before the rebels could organize sufficiently to overthrow the government, the land was plunged into crisis by a far more terrifying adversary than a crew of political agitators. The Black Death made its inexorable progress through England, Scotland and Wales, as vividly described by the Welsh poet Jeuan Gethin (died 1349):

> We see death coming into our midst like black smoke, a plague which cuts off the young, a rootless phantom which has no mercy or fair countenance. Woe is me of the shilling in the arm-pit; it is seething, terrible, wherever it may come, a head that gives pain and causes a loud cry, a burden carried under the arms, a painful angry knob, a white lump. It is of the form of an apple, like the head of an onion, a small boil that spares no-one. Great is its seething, like a burning cinder, a grievous thing of an ashy colour. It is an ugly eruption that comes with unseemly haste. It is a grievous ornament that breaks out in a rash. The early ornaments of Black Death.[48]

The Black Death, which killed about half the population of England and one third to half of the population of London alone, inspired utter terror and desperation. Whilst one might be tempted to conclude that it also killed off sexual desire and put a temporary end to prostitution, nothing could be further from the truth. Instead of repressing desire, the Black Death created an extraordinary mood of sexual profligacy, with victims and potential victims giving themselves over to pleasure, despite the fact that crowding into taverns and brothels inevitably caused the plague to spread faster.

Many believed that victims of venereal disease could not catch the plague; others, that sexual intercourse prevented it. An obsession with marriage developed, with widows and widowers rushing to the altar while they still had the chance. And, since an urban myth sprang up that sex with a prostitute actually guaranteed immunity from this plague, trade had never been better.

Members of the oldest profession displayed a similar resilience in 1381, when years of unrest and economic decline following the Black Death finally culminated in the Peasants' Revolt. When the rebel leaders, Wat Tyler, Jack Straw and John Ball, arrived in Southwark preparing to march on London, they 'despoyled' a brothel in the neighbourhood run by a Flemish woman (who leased the house from Walworth, the mayor of London). This was despite the fact that these institutions provided the only possible income for many of their 'sisters'. The whores were not to be out-done, however. Just as, centuries later, such women threw in their lot with the French and Russian revolutionaries, the girls of the Bankside immediately grasped the potential of such a mass upris-ing. When, the following morning, on the feast of Corpus Christi, the rebels surged peacefully across London Bridge and into the city, the whores marched alongside them, offering comfort and support as they threw open the prisons. The revolt concluded in tragedy, of course. Richard II, having promised the rebels a pardon, arranged a meeting the following day with Wat Tyler at Smithfield; when he arrived, Tyler was seized and stabbed to death by Mayor Walworth, the latter receiving a knighthood for this act of betrayal.

As a response to the revolt, the climate of public tolerance towards all so-called sex crimes quickly began to erode. The streets teemed with spies, ready to apprehend 'strollers' and any woman who was not either handsome or rich enough to bribe the authorities to turn a blind eye was carted through the streets and publicly humiliated with great pomp and ceremony, her hair shorn as pipes and trumpets belted out. Later that same year, when John Kempe and Isabelle Smythe were found guilty of adultery, they were taken to the mayor's court and charged a heavy fine.[49]

In another move to control the sex trade, a new dress code was enforced, designed to distinguish 'ladies' from 'women'. Just as the Roman whore was officially banned from wearing the *stola* of her respectable counterpart, so 'women' were informed that they must not ape the dress of their female betters. 'No such lewd [proletarian] woman shall be so daring as to be attired either by day or night in any kind of vesture trimmed with fur such as miniver, grey work [badger], squirrel, or any other manner of noble budge [fur] or lined with sendale, bokerames, samytes [rich silk] or any other noble lining, on pain of forfeting the said vestments.' Instead, they were ordered to wear a hood of ray (striped cloth) and plain undecorated clothes, 'that all folks native and strangers may have knowledge of what rank they are'.[50] As Burford notes, this early form of apartheid operated for another couple of centuries and served to safeguard the status quo by prescribing in minute detail what might be worn by the nobility and the lower orders.

Despite the income derived from prostitution, the ecclesiastical authorities felt compelled to crack down on the sex trade, as did a succession of reigning monarchs. Henry V attempted to abolish the stews in a fit of self-righteous bigotry, while his son, Henry VI, ordered a commission of inquiry in 1460, during one of his last periods of lucidity before succumbing to insanity. The report of this commission of inquiry concluded that the stews were a social menace and attracted violent antisocial behaviour: 'the number of prostitutes in Southwark and other places adjacent' caused 'many homicides, plundering and improprieties' which the ecclesiastical authorities were incapable of containing.[51]

Within a year of this inquiry, Henry VI was dead, murdered in the Tower of London, and his son Edward IV, the pleasure-loving 'sun in splendour', took the throne. And once again, London's moral climate changed.

It is tempting to regard this period as a grim catalogue of cruelty and abuse, but it is worth reminding ourselves that not every good-time girl came to a bad end. Indeed, many 'whores', amateur and professional, made enough of a success of their life on the game to retire and enjoy a healthy, wealthy old age. Their stories are untold: personal discretion, lack of historical records and the fact that until recently the lives of women were not considered worth recording account for this. But one documented case is the story of London's first courtesan, Jane Shore, 'harlot and heroine', mistress of Edward IV, victim of Richard III, and resourceful survivor of one of the darkest periods of English history.[52]

Jane was not potential harlot material. Born Elizabeth Jane Lambert in 1445 to the London merchant John Lambert and his wife, Amy, Jane seemed destined to become a prosperous nonentity. She was married 'ere she were ripe', to a goldsmith, Matthew Shore, who was considerably older, but the marriage was not a success. According to Sir Thomas More, Jane was 'not very fervently loved by her husband' and the marriage was eventually annulled on the grounds of his impotence.[53] Petite, curvy and round-faced, Jane was celebrated more for her personality and wit than her looks. But it was not long before she caught the eye of the king, Edward IV, and became his mistress. Edward was married, of course, and had a selection of mistresses, but his wife, Elizabeth Woodville (another great survivor), accepted her as the king's chief mistress, and it is at this period that she took the name 'Jane', to appease Elizabeth and avoid confusion with the queen. Jane's status changed with the death of Edward IV in 1483 and the accession of Richard III, who promptly consigned her to the Tower of London. Accused of being a harlot, Jane was sentenced by the Bishop of London to perform the traditional penance for that offence: she had to walk barefoot through the streets from St Paul's in a procession led by a choir and a priest carrying a cross. Dressed only in her petticoats with her hair hanging down, she carried a lit candle and had to endure the attentions of a noisy and ogling crowd, something which she managed with great dignity. She won over the onlookers with her 'womanliness and patience' during this ordeal. Following her penance, Jane was incarcerated in Ludgate prison, where she met the king's solicitor, Thomas Lyneham, who was so smitten that he proposed to her.

A question mark hangs over Jane's subsequent fate. The popular perception is that she lived on, 'lean, withered and dried up', according to Sir Thomas More, and ended her days begging on the streets of London, and gave her name to 'Shoreditch', the spot at which she died. But it seems unlikely that Jane died in poverty. Thomas Lyneham was a wealthy man, and even Sir Thomas More, when he met Jane in old age, reported that she had a soft tender heart and that the remnants of her beauty still shone through the ravages of time. The less sensational facts are these: Jane died at the age of eighty-two, a considerable age in those days, and was buried in Hinxworth Church, Hertfordshire, where her effigy remains to this day. She was a remarkable woman, having survived the back-stairs politics of a savage age, when Richard III cut a murderous swathe to the throne and the first Tudor monarch, Henry VII, subsequently dispatched all Plantagenet opposition. To have married again, died of old age and be buried in a quiet country church was quite an achievement for our demi-mondaine, first of a long and fascinating line of celebrity mistresses.

As Jane breathed her last peacefully, far from London and the court, a new and terrifying development in London's sexual history had made itself manifest: a mysterious, disfiguring and potentially lethal disease, against which the forces of both Church and state seemed powerless.

3

'THE BURNING' AND BUGGERY

'Detestable Vice and Synne'

Henry VIII has never been associated with piety or sexual abstemiousness. Indeed, the notorious Tudor's name is still synonymous with self-indulgence: hunting, dancing, eating, drinking and, most famously of all, wenching. And yet, in a move which now seems extraordinary, King Henry introduced two draconian pieces of legislation ostensibly aimed at curtailing the pleasures of the flesh. In 1546, he ordered the closure of London's brothels. And prior to this, in 1533, he ensured that the Buggery Act would be steered through Parliament. In this chapter, we will examine Henry's motivation for this legislation, and the success, or otherwise, of the venture.

First, let us turn to the attempt to close the brothels. In April 1546, Henry VIII issued a strict edict 'putting down the stews'. This was announced in the streets by a herald at arms, accompanied by blasts on a trumpet. The proclamation stated that any brothel keeper who ran one of the distinctive whitewashed houses must cease trading immediately. He or she was banned from entertaining clients or selling victuals.[1] And allied trades were destined to feel the pinch: in order to deter punters pouring into Bankside, Moorgate, Fleet Street and Chancery Lane, Henry VIII outlawed bear-baiting and dog fighting and closed the establishments where these entertainments took place. Bearing in mind Henry's permissive personal life and taste for cruelty, it seems extraordinarily hypocritical to have deprived Londoners of their traditional pleasures, however barbaric these seem to modern readers. It appeared unlikely that Henry was bowing to pressure from his subjects regarding lawlessness and antisocial behaviour. He had not been noted for listening to the wishes of his people, let alone acting on them, and at that historical period it was unlikely that his decision was informed by a sudden revelation concerning the issues of sex slavery or animal rights. Moreover, Henry himself was a veteran of 'Winchester Garden', never missing an opportunity to frolic with the 'geese' procured for him by his pimp, the devious Archbishop Gardiner. So what was the real explanation for Henry's decision to close the stews?

For the answer, we must travel to Renaissance Italy and enter the consulting rooms of Dr Pedro Pintor (1423–1503), physician to Pope Alexander VI, the 'Borgia Pope' (who, you will recall, was in the habit of getting prostitutes to crawl around the floor of his palace, squabbling over pieces of jewellery). Dr Pintor had identified an horrific sexual plague, the victims of which 'languished' with 'an obscene disease: dire flames upon their vitals fed within, While Sores and crusted Filth prophan'd their Skin'.[2] Whilst Dr Pinto would have been familiar with gonorrhoea, or 'the burning', characterized by severe inflammation of the urethra causing severe pain on urination (hence the name), he now encountered a ruthless and ultimately deadly condition.

In March 1493, Dr Pintor had noted the first case of the *morbus gallicus*, or 'French disease', in Rome, and claimed that the French army had brought it into Italy. Over the next two years, the disease spread like wildfire across Europe, as the inevitable consequence of military campaigns. When the French army occupied Naples in February 1495, many French soldiers were infected, so they in turn decided to call it *mal de Naples*, 'the sickness of Naples'. In August 1495, the Emperor Maximilian issued an edict referring to the disease as *malum franciscum*, and, when the French returned home in 1495, they spread it across their homeland. As Voltaire put it: 'when the French went hotfoot into Italy they easily won Naples, Genoa and the Pox. When they were driven out they lost Genoa and Naples, but they did not lose everything, for the Pox stayed with them!' 'Pox' (from 'pocks' on the skin brought about by the ravages of infection) remained the popular name for the disease for years after.[3]

The disease was officially recorded in Naples in January 1496; eight weeks later, the authorities in Paris made the first bid to control this menace to public health. But this proved impossible with promiscuous armies rampaging their way across Europe. Cesare Borgia caught it in France, and Pope Julius and many cardinals were also infected. The disease arrived in England around 1500. When it first occurred, doctors assumed this particularly vicious strain originated in the new American colonies, and had been brought back to Europe by Columbus's sailors. But, in 1521, the Veronese physician Girolamo Fracastoro gave the condition a name in his poem *Syphilis sive morbus gallicus* ('Syphilis, or the French disease'), which concerns the ordeal of a Greek peasant named Syphilus. Syphilus had angered Apollo and was punished with ill health and dreadful ulcers all over his body, which were later cured by Mercury, the god of medicine.

Fracastoro expressed doubt that the disease had come from America, and the controversy over its origins continues to this day, with some experts claiming that it originated in pre-Columbian America, whilst others argue that it originated in Africa and spread as the result of the slave trade. A third theory suggests that the disease mutated at the end of the fifteenth century and became virulent due to the unusual movements of populations in the Age of Discovery.[4] Renaissance thinkers postulated a number of theories as to the origins of the disease, ranging from astrology to leprosy. The most bizarre theory of all was proposed by Francis Bacon in *Sylva Sylvarum*. According to Bacon, 'the French do report, that at the siege of Naples [1495] there were certain wicked merchants that barrelled up man's flesh (of some that had been lately slain in Barbary) and sold it for tunney [tuna fish]; and that upon that foul and high nourishment was the original of that disease. Which may well be; for that it is certain that the cannibals in the West Indies eat a man's flesh; and the West Indies were full of the pocks when they were first discovered.' In other words, Bacon is suggesting that syphilis originated from cannibalism.[5]

Whatever its origins, syphilis spread with deadly rapidity among a population with a low degree of immunity. This was compounded by the fact that it could be spread without sexual contact. A syphilitic barber, an infected cup or a kiss from a diseased person were all enough to pass on the disease.[6] Tragically, it could also be spread by breast feeding, which in an era of wet-nursing presented a grave risk to infant health, and to the health of a nurse, who could be infected by a syphilitic baby.[7] The strain of syphilis decreased in severity over the course of the sixteenth century, most likely, Fabricius tells us, as a result of improved standards of living. But it was still a peculiarly unpleasant condition.

The physician Thomas Sydenham's description of the progress of the disease includes the graphic observations that the symptoms begin with a spot, about the size and colour of a measle, which appears in some part of the glans, followed by a discharge from the urethra. As the pustule becomes an ulcer, the patient experiences great pain during erections, followed by the development of buboes, swellings of the lymph nodes, in the groin. Then come splitting headaches, pains in the arms and legs, while crusts and scabs form on the skin. The bones of the skull, shin-bones and arm-bones are raised into hard tubers, and, worst of all, the cartilage of the nose is eaten away so that the bridge sinks in and the nose flattens.[8] One author noted the case of a man who 'being long sicke of the poxe had two tumours and an ulcer in his nose, at the which everie day there came foorth great quantitie of stinking and filthie matter'. This grim description depicts one of the most horrible lesions of syphilis, in which nasal bones are destroyed by *gumma*, or gummy tumours. Syphilis attacks the mucous membranes and soft tissue, eating away the nose and in serious cases exposing the brain to the air.[9]

This was an extreme example of syphilis; just as disturbing were the symptoms that went undetected. Victims were not always aware that they had been infected, and the disease took time to reveal itself: patients might feel well for up to four months before the syphilitic symptoms appeared, in the form of a 'dosser' or syphilitic bubo, agonizing ulcers that ate away the skin. But treatment was just as

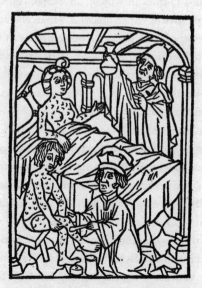

Treatment of a syphilitic couple with mercury balm,
a common medication during the fifteenth century.

painful. The traditional remedy for all skin diseases such as scabies, psoriasis and leprosy was mercury, or *Unguentum Saracenium*, an ointment invented by the Arabs (hence the name 'Saracen') and readily available in Europe.[10] This was a primitive form of chemotherapy, in which the mercury burned off the skin tumours, although it was not an effective long-term cure, as it did not destroy the infection and it was highly toxic.

An alternative treatment came in the form of guaiac, a wonder drug from the New World which sailors claimed would cure syphilis without the gruesome side effects of mercury. This substance derived from the guaiacum tree, a heavy, ebony-like wood, as black as ink, and was administered in a tincture in a sweat room, with the patient confined in stinking conditions for up to a month. The other remedy, which involved excising the sores and cauterizing the wound, would have been excruciating. If the disease had got a hold, it became essential to seek out an expert surgeon for help. Dr Andrew Boord, a famous physician, advocated celibacy and abstinence: at the first stirrings of an erection, a man was advised to 'leap into a grete vessel of cold water or putte nettles in the Codpeece about the yerde [penis] and the stones [testicles]', an extreme but doubtless effective method of cooling one's ardour.[11]

Scapegoats for the spread of syphilis were not hard to find. In 1530, Dr Simon Fish, a Protestant divine, even told Henry VIII that promiscuous 'Romish priests' were responsible for the spread of the disease, claiming that they 'catch the Pockes of one woman and bear them to an other; that be BURNT with one woman and bare it unto an other; that catch the Lepry of one woman and bare it to another . . .' The use of the word 'lepry' is significant here, as doctors at this time had difficulty in distinguishing the symptoms of syphilis from those of leprosy. Meanwhile, Dr Boord had established that 'if a Man be BURNT with an Harlotte and doe meddle with an other Woman within a Day he shal BURN the Woman that he shal meddle withal'.[12]

Nobody was safe. Henry VIII himself was a sufferer, and many historians have attributed his volcanic rages and outbursts of paranoia to tertiary syphilis (end-stage syphilis). The pox was no respecter of persons, and men of the Church were not immune. In 1553, Henry's pimp, Archbishop Gardiner, was afflicted with 'the Burning' while in 1556, Dr Hugh Weston, Dean of Windsor, was sacked for adultery, after being 'bitten by a Winchester Goose and not yet healed thereof'. The gossip writer John Aubrey tells us that Francis Bacon's mother made Sir Thomas Underhill 'deafe and blinde with too much of Venus'[13] when she married him, those symptoms being synonymous with sexually transmitted disease. And as for Sir William Davenant, the dramatist, the unfortunate gentleman 'got a terrible clap of a Black handsome wench that lay in Axe-yard, Westminster, which cost him his Nose', although the episode was not without its consolations, as the woman in question inspired the character of Dalga in the play *Gondibert*.[14]

Prostitutes were inevitably held responsible for the spread of syphilis and condemned as 'rotten filthy harlots' by the male medical establishment. For the whores, sexually transmitted disease was an unavoidable consequence of their trade, given that they might have intercourse with over thirty men in a day. Regular inspections by the likes of Dr Boord did nothing to protect them. Perfunctory examinations, lasting only a few minutes, were carried out with unwashed instruments by doctors with dirty hands. These health checks probably did as much to spread syphilis as the sex act itself. As it swept through London, Henry VIII had only one option: to close the brothels in an attempt to contain the epidemic. Sadly, this early example of gesture politics was ineffectual. Behind closed doors, Jack continued to have Jill, the sex trade flourished, and Henry's court became one of the most notorious in Europe, throbbing with intrigues, conspiracies and secret marriages. There was also a notable degree of male homosexuality. And yet, in 1533, Henry had instructed his adviser, Thomas Cromwell, to steer a new act through Parliament: it was referred to as 'the Buggery Act' and would make 'buggery' a capital offence, 'because there was not sufficient punishment for this abominable vice, committed with man or beast'.[15]

To achieve some insight into Henry's motivation, let us look at 'buggery' in its historical context. From the time of Henry I, 'buggery' had been downgraded from a criminal offence to a moral one, which required to be dealt with by the ecclesiastical courts rather than the judiciary. And to all accounts the offence was treated leniently, no doubt because buggery was so common amongst the priesthood, and was also prevalent at court. The Italian author and diplomat Castiglione, who had visited the court of Henry's father, Henry VII, noted the 'womanish' men who, 'seeing nature hath not made them women ought to be banished not only out of princes courtes but also out of the company of gentlemen', while another commentator argued that sodomy was associated with following French fashion trends, and that courtiers in French dress were transvestites, proud and drunken 'progeny of Lucifer' who flew in the face of nature by committing lechery, abuse and other abominable acts.[16]

This condemnation derived from the biblical edict on same-sex activities: 'If a man also lie with mankind, as he lieth with a woman, both of them have committed an abomination; they shall surely be put to death' (Leviticus 20:13). Castiglione doubtless was aware that the vice was associated, as were other sexual peccadilloes, with his fellow countrymen; the Italians were regarded as being particularly given to buggery, hence the common insult of 'back door Italian', meaning one who enjoys anal sex ('buggery' derives from the Italian *'buggerare'*). Anal sex was also routinely practised by heterosexual couples as a form of contraception, as in the poet Guilpin's observation that 'Since marriage, Faber's prouder than before, Yfaith his wife must take him a hole lower.'[17]

While Castiglione and his associates may have had certain reservations about homosexual practices, a reasonable degree of tolerance prevailed while England was still controlled by the Church of Rome. This tolerance was analogous to the acceptance of prostitution, a manifestation of the Roman Catholic belief that man was essentially impure and susceptible to the temptations of the flesh. However, after the Reformation, the climate of tolerance changed. To gain some idea as to the implications of this, let us analyse the meaning of the term 'buggery' in Reformation England.

For the modern reader, buggery means anal sex, but the Tudors interpreted buggery as any form of sexual deviation, including incest, bestiality and even witchcraft. This product of the peculiar Tudor mentality consisted of lingering medieval superstitions and ill-informed beliefs, including the idea that stillborn or deformed children were evidence of copulation with the devil. Bestiality was included because it was believed that buggery was not merely a sexual preference but associated with witchcraft and devil worship, the buggers in question copulating with the Prince of Darkness himself in animal form.

So, for the Tudors, buggery became a blanket term for sex crimes. The Buggery Act even contains one fascinating and bizarre reference to a noblewoman who, it was claimed, committed bestiality with a 'Barbary ape' and gave birth to a mutant offspring. Her crime was, it appears, too early for her to be prosecuted under the statute. Buggery was held to be such a vile crime that it actually constituted a form of treason. Committing buggery was a *crimen laesae Majestatis*, or a crime against the king, for which the only fitting punishment would be death followed by burial without religious rites. The Buggery Act was not a means of persecuting homosexual men. Instead, it represented a convenient method for disposing of anyone who represented a threat to the king, and its most famous victim died at the Tower of London on 19 May 1536. Executed as a heretic and a witch, she was Anne Boleyn, one of London's greatest *grandes horizontales* and the most tragic.

Anne had been the star of the court during her affair with Henry. The original 'It girl', right down to the initial necklace (a golden 'B' for Boleyn surrounded by pearls), Anne was celebrated for her vivacity, intelligence, political acumen and dark good looks.

Anne had married Henry VIII secretly in January 1533, following his divorce from Catherine of Aragon, but the marriage was not officially announced until June. The populace took against Anne, and soon allegations circulated that she was a witch with six fingers. Anne gave birth to one healthy child, the future Queen Elizabeth I, but then came two miscarriages; rumours flew around that the second foetus was hideously deformed.

By this time Henry was suffering bouts of impotence, which he blamed on Anne, since witches were believed to cause impotence by 'overlooking' unfortunate men. Meanwhile, Henry and his adviser, Thomas Cromwell, who had fallen out with Anne over policy issues, conducted a character assassination on a grand scale, discrediting Anne with allegations of 'buggery'.

Towards the end of April, Anne's musician, a young Flemish boy named Mark Smeaton, was arrested and tortured until he 'confessed' to having had sex with her, as were three other men, Henry Norris, Sir Francis Weston and William Brereton, despite the fact that the latter two were exclusively homosexual in their orientation. Finally, Anne's own brother, George, was charged with incest, the stillborn baby being considered evidence of an unnatural union. The 'evidence' for these allegations would not withstand the scrutiny of a modern legal team, but the trumped-up charges were sufficient to see Anne's four alleged 'lovers' executed on 17 May, while Anne herself went bravely to the scaffold two days later, and submitted to her fate with considerable dignity.[18]

Anne's real crime was not 'buggery' in any of its manifestations. She did not commit adultery, or incest, or dabble in witchcraft. The mundane facts are that she fell out of favour with her husband, and alienated the powerful political operator Thomas Cromwell by opposing his proposals for the funds confiscated during the dissolution of the monasteries. In short, Anne was executed for being an infertile woman whose husband had tired of her, and who meddled in affairs of state.

The Buggery Act received royal assent in 1533 and became

enshrined in English law as the Buggery Statute, with buggery remaining a capital offence until 1861. Four days later, 'Walter', Lord Hungerford (1503–40) was executed for infringing it. By all accounts Hungerford had been a violent and despicable man. He tried to starve his wife, Elizabeth, to death by locking her up in a castle for four years, and then tried to poison her.

Elizabeth wrote to their mutual friend Thomas Cromwell, concerning Hungerford's physical and mental cruelty, saying she was willing to testify against him in court. Cromwell had previously ignored her pleas, finding it expedient to take Hungerford's side. Subsequently, however, Hungerford found himself charged with exercising the 'abominable and detestable vice and synne' of buggery with his servants; William Maister and Thomas Smyth (his sons-in-law); and others at his house in Heytesbury, Wiltshire, and at 'divers other places within the same county'. Hungerford also stood accused of having sexual relations with his own daughter, and practising witchcraft, 'being seduced and led by the Devil, willing and desiring by all his wicked wit and power the mortal death and utter destruction of Your most royal person'. This consisted of attempting to predict how long the king had to live, with the help of Mother Roche, a notorious witch.

Another charge of treason stated that Hungerford had taken in a young priest and employed him as his chaplain. As the priest, William Byrde (a relative of the composer of the same name), was an outspoken critic of King Henry, Hungerford was also guilty of treason. So, although the church registers kept by the Grey Friars record that Hungerford was beheaded for 'bockery', the real cause was treason.

Hungerford was executed on Tower Hill, and he did not die with dignity. According to Holinshed, at the time of his death, 'he seemed so unquiet, that many judged him rather in a frenzy than otherwise'. As for Elizabeth, once her husband had been executed, she married Sir Robert Throckmorton, 'with whom she spent many years of presumably happy life, and by whom she became the mother of several children'.[19]

Executed alongside Hungerford was the original instigator of the Buggery Statute, the very man who had led the plot against Anne Boleyn. Thomas Cromwell himself had fallen out of favour with the king, following the latter's disastrous marriage to Anne of Cleves, and he now fell victim to the volatile monarch's terrifying destructive rage.

Not every charge of buggery resulted in execution. Nicholas Udall (1504–56), a cleric and poet who had written celebratory verse on Anne Boleyn's entry into London as a newly crowned queen, was also a Latin teacher at Eton College. By 1534, Udall had risen to the position of headmaster. But in March 1541, less than a year after Hungerford's execution, Udall was accused of physical and sexual abuse and admitted buggery with two of his pupils. Udall was lucky to escape execution – thanks to the intervention of the Earl of Southampton. Because he had not committed treason, Udall's sentence was commuted to imprisonment, and he was free within a year, but with his career in ruins. Who would employ a master who had sexually abused his pupils? However, after a period of rehabilitation which saw Udall as vicar of Braintree and vicar of Calborne, Isle of Wight, he returned to teaching, and ended his career as headmaster of Westminster School in 1555.[20]

The Buggery Statute was repealed by Queen Mary during her brief reign of 1553–8. As a Roman Catholic, Mary demonstrated tolerance towards sexual peccadilloes such as homosexuality and prostitution, but more than made up for this apparent leniency with her fanatical religious persecution.

When Elizabeth I took the throne, she renewed the law against buggery on the grounds that 'divers ill-disposed Persone have been the more bold to commit this most horrible detestable vice to the High Displeasure of Almightie God'. One suspects, however, that Elizabeth, like her father, was using the Buggery Statute as a political measure, rather than a method of persecuting homosexual men. After all, the atmosphere at court was one of high camp, as the bewigged, bejewelled, enamelled Elizabeth peacocked about like a drag queen, surrounded by her coterie of mincing ministers. These included such notable homosexuals as Sir Francis Bacon and Henry Wriothesley, Earl of Southampton. The latter was Shakespeare's most famous patron, dedicatee of 'Venus and Adonis' and 'The Rape of Lucretia' and possibly the mysterious male lover referred to in the *Sonnets*.

Elizabeth presided over one of the most magnificent outpourings of poetry and drama ever witnessed, in England or elsewhere, a considerable amount of which was composed by homosexual men. Much of Elizabethan literature is blatantly homoerotic, whether it be the passionate sonnets addressed by Shakespeare to the enigmatic Mr W H or the sex comedies with their innuendo-laden titles such as *As You Like It*, *All's Well That Ends Well* and even *A Midsummer Night's Dream*. Add to this titillating mix the fact that boys performed the role of girls dressed as boys and you have a plethora of transsexual teasing. No wonder the Puritans closed the theatres down.

Poets such as Richard Barnfield and William Drummond published manifestly erotic odes to Arcadian shepherd boys in the classical tradition, while Christopher Marlowe's famous invitation to 'come live with me and be my love' was addressed to one of London's 'golden lads', Lord Hunsdon, a favourite cousin of the queen, who was notorious for keeping a male brothel, described as a 'bawdy house of beasts', in Hoxton.[21]

This climate of happy tolerance existed in an era when there was no formal definition of male homosexuality, or a gay scene as it is understood today. Instead, behaviour which we would now categorize as homosexual was accepted as part of the spectrum of male sexuality, if it fell within certain socially acceptable boundaries. No shame attached to the young man about town who stepped out with his plump mistress on one arm and his 'Ganymed', or boyfriend, on the other.

Derived from the classical Greek tradition, it was permitted for a young man to have a pederastic relationship with an older mentor, which would then be discarded on marriage. George Villiers, for instance, was referred to by James I as 'my sweetheart' and shared James's bed, although he was twenty-five years younger than the king. Francis Bacon (1561–1626) was a good example of an establishment homosexual, celebrated for his intellectual and artistic achievements and tolerated because of his privileged status. Even when his political career ended in disgrace, he spent only a few days in the Tower of London before re-inventing himself as a popular scientist and writer.

A fascinating and witty man, Bacon had 'a delicate, lively, hazel eye, like the eye of a viper'[22] and was excellent company. Despite being engaged to a young widow, Elizabeth Hatton, who called off the marriage, and later marrying Alice Barnham, a girl of fourteen, Bacon was 'a Pederast'. According to John Aubrey, he was surrounded by his 'Ganymeds', who took bribes.

Bacon escaped censure in England, unlike his older brother, Anthony, who faced prison in France for buggery, after it emerged that he kept a houseful of young boys, one of whom penetrated another so forcefully that the victim screamed in pain. Anthony Bacon was lucky to escape with his life, as execution for sodomy was common across the Channel. An engraving by the Flemish artist Franz Hogenberg (1540–90) shows the execution of a group of Franciscan monks for 'sodomitical godlessness' in the town square at Bruges in 1578, and the same engraving comes with the inscription that three other friars had been burned for the same crime.

Prosecution for male rape in England was rare; the most notable instance was that of Humphrey Stafford, executed for this offence in 1608. Stafford's trial and subsequent execution were sensational, attracting 'a great throng and mass of people'. It will never be known whether Stafford was the unfortunate victim of a blackmailing scheme gone wrong, or a rapist, but his case caused a stir largely because it was so unusual. There are just two sources for this case; it was cited by Sir Edward Coke (1552–1634), the noted jurist, and became the subject of an anonymous pamphlet which circulated soon after Stafford's execution.[23]

The two accounts differ wildly. Coke's version rings with moral indignation and has the weight of Church and state behind it: 'that Humphrey Stafford, Knight, a known *paederastes* (lover of boys) on 12 May 1606 in the parish of St Andrew, High Holborn, led astray by the instigation of the devil, did with force and with arms assault a certain R B a lad of about 16 years of age and at that time he did wickedly and in a manner diabolical, felonious and contrary to nature have sexual relations with R B and at the same time had sex with R and did perpetrate with R that detestable and abominable sin of sodomy'.[24]

The pamphleteer goes for a more factual approach, noting that Stafford was charged with raping two youths at once, which must have been difficult particularly as Stafford's defence was inebriation. But the pamphlet provides more information about the boys themselves, naming them as Richard Robinson and Nicholas Crosse, aged seventeen and between thirteen and fourteen years respectively. According to the pamphlet, their parents complained to the law because the boys' injuries were so severe that they 'were forced to use the help of a surgeon for their care', in other words needed to have their anuses sewn up. The parents would have been keen to claim that the boys had suffered injury, as otherwise they would have faced the death penalty for buggery themselves.

Once again, one is left wondering what really happened. In the absence of witnesses, one can speculate that if Stafford was as drunk as he claimed, how did he manage to control two fit and able young men, let alone assault them? Stafford maintained his innocence and argued that 'if he had offended, it was in wine' and that he had been too drunk to penetrate either boy: 'I acknowledge that I have deserved death, but yet I could not perform mine intention,' he claimed. His real crime, if anything, was making the boys drunk. It will never be known whether Stafford was a harmless homosexual who fell out with a pair of rent boys, or a dangerous rapist. Whatever the truth, his defence did not serve Stafford well. He was hanged in front of a huge crowd in June 1608. His death also marks a period when public attitudes towards sexual morality were changing, and punishment becoming harsher.

Female homosexual activity remained almost invisible at this time, at court and in the street. Although the modern reader will detect lesbian connotations in plays such as *As You Like It* and *Twelfth Night*, where young women fall in love with other girls, these episodes of gender confusion are always resolved in the last act, when it transpires that these 'girls' are actually boys in disguise and the heroines are revealed as reassuringly heterosexual.

A classical precedent for the love between women certainly existed in the poems of Sappho, the Lesbian writer whose native Greek island, Lesbos, gives this form of sexuality its name. Sappho's poetry was translated by Renaissance scholars and inspired French poets such as Pierre de Ronsard (1524–85) and Pontus de Tyard (1522–1605), author of the 1573 'Elegy for One Woman Enamoured with Another'.[25] Sappho was also introduced to an English audience through Turbeyville's translations of Ovid, although in some accounts her biography was tweaked to appease male sensibilities. Although the poet was originally believed to have committed suicide on account of a female lover, the Renaissance chose to portray her as a woman finally driven over the edge, in Sappho's case the edge of a cliff, for love of a young boy, Phaon. However, the poet John Donne, during his early, erotic phase, gives Sappho her due in the following lines. It is tempting to dismiss 'Sappho to Philaenis' as conventional girl-on-girl action pandering to the voyeuristic appetites of heterosexual men, but nevertheless Donne effectively conveys the power of same-sex desire:

> Thy body is a natural Paradise
> In whose self, unmanured, all pleasure lies,
> Nor needs perfection; why shouldst thou then
> Admit the tillage of a harsh rough man?
> Men leave behind them that which their sin shows,
> And are as thieves traced, which rob when it snows.[26]

'Sappho' then proceeds to tell her lover that they are so alike that making love to her is like looking in a mirror:

> And oh, no more, the likeness being such
> Why should they not alike in all parts touch?
> Likeness begats such strange self flattery
> That touching my self all seems done to thee
> My self I embrace and my own hands I kiss
> And amorously thank my self for this.[27]

Beyond the world of the court and neoclassical poetry, the nearest to anything approaching a recognizable lesbian role model is Mary Frith, or the 'Roaring Girl', immortalized in the 1611 play of the same name by Middleton and Dekker. ('Roaring' in this context meant a well-born but uncouth person, similar to today's 'Hooray Henrys'.) Mary was a boisterous ladette who dressed like a man,

Mary Frith, aka Moll Cutpurse, 1589–1663,
a notorious thief who dressed as a man.

carried a weapon and embarked on a career as a petty criminal in direct competition with her male counterparts. This gloriously swashbuckling dyke was fêted in a number of broadsheets and dramas, turning the tables on the men and on one occasion even 'getting the girl' by marrying the female lead, who does not raise any objections when she discovers Mary's true identity. Mary Frith was fortunate to be so celebrated; other cases of women caught cross-dressing resulted in a whipping or a spell in Bridewell, the assumption being that they were whores.

Back at court, heterosexual sex flourished, behind closed doors. Whether Queen Elizabeth I enjoyed the benefits of sex, recreational or otherwise, will remain one of the great mysteries, but Elizabeth did take the precaution of branding herself as 'The Virgin Queen', an inspired piece of spin. Elizabeth was a political survivor, driven to extreme self-preservation following the fate of her mother, Anne Boleyn, and the constant reminder of mortality in the form of other noblewomen either murdered or killed by childbirth. Elizabeth's actual virginity must be a matter for conjecture. Henry IV of France joked that there were three things that nobody believed: that Archduke Albert was a good general; that he, Henry, was a good Catholic; and that the Queen of England was a virgin. Elizabeth certainly experienced a series of passionate crushes on courtiers such as Dudley, Earl of Leicester, and Robert Devereux, 2nd Earl of Essex. How close these encounters came to consummation cannot be determined, but the fact remains that Elizabeth always slept alone.

Queen Elizabeth's celibacy did not extend to the rest of her circle. While every man at court had to profess adulation for Elizabeth (or face the consequences), her admirers enjoyed tumultuous, indiscreet affairs. One such was Sir Walter Raleigh, whose company Elizabeth enjoyed because he was graceful and lively. As Aubrey tells us, 'he was no Slug, without doubt he had a wonderful waking spirit'. Raleigh was popular with the ladies, and 'he loved a wench well'.[28]

On one occasion, '[Raleigh] got one of the Maids of Honour up against a tree in a wood. This was his first Lady' – as opposed to commoners, presumably. Initially, the young woman had reservations, and wished to preserve her honour. 'Sweet Sir Walter,' she exclaimed, 'what do you ask of me? Nay, sweet Sir Walter! Sweet Sir Walter!' But Raleigh proved a skilful seducer, and 'as the danger and the pleasure at the same time grew higher, she cried, in the ecstasy, "Swisser Swatter, Swisser Swatter!"'[29]

Mary Herbert, Countess of Pembroke (1561–1621), came perilously close to infringing the Buggery Statute with her particular fetish. This noblewoman, a 'beautiful Ladie with a pretty sharpe-ovall face' whose 'haire was of a reddish yellowe', was very salacious. Her favourite activity took place during the springtime of the year: 'when the Stallions were to leap the Mares, they were to be brought before such a part of the house, where she had a *vidette* (a hole to peepe out at) to looke on them and please herself with their Sport; and then she would act the like sport herself with *her* stallions'.[30] There were also rumours that Mary had an incestuous affair with her brother, Sir Philip Sidney. 'There was so great love between him and his faire sister that I have heard old Gentlemen say that they lay together, and it was thought the first Philip Earle of Pembroke was begot by him, but he inherited not the wit of either brother or sister.'[31]

Mary Herbert is a fine example of the type which Alan Haynes has described as 'the privileged wanton' in his fascinating study, *Sex in Elizabethan England*. Mary's independent wealth and raft of supporters at court rendered her impervious to criticism. Although even this degree of freedom had its limits, as can be seen from the life of Venetia Stanley, who arrived at court at a slightly later date, during the reign of James I.

Venetia Stanley (1600–35), a 'most beautiful and desireable Creature' according to Aubrey, was a young beauty from Oxfordshire with a sweet face, brown hair and, most importantly, a strong constitution, an essential requirement for surviving life at court. When she arrived in London, Venetia caught the eye of the

Earl of Dorset and they had at least one child together, for which he settled an annuity of £500 on her. Venetia soon developed something of a reputation, but this did not deter Sir Kenelm Digby, who married her secretly in the spring of 1625, against the advice of his mother, who insisted you could not make an honest woman out of a whore.

But, to all intents and purposes, the marriage was a happy one. Kenelm celebrated his wife's beauty by commissioning portraits from Van Dyke and his contemporaries and having her face, hands and feet cast in plaster. Ben Jonson immortalized Venetia in verse, 'sitting, and ready to be drawne . . . in Tiffany, silks, and lawne'. In return, Venetia provided Kenelm with three children and appeared to be a reformed character, even restraining herself when they dined with her old lover, the Earl of Dorset, who would stare at her passionately across the table but manage to restrict himself to kissing her hand. Aubrey's own cousin Elizabeth stated that Venetia had redeemed herself by her strict living.

And then, at thirty-five years of age, Venetia was found dead in bed. Some people suspected she had been poisoned. 'When her head was opened,' Aubrey tells us, 'there was found but little braine', a condition which Kenelm put down to Venetia drinking 'viper-wine', which he believed would preserve her beauty. This is when the rumours started. Although Venetia might quite legitimately have been taking viper wine, a popular restorative made from adders and recommended for a range of ailments including hair loss, Venetia's friends were convinced that Kenelm had murdered her with this substance, because he was 'a viper husband who was jealous of her that she would steale a leape' (have extramarital sex).

There is a sad little postscript to this story. Around 1667, Aubrey was walking through Newgate Street when he saw the bust from Venetia's tomb for sale on a second-hand stall. It was in a wretched condition, the gilt ravaged by the flames of the Great Fire a year previously. Aubrey commented on the sight to his companion, but they never saw it again. Like Venetia, the bust suffered an ignoble fate. 'They melted it downe,' Aubrey noted, sadly. 'How these curiosities would be quite forgot, did not such idle fellowes as I am putte them downe.'[32] A sad end to the life of a beautiful and sophisticated court lady.

But what of the world beyond the court? For a taste of this, let us venture out into the streets of London.

4

THE SUBURBS OF SIN

'A Cunny is the deerest Peice of Flesh in the World!'

During the reign of the Tudors, London was the fastest-growing city in the world. By 1600, it had become the world's greatest metropolis, establishing its lead in overseas and domestic trade and setting itself up as the economic centre of Western Europe. Writers professed themselves awestruck by its glory: 'London is a place both for the beautie of buyldinge, infinite riches, varietie of all things, that excelleth all the Cities in the world: insomuch that it maye be called the Store-house and Marte of all *Europe*,' declared John Lyly;[1] while Daniel Lupton marvelled that London is 'the great Bee-hive of Christendom' and praised the Thames, which, with its swans and its bobbing vessels, was 'the glory and wealth of the City, the high way to the Sea, the bringer in of wealth and Strangers'.[2] This was the 'Sweet Thames!' which Edmund Spenser implored to 'run softly, till I end my song'.

But London had a less glamorous side. Orazio Busino, an Italian ambassador, observed that London was the filthiest city in the world:

'Its Italian name, *Londra*, should be changed into *Lorda*, or filthy, which would be well merited by the black, offensive mud which is peculiar to its streets, and furnishes the mob with a formidable missile whenever anything occurs to call forth their disapprobation.'[3]

This was a London of two halves, the affluent and the abject. In the most prosperous areas, streets had been widened and roads paved with cobbles; water was being piped into the city from an arch under Old London Bridge, courtesy of the Dutch engineer Pieter Mauritz, who had persuaded the City Corporation to install his water engines so that thousands of households had access to fresh water. The population had expanded and its citizens now numbered over 200,000; the city's boundaries spread north, west and south, while south-east London became home to thousands of Dutch and European Protestants seeking asylum from Roman Catholic persecution. These immigrants brought with them trades and skills, and a strict work ethic.

This was the London that so delighted a German traveller around 1602 that he commented that 'England is a paradise for women, a prison for servants, and a hell for horses'[4] where 'the females have great liberty and are almost like masters, whilst the poor horses are worked very hard'.[5] Another visitor, the Swiss physician Thomas Platter, was impressed with the *joie de vivre* of Englishwomen, and their habit of frequenting London's many taverns in an Elizabethan equivalent of a girls' night out: 'they count it a great honour to be taken there and given wine with sugar to drink; and if one woman is invited, then she will bring three or four other women along, and they gaily toast each other'.[6]

Englishwomen were considered particularly desirable, with foreign commentators remarking upon their beauty and easy manner, and their habit of greeting guests with kisses on all occasions. Others were impressed by the way English girls dressed, in tight-fitting gowns with deep cleavages, 'laying out their naked breasts after a whorish manner to be seene and touched', some even

An Elizabethan woodcut showing the interior of a whorehouse.

displaying their nipples, which were tipped with rouge for the purpose.[7] The women of London had a reputation for disrepute; just as in certain holiday destinations today, English girls are regarded as being 'up for it', so the girls of Tudor London were notorious creatures of appetite, 'more hotte than goates' and 'more desirous of carnall luste thane man'.[8]

This is the London of 'Merrie England', where buxom wenches raised a frothing tankard to their gallants, and jolly whores in the tradition of Shakespeare's Doll Tearsheet and Mistress Quickly happily plied their trade. Southwark and the Bankside were still the dominant areas for the sex trade, but by this period there were plenty of others, named in the literature of the time. Henry Savile refers to: 'Milford Lane, near to St Clement's Steeple, [where] lived a nymph, kind to all Christian people', while a ballad provides a useful guide to other areas of London:

> In Whitecross Street and Golden Lane
> Do strapping lasses dwell,

> And do there do in every street
> 'Twixt that and Clerkenwell.
> At Cowcross and at Smithfield
> I have much pleasure found,
> Where wenches like to fairies
> Did often trace the ground.[9]

Lying alongside this version of London was another London, a shadowy parallel universe of narrow, badly paved lanes, darkened by overhanging houses, and rendered insanitary by the citizens' tendency to fling their garbage, from cabbage leaves and chicken carcasses to the contents of their chamber-pots, straight out into the street. This was the London of 'small chambers, cottages and lodgings for sturdy beggars, harlots, idle and unthrifty persons, whereby beggary, vagabondcy, unthriftyness, theft, pox, pestilence, infections, diseases and infirmities do ensue and daily grow to the defacing of the beauty of the said city'.[10]

The population had been swollen by a vast army of beggars consisting of disenfranchised peasants. In an early form of the enclosures, entire villages disappeared as wealthy landowners fenced off their estates and kicked out the locals, meaning that the peasantry no longer had common land upon which to graze their animals and raise crops. Robbed of their livelihood, and in many cases their homes, these 'vagabonds' descended on London desperate for work, drawn, as ever, by the promise of the bright lights and the good life. According to Sir William Periam (1534–1604) there were around 30,000 'idle persons and masterless men' in the city, 'the very scum of England, and the stink of iniquity'.[11]

While some would have found employment as unskilled labourers, working on the docks or as porters, carrying goods about the city, many ended their days as vagrants. In 1587, one citizen observed that the streets of London 'swarm with beggars, that no man can stand or stay in any church or street, but presently ten or twelve beggars come breathing in his face, many of them having the plague sores and other contagious diseases running on them, wandering from man to man to seek relief'.[12]

But not all these vagabonds were male. Young women, unwanted at home where they were a drain on their poverty-stricken parents, streamed into the capital in their hundreds every day, on carts, in boats, most commonly on foot, all in search of a fresh beginning and a new life. Some were fortunate enough to find jobs as servants, but many gravitated to the one profession where they could be certain to find employment: prostitution. Just as it led the world in every other form of commerce, London dominated the sex trade, and there was an insatiable demand for new blood.

Imagine the fate of one such new arrival. Let us call her Kate, a fresh-faced country girl. Growing up on a farm, surrounded by animals, sharing a one-roomed cottage where she has frequently overheard her parents having sex, Kate is scarcely naive. But she is shortly to be appalled by the harsh realities of the sex trade. Unable to find work as a lady's maid, starving and footsore, she has been enticed by an ageing bawd into what appears to be an inn, with an offer of work in return for a roof over her head.

At first glance, this 'inn' seems reassuringly familiar, with a gateway leading into a stable yard, where horses can be fed and watered. The entrance, on the ground floor, leads to a reception area, attached to a dining room, with the kitchens at the rear. Downstairs, the rooms are full of men, gambling or drinking with flirtatious, giggling young women. Upstairs, she finds a bedroom overlooking the stable yard (and the dunghill). The floors are strewn with rushes and infested with fleas and other vermin but the room is pleasantly decorated, with a comfortable bed, pictures on the wall and little bottles of potions and powders. It is only once Kate flicks through the books and glimpses the illustrations that she realizes where she is. These amorous pamphlets are here to revive the jaded appetites of her clients. Kate is in a brothel.

To be honest, conditions here at the 'trugging-house' are better than those of the tiny cottage she left behind. As well as a clean white smock, she sees a 'groaning chair' or commode, and two piss-pots, his and hers. She will learn that her task is to hold the pot for her client to urinate into, in the belief that this served as a protection against gonorrhoea or 'the clap'. She will then use the other one, as graphically described by one ex-whore, urinating 'till I made it whurra and roar like the Tyde at London Bridge to endangering the breaking of my very Twatling-strings with straining backwards for I know no better way or remedy more safe than pissing presently to prevent the French Pox, Gonnorhea, the perilous infir-mity of Burning or getting with Childe which is the approved Maxim amongst Venetian Curtizans'.[13]

Pressed into service in this trugging-house, Kate learns that everyday life mirrors the hierarchy of a more conventional middle-class household. At the head of the house is the madam, or 'pandarelle', who supervises the 'apple squires', or male employees, whilst the whores are at the bottom of the food chain, even referring to their own genitals as 'the commodity', as this is what they are trading.[14]

After the enterprising bawd has auctioned off Kate's virginity to the highest bidder, and Kate has been initiated into the sex trade, she is granted clothes and victuals in exchange for a gruelling work-load satisfying the lusts of London's men. The work is harder because she is expected to be available day and night, entertaining all companions, sitting or standing at the door in her bright taffeta dress to entice the clients in, refusing nobody, drunk or sober, dis-eased or vile.[15]

Kate runs the constant risk of sexual violence, and has to pander to every requirement, from the lusty young lad to the ageing *roué* with whom she must be particularly tactful, offering aphrodisiacs such as asparagus, coriander seeds steeped in white wine, saffron boiled in red wine, and lettuce, the Viagra of its day.[16] If this is not enough to stir the ageing member, Kate must resort to one of the popular male fetishes, very likely flagellation, as in this epigram by the satirist Sir John Davies:

When Francus comes to solace with his whore
He sends for rods and strips himself stark naked
For his lust sleeps, and will not rise before,
By whipping of the wench it is awakened.
I envie him not, but wish I had the power,
To make myself his wench but one half hour.[17]

In addition to all this, Kate is expected to be polite, friendly, to keep herself 'free from all vicious diseases and all ill-smells from breath or under the arms or elsewhere'.[18] Her bed must be clean and so must she in her 'Holland's Smocke' or fine linen night-gown. Any spare time the poor young woman has left is to be spent leafing through volumes of pornography to brush up her technique; illiterate as she is, she can still look at the pictures. If she chooses to leave, it will be with nothing but her smock, but there is little incentive to do so.

After a short period, the irregular hours, the heavy drinking, the need to be constantly obliging to large numbers of clients will take its toll on her mental and physical health. Some girls find a way out: they are fortunate enough to meet a rich protector or marry a forgiving man who understands why they were driven into the trade in the first place.

The more enterprising girls embark upon a career as bawds or madams themselves, but most sink into menial work when they lose their charms, or become broken-down wretches scraping a living in Gropecunt Lane. This is, if they do not end up in Bridewell prison or the madhouse of Bedlam or die prematurely through suicide or murder. And yet, as will be revealed in the remainder of this history, generation after generation of young Kates flock to London, searching for romance and adventure, and there is never any shortage of customers.

Many contemporary writers, such as Dekker, Middleton and Greene, frequented the stews, and wrote about them, providing us with a rich seam of anecdotes about Elizabethan low life, whilst these dens of iniquity were also a constant source of inspiration for Ben Jonson, Christopher Marlowe and one author who rejoiced in the name of Shakerley Marmion. The most famous dramatist of all, William Shakespeare, lived close to the White Boar, one of the most notorious Bankside brothels, overhearing many phrases and scenarios which provided a rich source of material for his plays. These writers also demonstrated some sympathy for the whores, seeing in these women's lives a parallel with their own precarious efforts to live by the pen, embracing the life of near-vagabonds despite their elevated birth and university education, throwing in their lot with the strolling players, the tumblers and the minstrels who performed in taverns and the yards of inns.

John Marston, in particular, favoured an honest whore: in *The Dutch Courtesan* (1605), he claimed that if you pay your women regularly, 'they shall stick by you as long as you live. They are no ungrateful persons; they will give you quid for quo.'[19] Unable to provide the financial stability or regular hours required by a traditional wife, these men found sympathetic partners among the prostitutes, and there was an inexorable link between the theatre and the oldest profession, not least geographical.

The great theatres, the Globe Playhouse, the Swan, the Hope and the Rose, were located on Bankside, adjacent to the famous brothels such as the Cardinal's Cap, making Bankside the Elizabethan equivalent of Soho. The influential actor-managers all owned brothels as well as theatres. Take Edward Alleyn, manager of the Rose Theatre. An actor who also flourished as a property speculator, he began his career running a bear garden at Bankside and ended his days as the founder of Dulwich College, the public school. Alleyn's own wife, Joan Woodward, was 'carted' (driven around London and publicly humiliated) for prostitution in 1593, probably because she had inherited a number of brothels from her father, Philip Henslowe, and had failed to close them during an outbreak of the plague.

Enjoyment of the theatre was often the precursor to another form of entertainment, as many of the most popular plays were unabashedly bawdy. Once one's appetite had been whetted by the spectacles on show, repairing to the nearest brothel was an inevitable consequence. Playgoers could stroll out of the Globe and into Maiden Lane (an ironic name, clearly, as maidens were in short supply there) or take one's chances across the road in Rose Alley. Far from being an innocuous botanical reference, 'rose' was a euphemism for a harlot: going to 'pluck a rose' meant visiting a prostitute.[20]

For those who sought their entertainment alfresco, sexual release was also available in the shady streets nearby, such as Horse Shoe Alley, Unicorn Alley and Bear Gardens Alley, or in the appropriately named 'pleasure gardens' which sprang up around the theatres. The poet Everard Guilpin tells us of one citizen who, 'coming from the Curtain' (a London theatre which opened in 1576), 'sneaketh in to some odd garden, noted house of sin'.

According to the puritanical Stephen Gosson, writing in 1579, the Curtain was little more than a warm-up for the brothel and served as a general market of bawdry. Whores cruised the crowded auditorium as the plays unfolded, making it clear that they were available, often without saying a word. 'Not that any filthiness in deed is committed within the compass of that ground, as was done in Rome, but that every wanton and his paramour, every man and his mistress, every John and his Joan, every knave and his queen, are there first acquainted and cheapen [bargain for] the merchandize in that place, which they pay for elsewhere as they can agree.'[21]

The pleasure gardens were particularly popular with the new contingent of amateurs who had entered the scene, a group who proved very unpopular with the seasoned prostitutes. According to a balladeer of the time:

> The stews in England bore a beastly sway
> Till the eight Henry banished them away.
> And since the common whores were quite put down
> A damned crew of private whores are grown.[22]

These women had a variety of motives, ranging from the housewife 'that, by selling her desires, buys herself bread and clothes'[23] to the highly sexed wives and widows offering their favours in exchange for the excitement of tasting forbidden fruit.[24] In Ben Jonson's play *Bartholomew Fair* the prostitute Punk Alice berates Judge Overdo's wife for just such behaviour: 'A mischief on you, they are such as you that undo us and take our trade from us, with your tuft-taffeta haunches! The poor common whores can ha' no traffic for the privy rich ones; your caps and hoods of velvet call away our customers, and lick the fat from us.'[25]

Boys, too, were drawn into prostitution, then as now. There is little record of organized male brothels, although John Marston accused Lord Hunsdon of running a male brothel in Hoxton. Gigolos were always in demand; opportunistic and charming young men frequented the bath houses where women congregated, picking off available older women, and enjoyed a better quality of life than their female peers, or at least those women at the rough end of the market.

Not only was the sex trade a wretched way of life for most women, but the threat of punishment was ever present, in the form of the 'Clink' prison and other establishments. The 'Clink' prison, administered by the Bishop of Winchester, was conveniently located *underneath* his notorious stews, so that at least the poor girls did not have far to go. We have already learned, in the previous chapter, of the various stocks and pillories which were employed as a means of public humiliation for these unfortunate women.

During the reign of Mary Tudor (1553–8), another form of punishment became popular. 'Small houses' were set up in every ward of London, with one installed on London Bridge. 'Small house' was a deceptively bland euphemism for what can only be described as a method of public torture. Derived from the Near East, the 'small house' originally consisted of a cage where the victim was locked up like an animal, and put on show on the city walls, for all to see. Its first use in the British Isles appears to have been when Edward I

(1239–1307) hung Isobel, Duchess of Fife and Buchan, in a wooden cage on the walls of the City of Berwick, as a punishment for her part in crowning Robert the Bruce King of Scotland. Isobel was incarcerated for four years, a hardship which hastened her early death.

But London's city fathers devised a further refinement, by placing a pillory *inside* the cage. Men, as well as women, were locked in tiny pens, too small to lie down or turn around in, condemned to wallow in their own faeces, while the mob jostled and flung rubbish and insults at them. Many went mad; others suffered a merciful early death.[26]

Before going to the stocks, or the house of correction, prostitutes were publicly humiliated, stripped to the waist and their heads shaved bald, before being carted around London while a jeering crowd threw rotten vegetables and clattered barbers' basins, to create a mocking 'rough music'. Given the high number of prosecutions for prostitution, London's barbers had a profitable sideline hiring out these basins.[27] Particularly unlucky prisoners were tied to the cart's arse and whipped. But this was as nothing compared with Bridewell, which is where their troubles really began.

Bridewell, or the 'Palace of Bridewell' as it was originally known, became a prison during the reign of young Edward VI, and was soon anything but palatial. Located on the banks of the River Thames between what is now Fleet Street and Blackfriars Bridge, Bridewell had been rebuilt by Henry VIII for the reception of the Emperor Charles V. The origin of its name lay in its proximity to the Church of St Bride's. Remaining images show a magnificent red-brick palace in the style of Hampton Court, with imposing turrets and bay windows seventy feet wide, resting in landscaped gardens that sloped down to the river.

Like so many of London's grand houses, Bridewell must have been the perfect home for an embassy. Nevertheless, in 1552, Edward VI agreed to donate Bridewell to the city as a workhouse, in an attempt to abolish London's vagrancy problem by providing accommodation and training. The aim was laudable: orphaned children could be apprenticed to various trades while the sick and infirm were set to making mattresses and bedding. Stubborn and unregenerate low-lifes, meanwhile, would learn blacksmiths' skills in the smithy and grind corn, while women would card wool and spin yarn.[28]

The change of use, from royal palace to beggars' workhouse, meant that structural alterations were necessary. The eighty-foot Long Gallery, with its long windows, was partitioned, to make cells. Workshops were equipped, and all the inevitable trappings of prison life were delivered – the stocks and manacles, a treadmill and a block, upon which women beat out hemp with heavy mallets.[29]

This regime, whilst harsh, was humane by the standards of the time; which is more than can be said for the punishment meted out to prostitutes. The process of 'correction', designed to make the women repent, consisted of repeated whippings. These whippings were a very ceremonial affair, conducted before the board of governors. The hypocrisy, not to mention the connotations of sexual sadism that attended such events, reminds one irresistibly of King Lear's outburst:

> Thou rascal beadle, hold thy bloody hand!
> Why dost thou lash that whore? Strip thine own back;
> Thou hotly lust'st to use her in that kind
> For which thou whip'st her.[30]

Other forms of 'correction' included regular beatings, starvation and gang rape. There were no sentences, as such. Unless someone appeared to bail them out, these women could be detained indefinitely. Bridewell was enough to make a shiver run down a girl's spine, a chilling prospect to any young whore. But so was death by starvation. These women had little choice but to regard Bridewell as an occupational hazard, in the same category as syphilis. 'Bridewell' eventually became the generic term for 'houses of correction' throughout England, and lives on today as police terminology for a custody suite.

Southwark was already famous for its low life, from the functional shacks where whores serviced the Roman garrisons to the medieval stews. But, over the years, Southwark had its high-quality brothels, too, such as the Manor House of Paris Gardens, located on the wonderfully entitled 'Nobs' Island'.

Paris Gardens, referred to in the Domesday Book as 'Widflete', had not always been salubrious. In 1380, it was known as a rubbish dump, where butchers tipped their offal. Part of the land was given over to kennels for the Lord Mayor's dogs and the whole area stank, particularly in the summer. But it was ripe for investment. In 1542, William Baseley, the King's Bailiff of Southwark, bought the lease for the Manor House of Paris Gardens and turned it into a casino, with 'cardes and dyze and tabells'. There was already a bowling green outside, and it was from this period that the Manor House began to acquire an infamous reputation.

Elizabeth I granted the Manor to her cousin, Henry Carey, Lord Hunsdon, the 'golden lad' who so appealed to Christopher Marlowe. In turn, Hunsdon rented it out to pimps and madams. But these were no ordinary stews: this was a high-class club, catering for the nobility, the gentry, and the emerging affluent middle class, offering sex, gambling, wine and food.

At this period, the legendary 'Long Meg' of Westminster, an Amazonian Lancashire lass cast in the same mould as the 'Roaring Girl' Mary Frith, stepped in and ran the Manor House as a brothel. The house then changed hands several times until it was acquired by one Donna Britannica Hollandia, whose typically preposterous *nom de guerre* testified to the fact that she was an experienced madam.

Donna Hollandia had impeccable credentials: she had already worked the 'Italian quarter' in Cripplegate, as a whore, then promoted herself to the role of madam at St Andrews-by-the-Wardrobe. Arrested and sent to Newgate gaol, she soon escaped thanks to her contacts at court. A few words threatening to expose the sex secrets of the royals was enough to ensure Donna was smuggled out of prison, and once she had paid off the judiciary, she started to look around for pastures new, free from the restrictions of the city fathers. At length, Donna was directed to the Manor House of Paris Gardens, where she would find 'a place fit for her purpose being wonderous commodiously planted for all accomodations [*sic*]: it was oute of the cite onlye divided by a delicate river' and boasting 'an abundance of naturall and artificiall entrenchements'.[31]

The Manor House itself was securely fortified. Not only was there a gatehouse and a deep moat, but the surrounding pastureland had an elaborate system of ditches which filled with water according to the ebb and flow of the Thames. 'Ere any foe could approache it, hee must march more than a musket shotte on a narrow banke, between two dangerous ditches', according to one contemporary. And that foe would then have to contend with 'a drawbridge and sundry pallysadoes' (earthworks, from the Portuguese '*paliçadas*').[32] The gardens were elaborately landscaped, with pleasant walks and shrubberies and fine views across the river. A contemporary sketch depicts the front door of the Manor House secured by a guard armed with a musket, while the ladies of the house amuse themselves in the garden. Donna wasted no time. This suburban paradise was the ideal location for a discreet, high-class gentlemen's club, with the judiciary persuaded to turn a blind eye in return for a fresh young whore.

Donna soon became one of the most famous madams in London, with a host of celebrity patrons, including King James I and George Villiers. Regardless of their alleged homosexual relationship, they loved to disport themselves among the whores. James was a notorious libertine who enjoyed all the pleasures of the Bankside from theatres and horse-racing (which he is credited with inventing) to whores, and brothels such as Paris Gardens flourished during his reign. Luxuriously furnished and offering every comfort known to man, it was also staffed by girls who were experts in squeezing every penny out of their clients. But those men got what they paid for: they left exhausted and satisfied, well fed and entertained. Donna offered nothing if not value for money. A small woman but with a strong character, she ran her house with great efficiency, backed up by draconian security.

As with any private club, membership was stringently enforced. Potential punters had to present their credentials at the gatehouse, then face further questioning before being escorted across the drawbridge to the Manor. Donna greeted each client personally, to ask him his requirements and size him up. The safety of her girls was paramount: nobody was allowed to shout at or ill-treat them. Any wild or unruly behaviour meant instant and permanent expulsion, whatever the rank and station.

By the same token, Donna did not allow anyone in without money. There was no credit, no matter how famous the client. This policy ensured that the Manor House remained exclusive, as only the most affluent could afford to enter. As the years went by, so the coffers in Donna's basement filled up with gold. She had started out with just four girls, hand-picked for their special talents and much in demand: 'Beta Brestonia', a fiery beauty, 'impudent and insolent'; tiny Eliza Caunce, who was regarded as a nymphomaniac; Longa Maria, a gentle beauty with a sympathetic manner; and Maria Pettit, considered to be a real livewire.[33] As Donna's business expanded, so she took on more girls, and decorated the house in an ever more lavish style. Donna hired extra staff, including a doctor to look after the girls, and ensure that they were fresh and clean. The kitchen was run by professional cooks and the food and wine were abundant.

But, as the years passed, Donna's empire began to flounder. She had a high turnover of whores since she ran a strict house and many young women tired of the discipline. Standards started to slip. Lowlifes from the Globe, the Hope and the Swan were admitted. Instead of being a discreet suburban brothel, the Manor House became widely known for drinking and gambling and the subsequent noise which these activities produced. However carefully Donna may have screened her clients in the past, certain nobles enjoyed 'whore-bashing' which led to some bad publicity. In 1630, the pamphleteer Daniel Lupton produced a damning broadsheet in which he lambasted Paris Gardens as more of 'a foule Denne than a Faire Garden', filled with roaring boys, swearing drunks, rotten bawds and cunning cheats.

Donna remained safe while James I was still alive. But Charles I's first Parliament was committed to cracking down on prostitution, leaving her vulnerable to blackmailers and informers. She could no longer rely on bribing the local constabulary to leave her in peace, and rival madams were only too happy to see her brought down. Donna's luck was running out. Eventually, in December 1631, the authorities decided to intervene and dispatched a corporal and a stout band of pikesmen to arrest Donna and her girls. But it was at this point that Donna really showed her true colours. Thirty years as a madam had made her an excellent strategist and she greeted the law with defiance. When they demanded entry, she allowed them as far as the drawbridge, then let it fall down, tipping the soldiers into the stinking moat; as they floundered about in the freezing muddy water, the girls jeered at them and pelted them with missiles, including chamber-pots and their contents, while the Southwark mob, which had gathered to watch the fun, cheered them on. The soldiers attempted to regroup but all efforts to gain entry to the premises were repulsed. Eventually, they limped away, wet and exhausted, bested by a pack of whores.

A second attempt was made, and met with a similar lack of success. This 'beleaguering' of Donna Hollandia's house eventually gave it a new name: it gained immortality as 'Holland's Leaguer', a title which subsequently appears in conveyancing documents.

Eventually, the authorities triumphed, and two individuals bought the lease to the house, which was then scheduled for demolition. No more is known of the fate of Donna Hollandia, but 'Holland's Leaguer' passed into history. Shakerley Marmion's drama of the same name played to packed houses in 1631, the topical theme making it irresistible to London audiences, and Madame Hollandia's achievements were celebrated in a bawdy ballad.

The passing of 'Holland's Leaguer' heralded a dramatic change in London's landscape of sin. The sex trade was about to suffer a brutal backlash at the hands of the Puritans. It was as if Malvolio himself, the humiliated Puritan of Shakespeare's *Twelfth Night*, had appeared to shake his fist at the assembled drunkards, bawds and whores and repeat his terrible prediction: 'I'll have my revenge upon the whole pack of you!'

5

'THE PLAYHOUSE IS THEIR PLACE OF TRAFFICK'

Sex in the Restoration

In order fully to understand the relaxing of sexual morals during the Restoration, we need to put this remarkable period in the context of the fifty, often tumultuous, years which preceded it, years which witnessed a decade of civil war, the beheading of King Charles I and the enforcement of puritanical sex laws under the dictatorship of Oliver Cromwell, the Lord Protector.

To see how this course of events unfolded, let us visit the court of King James, one of the most outrageous courts in English history. James I was an enthusiastic visitor to Holland's Leaguer, as we already know. His regular trips to the Manor House of Paris Gardens reflected just one aspect of his appetite for life and the venal culture of his court, although in his defence it should be remembered that under his rule there was comparative religious tolerance (except in Ireland, where his legacy still proves turbulent today), and the lives of ordinary people were relatively calm and secure.

After a frugal and thankless period as King of Scotland, James arrived at the English court to inherit a wealthier and more organized kingdom. His response to this was to demand a higher level of personal attendance and service from his lords. The courtiers expected plenty of entertainment in return. James's court became 'extravagant and disorderly, frivolous and indecorous, with hard drinking common and immorality winked at'.[1] It was also filthy; one lady complained that she always returned home from court lousy. James himself drank heavily and gambled, and was often to be seen at the Bankside theatres and bear gardens, his arm around George Villiers, his incompetent administrator, best friend and, so rumour had it, lover. As for those with a taste for women, they were spoilt for choice. 'For concubines we need not travel as far as the Turk's Seraglio' wrote Heywood in his *Gynaikeion*. 'And to find such as we call Sweet Hearts, Friends or Good-wenches should we but search any citizen's garden houses and find plenty sufficient.'[2]

Under James's rule, London's sex trade expanded at a phenomenal rate, as the records indicate. Here are accounts of infamous characters such as Emma Robinson, who, in 1608, was described as 'a notorious Common Queane' and who sat outside her front door until midnight entertaining 'lewd persons'; Ellen Allen was fined for being a 'bad woman' and seducing a Dutchman while her maid stole his dagger. One Elizabeth Basse was charged with keeping 'a notorious bawdy house' where murder was likely to be committed. By 1613, the bulging casebooks of the Middlesex Sessions show that prostitution had spread beyond the walls of the city as far as Enfield and Barnet.

Even the Sabbath day was no exception. One Robert Cutler of St Bride's 'had the use of Isabella Sowth's bodie' one Sunday, while Alban Cooke of Hoxton was indicted for buggery with a man under twenty years of age and Richard Walker of Castle Baynard was taken late in the night, 'abusynge himself in an alehowse'.[3] London became so scandalous that even the tolerant James was forced to issue an ordinance on 4 December 1622, 'Touching on Disorderly Houses in Saffron Hill'. Saffron Hill, between Holborn and Clerkenwell, was particularly corrupt, teeming with 'divers immodest lascivious and shameless women' who sat outside their houses alluring and calling to passers-by, whom they would entertain in return for base and filthy lucre.

James also included a clause 'for the prevention of connivance' designed to prevent beadles being bribed by the prostitutes, but this ordinance made no difference. Despite mass raids, the situation deteriorated further and, in 1624, James was compelled to issue another ordinance. The extent of the red-light district is illustrated by the names of the areas which were raided: Cowcross, Cock's Lane, Smithfield, St John Street Clerkenwell, Norton Folgate (now Bishopsgate), Shoreditch, Wapping, Whitechapel, Petticoat Lane, Charterhouse, Bloomsbury and Ratcliffe Highway. Curiously, there is no mention of the Bankside, or Paris Gardens here: presumably because of the extent of provision for lecherous Londoners without having to go south of the river.[4]

The following year Charles I became king. A man of high moral character, Charles made an attempt to address the issue during his first Parliament as an extract from the journals of the House of Commons on 9 July 1625 illustrates:

Mr Jordan moveth: *That divers places, viz., Clerkenwell, Pickehatche (in Finsbury), Turnmill Street, Golden Lane, Duke Humphreye's at Blackfriars are places of open bawdry.*

Resolved: *To acquaint the Lord Chief Justice with this complaint and to desire him to take some present Order for Reformation of it.*[5]

By 1641, the Long Parliament ruled that prostitution was no longer to be classified as a crime but as a public nuisance, or gross indecency if committed in public. By enforcing Common Law, Parliament abolished a raft of medieval tortures and punishments for prostitution, which was an enlightened move, but times were about to become difficult indeed for London's whores, thanks to the new Member of Parliament for Cambridge, one Oliver Cromwell.

There had been nothing like this since the days of John Ball and Wat Tyler. Southwark was a hotbed of revolutionary fervour, with various sects meeting clandestinely in the inns and taverns. The essential aspect of this conflict was that it was a war of ideas, where taking sides was a matter for one's own conscience. Sir John Oglander reflected: 'thou would'st think it strange if I should tell thee that there was a time in England when brothers killed brothers, cousins cousins, friends their friends, when thou wentest to bed at night thou knewest not whether thou shouldest be murdered before day'.[6]

When the Civil War broke out in late 1642, Southwark supplied thousands of men for the New Model Army and routed Prince Rupert and his Cavaliers when they attempted to enter London. Rupert withdrew to Oxford, never to return. On 30 January 1649, the day that King Charles was executed, life in the city continued as usual; the shops were open and the king had few mourners.[7]

Cromwell's ascent proved disastrous for the sex trade. The Commonwealth's attitude towards 'sin' was decidedly intolerant, as exemplified by William Prynne's observation: 'it hath evermore been the notorious badge of prostituted strumpets and the lewdest Harlots to ramble abroad to plays and to Playhouses wither only branded whores and infamous adulteresses did usually resort'.[8] There was no understanding of the conditions which drove thousands of women into prostitution every year, or condemnation of the men who were their clients. The only concession to the view that prostitution provided a public service was the suggestion of one Dr Chamberlen who proposed to Parliament in 1649 that state-regulated bath houses with registered whores should be opened throughout the country.[9] But this pragmatic solution was overlooked as the Puritans set about the destruction not only of London's brothels but of all other forms of pleasure.

Parliament closed all the theatres and gaming houses and the actors were whipped at the cart's arse. Seven bears were shot dead near the Hope Theatre, and the theatre itself was torn down in 1655. Heavy fines were introduced for swearing. Maypoles were felled on the grounds that they were 'a heathenish vanity' and 'a stynkynge idoll'. Nude statues had their genitals covered with fig-leaves, and anything that profaned the sanctity of the Sabbath day was banned. The stews of Southwark, described as 'church lands', had already been sold off to developers for more than £4000. The whorehouses were being turned into warehouses by a rising afflu-ent middle class, while the alehouses and taverns which had always been a favourite haunt of whores and their clients were frequently raided by the army. An honest whore found it difficult to make a living. The 'doves of Venus' and 'birds of Youth' who had flocked around the watering holes and enjoyed £20 suppers before the Commonwealth were now forced to make do on a diet of cheese and onion. 'The ruination of Whoring was why the London Bawds hated 1649 like an old Cavalier.'[10] One or two brothels remained open, discreetly, such as 'Oxford Kate's' in Bow Street, chiefly because of their powerful and influential clientele.

As for the sexually promiscuous amateurs, they faced the death penalty. In 1650, the Commonwealth made adultery and incest felonies for which (on a second conviction) the penalty was death. To gain some idea of how sexual mores have changed, one has only to look at a conviction from the period: in 1653, a man of eighty-nine was tried and executed for adultery (these days he would be selling his story to the highest bidder). Eventually, even Puritan juries revolted against this draconian legislation, and subsequently refused to convict.[11] For all his efforts to police the morality of his citizens, Cromwell himself was no killjoy: he permitted 'music and frivolity and mixed dancing' at his daughter's wedding in 1657.[12] And far from taking a hair-shirt approach to his own private life, Cromwell had a mistress in the form of Bess Dysart, a Scottish beauty and self-confessed harlot, who survived political intrigue to end her days as Duchess of Lauderdale.

Puritan interference in the lives of ordinary people bred resentment; the populace were force-fed religion until it sickened them. Far from being a wholesome new Commonwealth of God-fearing fundamentalists, the Puritans created a groundswell of popular opposition against state intervention in private morals. When Charles II arrived in London to claim the throne on Tuesday 29 May 1660, the city erupted into one giant party which was to last for the rest of his life. The festivities and prevailing mood of anti-clericalism were such that it was said that if Cain, the first murderer, had returned from the grave and arrived in London, he would have received a hero's welcome. The most obvious manifestation of Swinging London was the erection of a giant maypole in the city. The draconian laws against prostitution and fornication were repealed and the court of Charles II and his entourage became one enormous brothel. There is no better summary of the decadence of court life than the Earl of Rochester's poem 'The Debauchée':

> I rise at eleven, I dine at two
> I get drunk before seven, and the next thing I do
> I send for my Whore, when, for Fear of the Clap
> I come in her Hand and I spew in her Lap.
> Then we Quarrel and scold till I fall fast asleep;
> When the Bitch growing bold, to my Pocket doth creep;
> She slyly then leaves me – and to Revenge my Affront
> At once she bereaves me of money and cunt.
> I storm and I roar and I fall in a Rage,
> And, missing my Whore, I bugger my Page.[13]

Charles II had been reared at the French court and was accustomed to the frivolous entertainment and constant debauchery considered appropriate to his royal birth. As a king, he deserved nothing less. To quote Rochester, Charles II was 'a merry monarch, who never said a foolish thing or ever did a wise one'.[14] To discover just how merry Charles was, we should read more of Rochester's satire, which earned him a temporary ban from court.

> PEACE is his aim: his gentleness is such
> And LOVE he loves, for he loves fucking much.
> Nor are his high desires above his strength,
> His *Sceptre* and his *Prick* are of a length,
> And she may sway the one who plays with t'other
> And make him little wiser than his Brother.
> Poor *Prince*, thy Prick, like thy Buffoon at Court
> Will govern thee because it makes thee Sport.
> 'Tis sure the sauciest Prick that e'er did Swive [fuck]
> The proudest peremptoriest Prick alive.
> Tho' Safety, Law, Religion, Life lay on't
> 'twould break through all to make way to *Cunt*.
> Restless he rolls about from Whore to Whore
> A Merry Monarch, scandalous and poor![15]

Charles was a compulsive womanizer, and his pathological appetite for sex saw him rolling from the most exquisite court lady to the commonest whore. William Chiffinch, the royal pimp, supplied him with a constant stream of girls plucked from the theatres and brothels, while his high-profile mistresses included the aristocratic Barbara Villiers, Duchess of Cleveland, the coy Frances Stewart, the French courtier Louise de Kéroualle, and her famous rival, Nell Gwyn.[16]

On one occasion, Barbara Villiers and the Earl of Rochester tricked Charles into visiting a whorehouse in Hosier Lane, arranging for the king to have his pockets picked while he was enjoying himself with the girls. Rochester departed, leaving Charles to discover that he was penniless. When Charles asked the bawd for credit, she understandably refused. So the king pulled a ring off his finger and told her to send for a jeweller and have it valued. She accepted it reluctantly, but when the jeweller arrived and examined the ring he gasped that there was only one man in England who could afford this ring, and that was the king himself! The jeweller and the bawd fell to their knees, trembling with fear. After all, they could have faced the death penalty for treason. But Charles retained his good humour, and left, although history does not relate what he said to the Earl of Rochester, or Barbara Villiers, when he eventually got home.[17]

Charles's affairs took up as much of his time as his affairs of state. As a result he often received his ministers while holding court with his whores, an arrangement which all parties had no choice but to accept. Charles's example meant that a mistress was the latest must-have; any courtier without arm candy risked ridicule and derision. Once Charles's philosophy was unleashed on the English court there was no vice or sexual peccadillo which was not encouraged. Chastity and virtue were considered to be hypocrisy: every man and every woman had their price.

This lax philosophy soon spread by example to all walks of life, and a climate of tolerance prevailed, as illustrated in this extraordinary anecdote from Samuel Pepys concerning the behaviour of Sir Charles Sedley MP, courtier and wit, who appeared naked on the balcony of 'Oxford Kate's' in broad daylight 'acting all the postures of lust and buggery that could be imagined', and claiming, like a quack doctor, that he could make a potion 'as should make all the cunts in town run after him'. As the crowd beneath swelled to over a thousand, Sedley 'took a glass of wine and washed his prick in it and then drank it off; and then took another and drank the King's health'.[18] While such an outrageous episode from an MP today would lead to instant resignation and questions in the House, Sedley had nothing more to fear than a few weeks' banishment from court, enabling him to sober up in the country in time for his next bender.

Londoners were more than robust enough to tolerate such antics with good humour. The 'City', in our modern understanding of the word, had arrived, in the form of an affluent merchant class to whom the government was forced to turn in times of crisis. This class made its own contribution to London, with gracious new houses filled with beautiful furniture; carpet, not rushes, covered the floor, and beds replaced straw mattresses. This class also required an army of domestic servants to tend it, consisting of women who were eternally at the mercy of their master, their master's sons and the male servants.

Following a hard day's trading, the new City men required relaxation and recreation, which they found at the theatre, revived after the long sleep of the Protectorate. The Theatre Royal Drury Lane and the Duke's Theatre opened, and for the first time, nubile young women replaced boy actors on the stage. With the arrival of actresses, the theatres once again developed a reputation for wanton behaviour, as every aspiring young thespian set out to secure a rich husband or lover to elevate her to the ranks of the aristocracy. 'Actress' became synonymous with 'whore', an inevitable development according to the satirist Tom Browne: ''Tis as hard a matter for a pretty Woman to keep herself honest in a Theatre, as 'tis for an Apothecary to keep his Treacle from the Flies in Hot Weather; for every Libertine in the Audience will be buzzing about her Honey-Pot.'[19]

The theatre auditorium was divided along traditional class lines, as were the girls. In the orchestra stalls sat the fashionable and the aristocratic men, alongside the most upmarket prostitutes. (Conventional married women were discouraged from attending, as both the drama and its location were considered far too disreputable.) The top theatre prostitutes were known as 'vizards' after the black masks they wore. One evening the diarist Samuel Pepys sat next to one, and concluded in his entry for that night that 'She is a whore, I believe, for she is acquainted with every fine fellow and called them by their name, Jack and Tom, and before the end of the play frisked to another place.'[20] The dress circle was home to the professional middle class, with a suitable grade of harlots. The upper circle, or the gods, was for hoi polloi, and the common rub 'n' tug whores also referred to as 'punks' and 'trugs'. Dryden summed up the scene admirably:

> The Playhouse is their Place of Traffick, where
> Nightly they sit to sell their rotten Ware
> Tho' done in Silence and without a Cryer
> Yet he that bids the most is still the Buyer!
> For while he nibbles at her am'rous Trap
> She gets the Mony: he gets the Clap![21]

These theatres were noisy, sensational places with as much action off stage as on: actors were heckled, fist fights broke out, and the audience was uninhibited in its criticism if the play was not to its liking. This all added to the entertainment and a good time was had by all – apart from the playwrights, of course, who were understandably dismayed by such anarchic scenes. 'Some there are,' observed one writer, bitterly,

> . . . who take their first Degrees
> Of Lewdness, in our Middle Galleries:
> The Doughty BULLIES enter Bloody Drunk,
> Invade and grubble one another's PUNK:
> They Caterwaul and make a dismal Rout,
> Call SONS of WHORES, and strike, but ne'er lugg-out . . .[22]

Among the turmoil, the 'orange girls' roamed with their baskets of fruit. The 'china' oranges were sixpence each, the girls a little dearer. They were organized, in a haphazard fashion, by an old bawd called 'Orange Moll', who sent them to trawl the new theatre at Drury Lane. Samuel Pepys had a weakness for orange girls, and one afternoon in January 1667 his actress friend Mrs Knipp introduced him to 'a most pretty woman'. Her name was Nell Gwyn. Nell's story provides one of the happier accounts of a whore's life,

The celebrated Nell Gwyn, mistress of Charles II (1777).

the rags-to-riches tale of an archetypal tart with a heart of gold, the original Pretty Woman.

Nell was born in a brothel in Covent Garden in 1650. Her mother, Eleanor Smith, was a bawd, and her father, Thomas Gwyn, had been a captain in the Cavalier army. Nell's father disappeared early from their lives, and Mrs Smith took to drink. Nell herself may have been a child prostitute; she certainly grew up in 'the life', serving brandy to the customers in her mother's house when still just a little girl. The Theatre Royal was just around the corner in Drury Lane, and by the age of thirteen she was working as an orange girl. Her good looks, charm and witty tongue were quickly spotted by the actors, and by the time she was fifteen, Nell had taken stage roles and her first lover, the actor-manager Charles Hart. Nell was a natural comedienne, and the sex comedies of the Restoration theatre provided the ideal vehicle for her talents. She was invariably cast as the attractive, sex-starved young wife of an impotent old man, romanced by a handsome young lawyer or parson, in productions such as *The City Lady, or Folly Reclaim'd*, *An Evening's Love, or The Mock Astrologer*, *The Husband his Own Cuckold* or *The City Bride*.[23] Samuel Pepys raved over Nell's performance as 'the Mad Girl' in *The Maiden Queen* in March 1667:

> so great performance of a comical part was never, I believe, in the world before as Nell doth this, both as a mad girle and then, most and best of all, when she comes in like a young gallant; and hath the motions and carriage of a spark the most ever I saw any man have. It makes me, I confess, admire her.[24]

Playing a masculine role gave young actresses the ideal opportunity to show off their figures in tight breeches. Since Nell had excellent legs, this proved to be a brilliant career move. King Charles had heard the rumours of her beauty and sex appeal, and soon he ordered her to give a private performance at the palace. After brief liaisons with Lord Buckhurst and his brother, the Earl of Dorset, Nell finally embraced her destiny in the form of the king and was installed as his chief mistress, regardless of the fact that, according to Bishop Burnet, she was 'the indiscreetest and wildest creature that ever was in court'.[25]

Despite this, Nell remained Charles's favourite until his dying day, and was maintained at great expense, receiving over £60,000 from the king. Valued for her high spirits and humour, Nell was 'such a constant diversion to the king, that even a new mistress could not drive her away'. All this despite the fact that she called her lover 'Charles the Third' because she had had two lovers named Charles previously.[26]

Nell even saw off her chief rival, Louise de Kéroualle, who had been created Duchess of Portsmouth by Charles II. On one occasion, when Louise cattily remarked that Nell was dressed richly enough to be a queen, Nell shot back, 'You are entirely right, Madam, and I am whore enough to be a duchess!' The two women eventually became friends, when Louise was ousted by a new love, Hortense Mancin. They met regularly for tea and cards, although Nell was exasperated with Louise's histrionic fits of despair, referring to her as 'the weeping willow'. Nell's wisecracks were legendary. When her coachman got into a fight with another man who had called her a whore, Nell broke up the fracas, saying, 'I *am* a whore. Find something else to fight about!' Nell's most famous remark came about when she was passing through the streets of Oxford one day in her coach and the mob, mistaking her for her rival, the Catholic Louise de Kéroualle, started hooting and shouting at her. Nell put her head out of her window, smiled at the crowd and declared: 'Good people, you are mistaken; I am the *Protestant* whore.'

Nell's relationship with the king lasted until his death, seventeen years after their first encounter, and they had one son, Charles, later created Duke of St Albans. Charles himself was eager to provide for her, entreating his dour brother, James II, 'let not poor Nelly starve'. Despite the fact that James had frequently been the butt of Nell's jokes, he oversaw the provision of a pension of £1500 a year for life, as well as paying off all her debts. She also retained the estates and incomes which Charles had granted her during their relationship, including houses in Pall Mall and Windsor. By the age of fifty, this whore's daughter from the backstreets of Covent Garden was worth £100,000.

Charles II's infatuation with Nell did not make her a favourite with everyone. John Wilmot, Earl of Rochester (1647–80), took against her and characterized her as a Cinderella on the make in a vicious satire. But Rochester, who saw all Charles's mistresses as potential rivals for his affection, offended every one of them, bribing palace officials to dish the dirt on Charles's love life. To her great credit, 'pretty, witty Nell' proved admirably tolerant towards Rochester, who eventually befriended her, taking her side against the dreadful Louise.

Rochester had become the embodiment of Charles II's court, and it is to Rochester that one must return for further insights into this extraordinary period. Tall, elegant and witty, he was wild even by contemporary standards. He graduated from Oxford at the age of fourteen, with a classical education that provided good training for his excoriating satires. Rochester served as a Royalist spy before the Restoration, and proved heroic in the war against the Dutch, when he rowed under heavy fire to deliver orders from the commander of the fleet after the latter was shot dead in his arms, an action which was 'commended by all who saw it'. Rochester's evident physical courage was as great as his wit; but, like many men of action, he missed the excitement of war in the dull days afterwards and compensated for it with a riotous lifestyle, drinking, quarrelling and fighting.[27]

Writing with 'passionate colloquialism',[28] Rochester gives us a vivid picture of London and sex in the 1660s, as the following lines illustrate. It will come as no surprise to the reader that Rochester was an unregenerate bisexual whose play *Sodom, or The Quintessence of Debauchery* (1684) was censored by the government on the grounds of obscenity, primarily because of its homosexual nature. 'There's a sweet, soft page of mine, Does the trick worth forty wenches,' he comments:

> Nor shall our love-fits, Chloris, be forgot,
> When each the well-looked linkboy strove t'enjoy,
> And the best kiss was the deciding lot
> Whether the boy fucked you, or I the boy.[29]

'Link boys', or torch bearers, ostensibly earned a crust by conducting the wealthy about the murky streets of London with flaming torches; an early form of rent boy, these lads frequently subsidized their meagre incomes by selling their sexual favours – and Rochester quite clearly enjoyed their attentions.

Rochester's vivid poem 'A Ramble in St James's Park', meanwhile, shows London in all its seedy glory; the author reflects on the action in this 'all-sin-sheltering grove', from buggeries to rape and incest, as Londoners of all conditions arrive looking for sex. Whores, great ladies, chambermaids, heiresses and drudges trudge towards the park to encounter 'divines, great lords and tailors, prentices, poets, pimps and jailors, footmen and fops'. Rochester is there stalking his mistress, 'Corinna' (a nod to Ovid's *Ars Amatoria*),who is being paid court by three men – a well-connected 'Whitehall Blade', a theatre critic and a young lad, enticed by 'the savoury scent of salt-swollen cunt'. As Corinna disappears in a hackney coach with all three of them, Rochester reflects that she will come home later that evening, with her 'lewd cunt drenched with the seed of half the town'.[30] If this appears to be the embodiment of aristocratic misogyny, it is worth considering that these lines represent the shadow side of Rochester's extraordinary talent. He could also prove sympathetic and insightful as in this observation of Corinna's fate after he has discarded her:

> Now scorn'd of all, forsaken and opprest,
> She's a *Memento Mori* to the rest:
> Diseas'd, decay'd, to take up half a crown
> Must mortgage her long scarf and manto gown:
> Poor creature, who unheard of, as a fly
> In some dark hole, must all the winter lie:
> And want, and dirt, endure a whole half year,
> That, for one month, she tawdry may appear.[31]

And Rochester could also write from a female perspective, as in this witty and sentimental declaration from 'A Young Lady to her Ancient Lover':

> Ancient Person, for whom I
> All the flattering youth defy,
> Long be it e'er thou grow old,
> Aching, shaking, crazy cold;

But still continue as thou art,
Ancient Person of my heart.

On thy withered lips and dry,
Which like barren furrows lie,
Brooding kisses I will pour,
Shall thy youthful heart restore,
Such kind show'rs in autumn fall,
And a second spring recall;
Nor from thee will ever part,
Ancient Person of my heart.

Thy nobler parts, which but to name
In our sex would be counted shame,
By ages frozen grasp possest,
From their ice shall be released,
And, soothed by my reviving hand,
In former warmth and vigour stand.
All a lover's wish can reach,
For thy joy my love shall teach;
And for thy pleasure shall improve
All that art can add to love.
Yet still I love thee without art,
Ancient Person of my heart.[32]

Sadly, the Earl of Rochester never lived to be an ancient person of anybody's heart. He was dead by forty, his constitution and talent destroyed by alcohol and disease. But he was not without redemption, as this observation from the playwright George Etherege illustrates. 'I know he is a Devil,' said Etherege, of this brilliant, conflicted man, 'but he has something of the Angel yet undefac'd in him.'[33]

Like Rochester, the diarist Samuel Pepys enjoyed London's low life to the full. But Pepys lacked the flamboyant Earl's self-destructive streak. He also lacked Rochester's patrician generosity and sexual charisma, arguing the toss with street whores and shamefully chronicling his many sexual failures. Pepys exemplified the middle-class approach to sex in Charles II's London. When not molesting the servants, such as Mary Mercer, who allows him to touch her breasts, 'they being the finest that I ever saw in my life; that is the truth of it',[34] or visiting his mistress, Betty Lane, with a bottle of wine and a lobster for dinner, Pepys was patronizing the dockyard brothels of the Ratcliffe Highway and singing along to bawdy ballads with lyrics such as 'Shitten-come-Shite the Way to Love is!'[35] An earthy attitude towards bodily functions is exemplified by a diary entry in which Pepys records that he was 'struck with a looseness of the bowels', dashed into a tavern, paid a groat for a pot of ale and defecated in the fireplace.

Pepys does not emerge as heroic or exemplary in his accounts of his sexual experiences, but, as his biographer Claire Tomalin has commented, his honest accounts of sexual failure and unrequited lust make him a sympathetic figure to modern readers. These exploits are written up with refreshing frankness, from an 'experiment' when he lay down on the floor of his boat while being rowed up the Thames and, by fantasizing about a beauty he had spotted at Westminster Hall, came to orgasm 'without use of my hand'[36] to a confession that he was so aroused by the queen and her retinue at Mass on Christmas Eve 1666 that he masturbated during the service.

Although Pepys was occasionally successful, as when he persuades young Betty Mitchell to touch his 'thing' on the pretext of securing promotion for her husband, he confesses that he is at a loss to emulate the sexual confidence of his colleagues and is shocked by the outrageousness of court life. The civil servant in him takes over as he is horrified not by Charles's affairs but by his lack of discretion about them, and views Charles's court as vicious, negligent and badly governed. King Charles plays with his dog or fiddles with his codpiece during meetings; chronic financial mismanagement means that on one occasion Pepys turns up to a meeting to find that there are no paper agendas on the table, because Charles has failed to pay an outstanding stationery bill for over £3000. On the same night that the navy is battling the Dutch fleet in the Medway, Charles and Barbara Villiers are more preoccupied with chasing 'a poor moth' around the dining room.

While living vicariously through the king's sexual excesses, Pepys deplores his lack of management skills. But, as Tomalin states, this is what makes Pepys such a credible witness; his sexual encounters and fantasies take place between committee meetings and home improvement schemes designed to pacify his wife. Relations with his wife, Elizabeth, were difficult, which explains why Pepys felt the need to look outside their marriage for companionship and sexual release. Elizabeth suffered with a genital abscess three inches deep,[37] which she found shameful and humiliating, and Pepys worried that he had infected her. This put a strain on their sex life; it was fourteen years into their marriage before Pepys could bring himself to put his finger 'into her thing, which did do her much pleasure'[38] but he confides in his diary that he hopes she does not get a liking for it. He had difficulty in accepting that women actually enjoyed sex, despite encounters with his robust mistress, Betty Lane, who brought 'an unabashed enthusiasm' to their love-making.[39]

Where Rochester was the ruthless rake, Pepys is a comical figure, lacking the self-confidence to woo the fine ladies he drools over, chasing the servants, finding fleeting satisfaction in a stolen kiss or slipping his hand under a petticoat, but not always with success:

18th August 1667: being weary, turned into St Dunstan's church, where I hear an able sermon of the minister of the place. And stood by a pretty, modest maid, whom I did labour to take by the hand and the body; but she would not, but got further and further from me, and at last I could perceive her to take pins out of her pocket to prick me if I should touch her again.[40]

While Rochester and Pepys may have had very different degrees of sexual success, there is one item to which both had recourse, and that is the condom, attributed to the apocryphal Colonel 'Condom' who promoted it in 1665, though he could scarcely be said to have invented it as condoms in some form or another have been with us for centuries as a method of preventing pregnancy and as disease control. While the Romans made them out of leather, the Egyptians preferred linen, the Chinese carved them out of tortoiseshell and the Japanese rolled oiled silk around the penis to prevent disease.

In his treatise on syphilis, *De Morbo Gallico* (1564), the Italian anatomist Gabriello Fallopio claimed to have invented a linen sheath which, when dipped in a solution of salt and herbs, formed a protection against the disease. The sheath fitted over the glans and under the foreskin, and appears to have been impractical and highly uncomfortable, but it was superseded by a larger sheath, still made of linen, that covered the entire penis.

Condom's breakthrough consisted of manufacturing sheaths out of animal gut. This process involved soaking sheep's intestines in water for a number of hours, then turning them inside out and macerating them again in a weak alkaline solution, changed every twelve hours. The intestines were then scraped carefully to remove the mucous membrane, leaving the peritoneal and muscular coats, and exposed to the vapour of burning brimstone. Next they were washed in soap and water, inflated, dried and cut into eight-inch lengths. Finally, the open end was finished with a ribbon that could be tied around the base of the penis, and the condom had to be soaked in water to make it supple before use. After use, it could be washed out and hung up to dry, ready for another excursion. Despite this laborious procedure, gut condoms soon proved hugely popular, and were celebrated by Rochester in his 1667 'Panegyrick Upon Cundums' which hailed this breakthrough as a protection against the horrors of venereal disease: 'happy is the man who in his pocket keeps a well-made cundum, nor dreads the ills of shankers or cordes or buboes dire' and as contraceptive, ruling out the appalling prospect of an 'unknown big belly and the squalling brat'. This development, he assures the reader, would rule both the chaste marriage bed and the filthiest stews, ensuring endless sexual pleasure without unhappy consequences and no need to have recourse to the mercy baths of Leather Lane, where victims underwent painful and protracted treatment for venereal disease.

While Charles II's court gained a reputation for profligacy, Restoration London proved its equal by offering an extraordinary catalogue of sexual pleasures. The sex trade, driven underground by Cromwell's Protectorate, flourished more vigorously than ever, offering something for every man, from the glamorous, top-drawer Venetian girls to the 'ambulant whores' who roamed the streets in the distinctive white aprons which indicated that they were available for business. The Venetian girls were so expensive that they catered only to the aristocracy, as may be seen from this itemized receipt from John Garfield's series of satirical pamphlets, 'The Wandering Whore':

Summa Totalis & Bill of Charges

FOR	Broaching a Belly unwemmed and unbored	£1.0.0
ITEM	For the Magdalena's Fee	10.0
ITEM	For the Hectors Fee	2.6
ITEM	For providing a fine Hollands Smock	10.0
ITEM	For Dressing, Perfuming and Painting	5.0
ITEM	For occupying the most convenient Room	5.0
ITEM	For Bottles of Wine	£1.0.0
ITEM	For Pickled Oysters, Anchoves, Olives	10.0
ITEM	For Sweet Meats, Sugar-cakes, Peaches, Walnuts	10.0
ITEM	For Musicke	£1.0.0

Summa Totalis £5.12.6d[41]

This does not include the courtesan's own fee, which would have been at least £5, and the Holland smock would have been a present. But this represented the top end of the market with the best available girls, managed by a redoubtable circle of madams known as 'the bawds'. These women, extraordinary characters in their own right, were quick to exploit their gullible clients and profit from the rich pickings available in the sex trade. The lives of the bawds are best illustrated by the stories of three forgotten women – Damaris Page, Elizabeth Cresswell and Priss Fotheringham – who met in prison and created an informal bawds' guild, supporting one another through the trials and vicissitudes of the sex trade.

Damaris Page was born into a life of abject poverty in the East End, around 1620. She first enters the record books in 1655, charged with assaulting Eleanor Pooley, 'she being with child, with an instrument from which the said Eleanor died'.[42] This 'instrument' was described as a fork or prong with two tines, which had been thrust four and a half inches into Eleanor's belly. In other words, Damaris had attempted to perform an abortion, and she was charged with manslaughter and sentenced to be hanged. Damaris pleaded for clemency on the grounds that she was herself pregnant. She gave birth to a stillborn child whilst in Newgate, before being pardoned by the Lord Protector, Richard Cromwell. Once freed, Damaris went back to the life and developed her own speciality, running brothels for sailors on the Ratcliffe Highway. There had been brothels in this location since Roman times, when the first galleys landed at Londinium and Damaris's premises continued this ancient tradition, earning her the accolade of 'The Great Bawd of the Seamen' from none other than King James II. Damaris's brothels offered basic fare of the sort enjoyed by Samuel Pepys: four girls on duty, taking each man as he came in on a 'first cab off the rank' basis and offering 'a sturdy cunt for two shillings'. Damaris died peacefully in 1669 in her own bed, leaving a handsome estate, a testimony to her long-held belief that 'Money and Cunny are the Best Commodities!'[43]

Elizabeth Cresswell was neither an aristocratic courtesan like Barbara Villiers, mistress of Charles II, nor a humble streetwalker like Damaris Page, and her origins come as something of a surprise.

Despite being born into a comfortable middle-class household in Aldgate in around 1625, Elizabeth inexplicably embarked on a career as a street prostitute, operating in Aldersgate, Clerkenwell and Shoreditch. As her looks began to fade, she became a bawd without rival in her wickedness, using all her diabolical arts of seduction to entice young women into the trade, and exploiting her family connections to set up an upmarket brothel.[44] Discretion was not Elizabeth's strongest suit, however, and she ended up in court and in prison several times for keeping a disorderly house. On one celebrated occasion her brothel was raided on a Sunday when the constables found a group of a dozen reprobates drinking wine on the Lord's day, the women stripped to the waist, and one young lady 'proposing a health to the privy member of a gentleman' and later 'drinking a toast to her own private parts'.[45] Once the Lord Protector, Richard Cromwell, had been replaced by Charles II, Elizabeth was free to pursue her career in an atmosphere of benign tolerance. Her most successful establishment was in Cripplegate, now the site of Moorfields underground station.

This was a house catering to the aristocracy, filled with girls of superior education, many of them the daughters of Cavalier families ruined in the Civil War. Known as 'Countesses of the Exchange', as they lived near the Royal Exchange, it was said of them that 'they master your britches and take all your riches'.[46] One commentator, Richard Head, an Oxford-educated conman, visited this establishment in 1663, and turned down the first girl he met there for being too expensive, even though she did touch his 'needle' and bartered with a second, bringing her price down to half a guinea, a considerable amount to pay for sex when two shillings was the going rate for a Ratcliffe Highway whore.

Elizabeth Cresswell's establishments survived the Great Plague of 1665, and the Great Fire of 1666. What they did not survive with impunity was the Shrovetide riots of 24 March 1668. This was the occasion when thousands of London's apprentices rioted and attacked the city's brothels in an excess of moral zeal later referred to as the 'Bawdy House Riots'. Such attacks were a typical feature of Shrove Tuesday, the day before Ash Wednesday, but on this particular occasion they also constituted a form of political rebellion against Charles II's decadent court and represented a growing public unease with the economy; the soldiers and sailors went unpaid while public money was siphoned into the excesses of court life – or even embezzled. The troops were mustered and the riots went on all night, with the crowd roaring slogans such as 'Reformation and Reducement', which, according to Pepys, made the courtiers apprehensive, because 'among the Rioters were many Men of Understanding that have been of Cromwell's Army!'[47] Ten years after Cromwell's death, the aristocracy were still unnerved at the mention of his name.

By daylight, Pepys was able to record the damage: 'a great many brothels have been destroyed or damaged', including the one belonging to Damaris Page, while two houses belonging to the Duke of York had been pulled down, which especially upset the duke as he had received £15 a year from each one for their liquor licences. As for the apprentices, their only regret was that they had attacked small brothels and not the great bawdy house at Whitehall: Charles II's palace.

Charles did not take these attacks lightly; eight of the apprentices were subsequently executed. One particular target for public rage was Charles's principal mistress at the time, Barbara Villiers, Lady Castlemaine, who was hated for being a Roman Catholic. Surveying the wreckage of the brothels, Elizabeth Cresswell took it upon herself to sponsor a seditious pamphlet directed at Barbara Villiers entitled 'The Poor Whores' Petition to Lady Castlemaine'.

This pamphlet, which may have been written by the diarist John Evelyn (who also hated Barbara Villiers), and was co-authored by Elizabeth's lover, the anti-Catholic MP Sir Thomas Player, begs Lady Castlemaine to help the poor whores, her less fortunate sisters from Dog and Bitch Yard, Lukener's Lane, Saffron Hill, Moorfields, Chiswell Street, Rosemary Lane, Nightingale Lane,

Ratcliffe Highway, Well Close, Church Lane and East Smithfield, whose homes have been destroyed by the apprentices, calling on her for support as a fellow whore who should show some feeling for her sisters.

Unfortunately, this pamphlet infuriated Barbara Villiers, who was horrified at being compared with London's common whores. It also catapulted Elizabeth into the limelight, the last place any self-respecting madam wishes to find herself. Elizabeth had bankrolled her MP lover, and suddenly all his debts were called in. Her girls were persuaded to give testimony against her by the authorities. As Elizabeth had been a cruel employer, this did not prove a hard task. After thirty years in the business, she was sentenced to Bridewell, where she died, aged sixty, in 1684. Elizabeth's last request was that a sermon be preached at her funeral, for which the preacher would receive £10, but only if he could say nothing bad about her. Eventually a preacher was found who managed to deliver the following lines:

> By the Will of the Deceased it is expected that I should mention her and say nothing but Well of her. All that I shall say of her therefore is this. She was *born well,* she *liv'd well* and she *died well*, for she was born with the name Cresswell, she liv'd in Clerkenwell and she died in Bridewell.[48]

The most notorious of our three bawds was undoubtedly Priss Fotheringham. Born in Scotland around 1615, Priss found her way to London and is first glimpsed in the records of Newgate gaol, after stealing some garments from a widow, Elizabeth Cragg. Already a prostitute, and scarred by smallpox, Priss was not without her charms. One acquaintance described her when young as 'a cat eyed gypsy, pleasing to the eye in her finery'.[49] Priss was also a highly resilient young woman: after being released from jail she set up as bawd of 'The Six Windmills' in Moorfields, which was to become known, infamously, as 'Priscilla Fotheringham's Chuck Office'. This is where

Priss performed her *pièce de résistance*, an 'abominable practice' dating back to the days of ancient Rome, whereby the prostitute stood upside down with her legs spread apart, allowing customers to throw coins into her vagina. This was known as 'chucking' and was a real money-spinner. It also required considerable gymnastic ability on the part of the whore, although clients could be relied upon to secure the girl's legs.

In her early days, Priss could perform this feat several times a day, standing on her head with 'naked breech and belly while four cully-rompers chuck'd in sixteen half-Crowns into her Commoditie'.[50] The Six Windmills drew a considerable clientele and proved wildly popular. As Priss grew weary with age and increasingly more disabled, she trained up new talent to perform, such as the Dutch prostitute known as 'Mrs Cupid', described here by Garfield:

> When French Dollars, Spanish Pistoles and English Halfe-Crowns were chucked as plentifully as Rhenish Whine into the Dutch Wench's two holes, the half crowns chuck'd into her commoditie did lesser harm than the Rhenish wine, for its smarting and searing quality, differing from the Sack poured in by such Cullies as at Priss Fotheringham.[51]

This episode led Garfield to conclude that 'A Cunny is the deerest Peice of Flesh in the World!'[52]

A speciality of another kind was available at the 'Prick Office' over in East Smithfield. This brothel, also known as the 'Last & Lyon', was run by a pimp called Hammond, and his speciality was fellatio. He employed a number of women and his interview technique consisted of a request for oral sex: any girl who wanted to work for him 'must buss the end of his Trapstick, as he lies naked upon his bed with his *Tarse* standing upwards'.[53] According to Burford, this is the only reference to fellatio to be found in contemporary writing.

Priss Fotheringham died around 1668, worn out by age and

disease, but wealthy, having made a small fortune from her exploits as a bawd and her extraordinary party trick. By this time, London's oldest profession was in transition. After the depredations of the Great Plague of 1665, the Great Fire the following year and the destructive apprentices of 1668, the landscape of London was shifting and changing, and inevitably so was its sex trade. The days of the old brothels of Moorfields and Clerkenwell were numbered, and the trade was heading west, to the fashionable new district of Covent Garden.

6

'THAT SQUARE OF VENUS'

Covent Garden and *The Harlot's Progress*

In 1630, the Duke of Bedford commissioned Inigo Jones to
develop his land at 'Convent Garden and the Long Acre' west
of the City. The architect responded by creating an imposing
square or 'Piazza' in the Italianate style, inspired by Palladio.
'Covent Garden', as it became known, thanks to the Cockney
glottal stop, swiftly appealed to the 'quality', who moved into
the elegant two-storey houses and flocked to the newly built
church of St Paul's on the west of the Piazza. After the Great Fire
of 1666, London's street markets were relocated here and Covent
Garden market became the most important in the country. Exotic
items were carried up the Thames by boat and put up for sale,
and taverns and coffee houses opened alongside the Piazza.
Inevitably, sex soon joined the list of goods for sale, and the Piazza
became London's premier flesh market, 'that great square of
Venus'.[1]

As early as 1709, the *Tatler* was telling readers that every house in

111

the district was inhabited by 'nymphs of different orders so that persons of every rank can be accommodated'.[2] By 1749, the keen student of vice could take a tour through London's illicit heartlands, like this anonymous author who walked up from Fleet Street, past Charing Cross, and on through Drury Lane to Covent Garden. Charing Cross, he declared, had 'little else but Concubines in all the Lodgings, and nothing but *Lascivious Looks* seen in the Chamber-Windows, from one end of the Verge to the other'.[3] The 'lodgings' were the rented rooms where the poorer whores took their pick-ups. The scene gets even worse as he makes his way through Drury Lane,

> where ev'ry half a dozen Steps he meets with some odd Figure or another, that looks as if the Devil had robb'd them all of their *natural Beauty* . . . for nothing can be read but *Devilism* in every feature; *Theft, Whoredom, Homicide and Blasphemy* peep out of the very Windows of their Souls . . . Turn your eyes up to the Chambers of Wantonness, and you behold the most Shameful Scene of *Lewdness* in the Windows even at Noon-day, some in the very act of Vitiation [copulation] visible to all the opposite Neighbours. Others dabbing their *Shifts, Aprons* and *Headcloths,* and exposing themselves just naked to the Passers by . . . *My Dear, will you give me a glass of wine; take me under your Cloak, my Soul, and how does your precious C do?* You hear at the Corner of every Court, Lane and Avenue, the Quarrels and Outcries of Harlots recriminating one another, Soldiers and Bullies inter-mixing, the most execrable Oaths are heard.[4]

This is an author who would have agreed with William Blake that 'the harlot's cry from street to street shall weave Old England's winding sheet', and echoed the same poet's sentiment that the harlot's curse would blight with plagues the marriage hearse, a reference, of course, to venereal disease.

The keen student of human depravity would then arrive at the

Piazza in Covent Garden, where there were enough lewd women to form a colony, and where 'the front windows of the Piazza are filled from seven at Night until four or five o'clock in the Morning with Courtezans of every description, who in the most impudent Manner invite the Passengers from the theatres into Houses where they are accommodated with Suppers and Lodgings, frequently at the expense of all they possess'.[5] These 'courtesans' were out in all weathers, at all seasons, 'sallying out' at dusk, dressed in the most gaudy colours, thronging the streets. While the more sedate whores contented themselves with walking around until they were addressed directly, the more desperate girls accosted every man they saw, offering to take them home, even standing around potential punters in a crowd, overwhelming them with 'caresses and entreaties'.[6]

A young German, Baron Zacharias von Uffenbach, was struck by the number of black women and men he saw 'hawking their bottoms round the Strand and Covent Garden, the females in European dress, with uncovered black bosoms'.[7] The majority of these black prostitutes had arrived in England as slaves, and been sold or abandoned by their white masters. Black girls were familiar enough on the scene for Hogarth to include a black prostitute in Plate 3 of *The Rake's Progress*, where Tom Rakewell is carousing the night away in the notorious Rose Tavern.

Another notable feature in this teeming den of vice was child prostitution. In 1777, 'Mother' Sarah Woods, a well-known bawd, was charged with 'harbouring young girls from eleven to sixteen, for the purpose of sending them nightly to parade the streets'. The charges came after the Watch had picked up a girl of twelve and the servant 'parading with her' to stop her running away with her clothes. Sarah Woods, it transpired, kept the girls hard at work all day cleaning her house, then sent them out as prostitutes at night, some half-naked and drunk.[8]

Given the desperate living conditions of the time, these children were easily coerced into prostitution. The writer George Alexander

Stevens noted that he often saw young girls of twelve and thirteen lying on stalls outside shops,

> in a most despicable condition; poor Objects with a Pretty face. A Pimp will pick them up and take them to a Bawdy-house wherein the poor Wretch is stript, washed and given Cloaths. These are called *Colts*. The Pimp gets paid a Pound or two for his trouble: the girls have thus been bought and must do as the Purchaser pleases. I have known a girl pay £11 [an exorbitant sum, equal to that paid by the highest class of prostitutes] for the use of a Smock and Petticoat which when new did cost only six Guineas. The girls are obliged to sit up every Morning until Five o'clock to drink with any straggling *Buck* who may reel in the early Morning and bear with whatever behaviour these drunken Visitants are pleased to use – and at the last endure the most Impure connexions.[9]

It was a desperate world of vicious cruelty for girls and boys alike. Those children who did not end up in the sex trade were forced into other criminal activities such as begging, stealing or working in sweatshops. Many were pressed into service as pickpockets, since Covent Garden was a den of vice. Criminals, big-time and small, from fraudsters and footpads to highwaymen, lived in the alleys off the Piazza, drawn to the area by the prospect of rich pickings. Their favourite haunt was the aforementioned Rose Tavern, near Drury Lane Theatre in Russell Street.

The Rose was notorious even by the standards of eighteenth-century London. Patronized by the most dissipated characters in town, from aristocrats to street whores, and from poets and playwrights to conmen and quacks, its clientele included Samuel Pepys (who enjoyed the excellent food) and the actors David Garrick and Sarah Siddons. It was a riotous venue, with bar-room brawls involving members of both sexes. Women would wrestle with each other, stripped to the waist, while customers placed bets on the likely winners.

The Rose was described by Thomas Brown as 'that black School of SODOM' where men paid a fortune to be flogged by a contingent of women known as 'posture molls'. These women, who were not prostitutes and were greatly offended if they were asked for sex, consented to flog and be flogged in public. They demonstrated their charms by stretching out naked on the floor, or performing a variation on the 'chuck office' trick pioneered by Priss Fotheringham. Plate 3 of *The Rake's Progress* joins our rake just as this variation is about to begin. In the background, the porter, Leathercoat, is carrying in an enormous pewter plate and a candle. In the foreground, a posture moll is stripping off in readiness. When the plate has been placed upon the table, the posture moll will dance naked, then lie down on her back with her hands clasped under her thighs, and simulate sex with the (lighted) candle as the customers crowd around; finally, she will snuff out the candle in a highly obscene and hazardous manner, to roars of approval from her audience.[10]

Although taverns were the traditional haunts of prostitutes, coffee houses had become a rival attraction since the late seventeenth century, when they had been introduced by the Puritans as an alternative to pubs, where men could meet to drink coffee and chocolate and share the news of the day. This new beverage was bad news for wives. In 'The Women's Petition Against Coffee!' a complaint is raised against the 'heathenish abominable liquor, the Puddle-Water' which it was believed turned their husbands into eunuchs. 'Men come home with nothing Stiff except their Joints!'[11]

Whatever the effect of caffeine upon potency, coffee houses offered great potential for whores, particularly the ambulant variety who, tired of traipsing through the streets on a bitterly cold day, could sit instead before a steaming cup of coffee and appraise the potential clients in this male preserve. 'The unfortunate strumpet who had been starving in a garret all day long while washing her only and last shift, upon making appearance here, might probably meet with a greenhorn apprentice boy who could treat her with a mutton chop and a pot of porter.'[12]

One of the most famous coffee houses in Covent Garden was Moll King's. Moll, or Mary, King opened her first coffee house around 1717, with her 'husband' Tom King, a Cambridge graduate who found the demi-monde of Covent Garden far more to his liking than the respectable professional career his parents had intended. The coffee house, initially a wooden shack along the side of the Piazza, soon proved so profitable that a second and then a third shack had to be built alongside, and even then business was so successful that it was difficult to accommodate all their patrons. Moll herself was a draw, 'a fat priestess' with an attractive voice and a jolly personality, and crowds flocked to admire 'Tawny Betty', her attractive black waitress. At Moll's insistence, there were no beds, apart from hers and Tom's in the attic. Moll had dabbled in prostitution in the past and the last thing she wanted was a visit from the law and a spell in Bridewell.

But curiously enough Moll King's was equal, if not superior, to the adjacent brothels in terms of takings. The coffee house was a magnet for young rakes and their mistresses, who could rendezvous there; it was said that 'every swain from the Star & Garter' (the aristocracy) 'could find a *Nymph* there'. It was here that one might meet anybody, high life or low, from the top whores, 'dressed up fine and pretty and elegantly as if going to a Box at the Opera', who were joined, after the performance, by the 'Bucks and Bloods' (Hellraisers and Hooray Henrys) the 'All-Night Lads' and the 'Peep o' Day Boys',[13] and the actress-whores who were known as the 'Toasts of the Town'. The theatre still represented a successful method of social climbing for clever, attractive women, a showcase where they could display their ample charms to capture a rich husband or long-term lover. One successful 'toast' was Kitty Fisher, 'indebted to nature for an uncommon portion of beauty, judgement, and wit, joined in a most agreeable and captivating vivacity'.[14] Kitty, who posed for Sir Joshua Reynolds as Cleopatra, was well aware of her value: she charged a hundred guineas a night and she was never without admirers, including the Duke of York, who left

£50 on her dressing table one morning, a tip she found so derisory that she refused to see him ever again, then stuck the banknote between two slices of bread and butter and ate it for breakfast.[15] As for Lavinia Fenton (1708–60), she was a social climber *extraordinaire*. Born a bastard and raised in a pub, she became the mistress of a nobleman at the age of seventeen and then took to the stage, which proved the making of her. In 1725, Lavinia secured the role of Polly Peachum in John Gay's *The Beggar's Opera* at Rich's theatre. The show was an overnight success, making 'Gay rich and Rich gay' and propelling Lavinia into the highest ranks of the 'toasts of the town'. By 1728, she had become the mistress of the Duke of Bolton and finally married him in 1751, when his wife died, becoming Duchess of Bolton and ending her days wealthy and respectable.[16]

Lavinia's was a success story; other 'toasts' were not so fortunate. Take the case of Sally Salisbury, born the daughter of a bricklayer in 1692. A beauty of considerable intelligence and wit, Sally was also a 'madcap', with a violent temper which was to prove her undoing. She was apprenticed to a seamstress at the age of nine, but ran away to be an orange girl in the Garden. By fourteen, she was working as a whore for the pious Mother Whyburn, a high-class bawd who had been seduced while at finishing school in Italy and completed her education in a more unorthodox fashion, by working in a seraglio. Mother Whyburn selected girls when they were little more than children and coached them in the social graces necessary to pull the gentry, dressing up her 'kittens' with paint and patches and claiming they were all parsons' daughters or young milliners.[17]

Sally soon became Mother Whyburn's star attraction, and her lovers included the Duke of Richmond, the Duke of St Albans (Nell Gwyn's son by Charles II), the poet Matthew Prior and the Prince of Wales (later George II). Sally's charges were so high that 'shee made Folks pay vastly Dear for what they had but they paid the greatest Price for the Greatest Pleasure'.[18] After a riot at Mother Whyburn's, Sally ended up in jail, but not for long: her judge, Mr

Justice Blagney, not only fell in love with her and secured her release, but was so infatuated he set himself up as her personal slave. When Mother Whyburn died in 1719, Sally went to work for the ill-famed Mother Needham. It was here, in 1722, that Sally stabbed her lover, Lord Finch, in a fit of temper. Convinced that he was about to die in her arms, his Lordship whispered, 'I die at pleasure by your hand,' although he later recovered. Sally was arrested and sent to Newgate, and, despite his injuries, her lover did all he could to console her with legal help and hampers of food. However, Sally developed 'brain fever', presumably as a result of venereal disease, and died in 1724. She was thirty-two years old.

With such a clientele at her coffee house, Moll King sailed pretty close to the wind. While not in effect a brothel, Moll King's was a meeting place for Covent Garden's bawdiest, such as Mother Needham and Mother Whyburn. In 1737 Moll and her husband Tom were charged with keeping a disorderly house but released on bail. A 'disorderly house', unlike a brothel, only merited a fine. But scenes such as the following did not help matters: 'you might see grave looking men half mizzy-eyed eying askance a poor supperless Strumpet asleep on a Bench, her ragged Handkerchief fallen, exposing her bare Bosom on which these old Lechers were doating. This was the Long Room.'[19]

Despite the success of their venture, Tom King had drunk himself to death by 1739, after which Moll King's became even more notorious, the haunt of the most outrageous and intemperate people from every walk of life; noblemen would appear in court dress with swords and richly brocaded coats and mix with chimney sweeps, gardeners and market traders. Widowhood altered Moll's personality, and her sweet, tolerant attitude to life disappeared for ever, to be replaced by a simmering rage which earned her the nickname of 'The Virago'. Moll's grasp of her affairs vanished along with her good temper and, charged again in 1739 with keeping a disorderly house, she was unable to put up bail and spent three months in Newgate gaol, although she had a reasonably comfortable time of it owing to her ability to bribe her jailers and receive distinguished visitors. Moll eventually retired to a villa in Hampstead, where she died peacefully in her sleep, leaving a considerable fortune. Much missed, she was commemorated in a broadsheet entitled 'Covent Garden in Mourning' and remembered with affection for a generation.

The Bedford Head was another famous coffee house, 'crowded every Night with Men of Parts, Politicos, Scholars & Wits',[20] who mixed with the stars and the low-lifes and the whores, decked out in their flamboyant clothes. The most outrageous coffee house was Weatherby's, which attracted 'rakes, gamesters, swindlers, highwaymen, pickpockets and whores'. According to the diarist William Hickey, Weatherby's was 'absolute hell on earth'; on his first visit, with friends and 'brimfull of wine', he observed with horror that:

the whole room was in an uproar, men and women promiscuously mounted upon chairs, tables and benches, in order to see a sort of general conflict carried on upon the floor. Two she devils, for they scarce had a human appearance, were engaged in a scratching and boxing match, their faces entirely covered with blood, bosoms bare, and clothes nearly torn from their bodies. For several minutes not a creature interfered between them, or seemed to care a straw what mischief they might do each other, and the contest went on with unabated fury.[21]

Tea gardens or pleasure gardens also offered opportunities for all sorts of frivolity, with a blind eye turned to bad behaviour. Designed to entice Londoners and visitors alike 'to linger beyond the calls of business soaking up the atmosphere of urbane and civilised living',[22] there were in the order of 200 pleasure gardens around London, celebrated for their fishponds, fireworks, musicians and masquerades. Famous pleasure gardens included Sadlers' Wells, Kilburn Wells, Bermondsey Spa, Hockley in the Hole (Clerkenwell), Pimlico,

Lambeth Wells and Vauxhall Gardens. Shady Vauxhall with its secluded arbours was particularly louche; even Samuel Pepys was shocked by the behaviour he witnessed there. On 27 July 1688, he noted: 'Over the water with my wife and Deb and Mercer . . . and eat there and walked; and observed how coarse some young gallants from the town were. They go into the arbours where is no man and ravish the woman there, and the audacity of vice in our time much enraged me.'[23] According to the historian of prostitution Fernando Henriques, 'those who purposely lost their way in the bushes did not bother to be discreet and made a tremendous uproar, no doubt added to by the screams of respectable women being raped'.[24]

The attractions of Ranelagh Gardens in Chelsea, opened in1742, included grottoes, fishing, cream teas, skittle alleys, fountains and formal walks, spa waters and even bear-baiting. The gardens were described by the rakish novelist Tobias Smollet as being like 'the enchanted palace of a genie, adorned with the most exquisite performance of painting, carving, and gilding, enlightened with a thousand golden lamps, that emulate the noon-day sun; crowded with the great, the rich, the gay, the happy, and the fair; glittering with cloth of gold and silver, lace, embroidery, and precious stones'.[25] The main attraction was a rotunda with an orchestra in the centre and tiers of boxes all round. The wit Horace Walpole declared: 'every night I constantly go to Ranelagh, which has totally beat Vauxhall'.

At 'English Castle' in Clerkenwell, visitors were promised a grand garden, golden and silver fish, an enchanted fountain and even a rainbow – and all for sixpence! At Lambeth Wells, one of the attractions was all-night music, resulting in the garden losing its licence in 1755 due to complaints by disgruntled residents and a series of drunken brawls. Inevitably, pleasure gardens became famous for pleasure of another kind. Cupid's Gardens in Lambeth were celebrated for their 'erotic ambience', and the proprietor of the 'Temple of Flora' received a prison sentence in 1796 for keeping a disorderly house. Spring Gardens, later known as Vauxhall, opened in 1660, and could be reached only by boat at its location on the South Bank, adding to the romantic ambience. Vauxhall was one of the most famous pleasure gardens, where, for just a shilling, the visitors could enjoy orchestras, dazzling firework displays, dancing and the opportunity to indulge in a little flirtation in the decorated alcoves set aside for just such a purpose. In 1749, a hundred musicians entertained an audience of 12,000, causing traffic jams as far away as London Bridge.

Back in the Garden, another development was taking place: the return of the bath house, or 'bagnio'. These bath houses were expensive, exclusive and devoted to anything but getting clean. The legendary Casanova tells us that during a trip to London he 'visited the bagnios, where a rich man can sup, bathe and sleep with a fashionable courtesan, of which species there are many in London. It makes a magnificent debauch, and only costs six guineas.'[26] The German historian Johann Wilhelm von Archenholz (1741–1812) provides a vividly detailed account:

> In London there is a certain kind of house, called bagnios, which are supposed to be baths; their real purpose, however, is to provide persons of both sexes with pleasure. These houses are well, and often richly furnished, and every device for exciting the senses is either at hand or can be provided. Girls do not live here, but they are fetched in sedan chairs when required. None but those who are specially attractive in all ways are so honoured, and for this reason they often send their address to a hundred of these bagnios in order to make themselves known. A girl who is sent for and does not please receives no gratuity, the chair alone being paid for. The English retain their solemnity even as regards their pleasures, and consequently the business of such a house is conducted with a seriousness and propriety which is hard to credit. All noise and uproar is banned here; no loud footsteps are heard, every corner is carpeted and the numerous attendants speak quietly among themselves . . . In every bagnio

there is found a formula regarding baths, but they are seldom needed. These pleasures are very expensive, but in spite of this many houses of the kind are full every night. Most of them are quite close to the theatres, and many taverns are in the same neighbourhood.[27]

James Boswell, biographer of Samuel Johnson, was one of the most famous enthusiasts of London low life. He expressed unabashed admiration for women such as 'the civil nymph with white-thread stockings who tramps along the Strand and who will resign her engaging person to your honour for a pint of wine and a shilling'.[28] A diary entry for 25 March 1763 reads:

> As I was coming home this night, I felt carnal inclinations raging through my frame. I determined to gratify them. I went to St James Park and picked up a whore. For the first time did I engage in armour [a condom] which I found but a dull satisfaction. She who submitted to my lusty embraces was a young Shropshire girl, only 17, very well-looked, her name Elizabeth Parker. Poor being, she has a sad time of it![29]

But he does not feel sorry for Elizabeth Parker for long. A few days later, on 31 March, he 'strolled into the park and took the first whore I met, whom I without many words copulated with free from danger, being safely sheathed. She was ugly and lean and her breath smelt of spirits. I never asked her name. When it was done, she slunk off. I had a low opinion of this gross practice and resolved to do it no more.'[30]

That didn't last long, either. On 17 May, Boswell picked up a girl called Alice Gibbs at the bottom of Downing Street and repaired to a shady spot down a lane, where he produced his 'armour'. Alice begged him not to put it on, 'as the sport was much pleasanter without it, and as she was quite safe'. On one famous occasion Boswell even had sex with a strong jolly young damsel on Westminster

Bridge, and found 'the whim of doing it there with the Thames rolling below us amused me much'.[31]

Despite his familiar use of prostitutes, Boswell was as vain and naive as the next punter. He recalls one girl, picked up on the Strand on 25 November 1762, who 'wondered at my size and said that if I ever took a girl's maidenhood, I would make her squeak'.[32] Boswell, like so many men, had obviously not realized that this is a stock line, a piece of harmless flattery intended to raise the spirits of all clients.

While Boswell was slumming it with pick-ups in St James's Park, the luxury market had established itself at the fashionable end of town, close to the royal palaces of St James's, the mansions of Mayfair, and of course the Houses of Parliament at Westminster. Further north, in Marylebone, the first generation of middle-class mistresses was being established. These women were the sexual carriage trade, catering to the higher echelons of society, attractive and accomplished girls from good families who had exchanged a life of genteel poverty for becoming the established companion of a regular, wealthy client. According to one commentator,

> In the parish of Mary-le-bone only, which is the largest and best peopled in the capital, thirty thousand Ladies of Pleasure reside, of which seventeen hundred are reckoned to be housekeepers [homeowners]. These live very well, and without ever being disturbed by the magistrates. They are indeed so much their own mistress, that if a justice of the peace attempted to trouble them in their apartments, they might turn him out of doors; for as they pay the same taxes as the other parishioners, they are consequently entitled to the same privileges.[33]

It is this ideal position of 'mistress' that the fictional Fanny Hill briefly achieves in her celebrated *Memoirs of a Woman of Pleasure*, and Moll Hackabout experiences equally briefly in Hogarth's satirical cartoon sequence, *The Harlot's Progress*. These girls were at the top of their game, and, if shrewd and pragmatic enough to retain their lovers' support and resist the urge to follow their hearts, they were as safely established as wives. Indeed, they had more security than wives, who at the time had no financial claim over their husbands.

One step down the scale from the mistresses were the 'seraglios' or high-class brothels of St James's and Soho. These were modelled on French 'houses' which were characterized by a 'seraglio', or great salon, in which the girls sat around in a state of *déshabillé*, ready to advertise their services to prospective clients by striking dramatic poses. The girls had been trained in all aspects of the trade, allowing the seraglios to cater for all varieties of sexual deviation, from pornography and 'slaves' who could arouse the latent passions of the older man to a peep-room for voyeurs, and even a 'chamber of horrors' for sado-masochists. That epithet might have taken another two centuries to develop, but the pragmatic, worldly-wise bawds were familiar enough with those who equated pain with pleasure. One Mrs Goadsby, a frequent visitor to Paris, was mightily impressed by the French seraglios and opened her own 'house' in Berwick Street, Soho, in 1750, catering to all tastes at the most exclusive prices.

Another bawd, Miss Fawkland, actually trained her whores rigorously before they were allowed to work at one of her three adjoining houses in St James's Street, decked out as 'temples'. The first was the 'Temple of Aurora', which specialized in very young girls, aged between eleven and sixteen, who were, disturbingly, handpicked from crowds of little girls brought to Miss Fawkland by their parents.[34] Here, elderly clients were permitted to fondle and slobber over the trainee whores, but officially go no further. After their training, the girls graduated to the 'Temple of Flora', which operated as a conventional luxury brothel, while the third house, or 'Temple of Mysteries', concentrated on more outlandish tastes and the sado-masochistic practices so popular with the upper classes.[35]

As one might have predicted, Miss Fawkland's establishments

were highly successful, and her clientele was drawn from the highest in the land, including as it did Lords Cornwallis, Buckingham, Hamilton and Bolingbroke, and the writers Sheridan and Smollet.

Mrs Charlotte Hayes's establishment, meanwhile, offered an entertaining line in theatrical reconstructions. Having heard that Captain Cook had just discovered Tahiti, and reported that their handsome young men and lovely maidens copulated in public, Charlotte invited favoured clients to a 'Tahitian Feast of Venus' which would start at seven prompt, when 'twelve beautiful spotless nymphs all virgins will carry out the Feast of Venus as it is celebrated in Oteite' [Tahiti]. Charlotte would play Queen Oberea, and the maidens would be aged eleven and over. An additional attraction would be tableaux based on the drawings of the Renaissance pornographer Pietro Aretino, and twelve attractive young men had been hired to flank the aforesaid maidens. Twenty-three gentlemen 'of the highest breeding' including five MPs arrived punctually. The proceedings opened with each youth presenting his nymph with a dildo wreathed in flowers, after which they copulated enthusiastically, accompanied by appropriate music, until the spectators were so overcome with excitement that they invaded the floor and joined in. This 'Cyprian Feast' ('Cyprian' alluded to Cyprus, island of Aphrodite, the Greek goddess of love) lasted for two hours, after which everyone sat down to a hearty supper. Charlotte never repeated this particular event, but it was much copied by other bawds.[36]

A satirical 'menu' designed to ridicule some of the top-brothel patrons of the day gives some idea of the high cost of these diversions and the price charged for specific services:

Sunday the 9th January
A young girl for Alderman Drybones.
Nelly Blossom, about 19 years old, who has had
no one for four days, and who is a virgin
20 guineas

A girl of 19 years, not older, for Baron Harry Flagellum.
Nell Hardy from Bow Street, Bat Flourish from Berners
Street or Miss Birch from Chapel Street
10 guineas

A beautiful girl for Lord Spaan. Black Moll
from Hedge Lane, who is very strong
5 guineas

For Colonel Tearall, a gentle woman.
Mrs Mitchell's servant, who has just come from the
country and has not yet been out in the world
10 guineas

For Dr Frettext, after consultation hours, a young agreeable
person, sociable, with a white skin and a soft hand. Polly
Nimblewrist from Oxford, or Jenny Speedyhand from Mayfair
2 guineas

Lady Loveit, who has come from the baths
at Bath, and who is disappointed in her affair with Lord Alto,
wants to have something better, and to be well served this
evening. Capt O'Thunder or Sawney Rawbone
50 guineas

For His Excellency Count Alto, a fashionable
woman for an hour only. Mrs Smirk who came from
Dunkirk, or Miss Graceful from Paddington
10 guineas

For Lord Pyebald, to play a game of piquet,
for *titillatione mammarum* and so on, with no other
object. Mrs Tredrille from Chelsea
5 guineas[37]

This menu covers almost the entire range of specialities available at a high-class brothel: masturbation, fondling without intercourse, defloration – of a *soi-disant* 'virgin' – flagellation and a stud for the female client, who is charged far more for this service than her male counterpart. This was by no means unusual: there was a demand for male prostitutes from wealthy female clients, and a well-run seraglio would offer them as well, so that man and wife could enjoy their pleasures without encountering each other.[38] The prices are accurate for a top-class seraglio, and some of the names are satirical references to real people. 'Lady Loveit' was the 'nymphomaniac' Lady Sarah Lennox, while her lover was Lord William Gordon. 'Alderman Drybones', the elderly civic with a taste for virgins, was Robert Alsop, Lord Mayor of London in 1752, while 'Lord Pyebald', so elderly that he can do little more than fondle girls' breasts, was Hugh, Viscount Falmouth.[39]

As for the *soi-disant* 'virgin', it was easy, through simply trickery, to persuade a punter that his girl was a first timer, as illustrated by this extract from *Fanny Hill*. Our heroine, directed by her bawd to spend the night with an elderly virgin hunter, puts up a convincing performance as a virgin with a sequence of complaints and refusals, until she finally allows the old man to have his way with her. While he sleeps, having become fatigued after his second 'let-go', Fanny's nimble fingers spring the lock of a secret drawer which contains a bottle of red liquid and a sponge. It is but the work of a moment to squeeze this sponge between her legs and return the bottle to its hiding place, having produced manifest proof of her client's 'victorious violence'. He is completely taken in: 'viewing the field of battle by the glimmer of a dying taper, he saw plainly my thighs, shift and sheets, all yet wet and stained with what he readily took for virgin gore, proceeding from his last half-penetration'.[40]

There were already black prostitutes working in London, including the curvaceous Miss Lowes of Upper Charlotte Street, Soho, and Miss Wilson of Litchfield Street, Soho, who was of very pleasing features and intelligence and frequently to be found at the theatre in the evening.[41] But 'Black Harriott' or Miss Harriott was the only black bawd in London. Born in Guinea, Harriott – she does not appear to have had a Christian name – was shipped to Jamaica as a slave, where her beauty and wit captivated William Lewis, a plantation owner and captain in the merchant navy. Lewis married Harriott, educated her and prepared her for high society. He brought her to England, where they lived just off Piccadilly and moved in the most exclusive circles, until Lewis died in 1772, leaving Harriott penniless.

For all her intelligence, looks and education, it seemed as if Harriott would languish in debtors' prison, but she was freed by a band of admirers and set up a brothel in St James's which became wildly successful. A brothel guide of the time rather insultingly commented that Harriott had 'attained a degree of politeness scarce to be paralleled in an African female'.[42] Harriott's top-drawer clientele included peers of the realm, and it was her proud boast that nobody spent less than 'a soft paper', in other words, a £20 note. Two of Harriott's most famous clients were the hellraiser the Earl of Sandwich, famous of course for inventing that invaluable snack, and his one-time friend, the radical MP and journalist John Wilkes. When they fell out, Sandwich shouted at Wilkes, 'Sir, you will either die on the gallows or of the pox', to which Wilkes replied, 'That, my Lord, depends on whether I embrace your principles or your mistress.'[43] Harriott, sadly, fell hopelessly in love with a Guards officer and neglected her business. Her girls sold off the contents of her brothel and she ended up in debtors' prison again, eventually dying of tuberculosis.

Despite regular moral panics and attempts to crack down on prostitution, a sentimental journalistic convention had developed by the 1730s which suggested that most prostitutes were innocent country girls, lured to the big city by the promise of fame and fortune and decoyed into immorality by wicked old bawds. This is the backdrop for both *The Harlot's Progress* (1733) by William Hogarth, and John Cleland's *Fanny Hill or Memoirs of a Woman of Pleasure*

(1749). These famous accounts of prostitution bookend the popular perception of sex in eighteenth-century London. At first glance, the two young protagonists, Moll Hackabout and Fanny Hill, appear to have much in common, but in fact their lives and destinies are very different, as we shall discover when we compare their experiences of the seamy underbelly of city life.

John Cleland (1710–89) was an educated but impoverished London hack who wrote himself out of debtors' prison with his genial erotic classic. *Fanny Hill* is essentially a titillating saga about a lively country girl who is forced to live on her wits in London by prostituting herself, and was accurately described by the lubricious James Boswell as 'a most licentious and inflaming book'. Hogarth's *The Harlot's Progress*, on the other hand, represented a harsh satirical critique of London morality and the fate which awaited poor, deluded young women who were lured into the sex trade. To make his point, Hogarth folded in vicious caricatures of actual people, such as the bawd Mother Needham and Colonel Charteris, 'Rape Master of Great Britain'.

The first plate of *The Harlot's Progress* shows young Moll Hackabout arriving at the Bell Inn in Cheapside, just up from the country. Fresh and healthy, in her plain peasant clothes, she is seeking employment as a seamstress or a servant. Moll is based on a real person, one Kate Hackabout, who worked for Mother Needham. Innocent and modestly attired, she stands before the bawd, who is examining her youth and beauty beneath a cracked bell, a medieval symbol of fallen chastity. Mother Needham is immediately recognizable, a handsome middle-aged woman, well dressed in silks, simpering beneath the patches on her face, which are placed there to conceal the symptoms of the pox. Moll may well have been duped by a bawd, such as Needham, or one of her operatives, whose task it was to scour the countryside for talent, inviting naive or newly orphaned girls to come up to town with the promise of a glamorous life in London. Sir Richard Steele, one of the founders of the *Spectator*, remarked in 1712 that on a trip to the Bell, he saw 'the most artful Procuress in Town examining a most beautiful Countrey girl who had just come up in the same Wagon as my Things', while Tom Brown described Needham as haunting taverns so that she could pick off 'fresh Countrey Wenches sound and plump & juicy'.[44]

Mother Needham was mentioned around 1710, running a luxurious brothel in Park Place, St James's, a rich and fashionable area only yards away from the royal palace. She was a well-born woman, related to the Earls of Kilmorey, and her aristocratic connections, good looks and considerable management expertise made her almost immune to prosecution. With neighbours such as George Hamilton, Duke of Orkney, husband of William III's mistress; George Montagu, Marquess of Halifax; and Barbara Castlemaine, Needham went unchallenged; the fact that the young Prince of Wales liked to drop by from time to time only enhanced her reputation. Needham was a strict and brutal employer, who hired out the very clothes on the girls' backs and was quick to dismiss any harlot who did not adhere to her punishing work ethic. Girls who grew old or sick, or fell into disfavour, were summarily ejected, to debtors' jail or the gutter.

Plate 1 of *The Harlot's Progress* implies that Mother Needham may be acting on behalf of Colonel Charteris, who stands in the doorway to the right, fondling himself and eyeing up the new arrival, accompanied by his valet, Jack Gourlay. Over the years, Needham had sourced 'above one hundred Maidenheads' for Charteris, 'which she picked up at the Carriers'. What Charteris liked were 'Strong lusty fresh country Wenches that would make a dint in a wooden Chair & work like a Parish Fire engine at a conflagration', and for which he was willing to pay £20 a time.

Charteris was a cashiered army officer who had prospered as a property developer and made a killing from South Sea stock. He owned several brothels, paid for with the proceeds of his gambling, and, of course, he cheated at cards. He once won £3000 from the Duchess of Queensberry by placing a mirror nearby so that he could read her cards. He was also a convicted rapist with a taste for young virgins. In collusion with his servants, he used false names and addresses to lure girls to his house, and he also arranged for the bawds to recruit suitable fresh-faced country girls. His methods were so violent and arrogant, even by the standards of the time, that he frequently came to the attention of the magistrates. In 1717, he raped a young virgin, Sarah Selleto, at the Scotch Arms Ale House in Pall Mall and was ordered to pay for her bastard child. Another victim of his was Isabella Cranston who fell into his clutches at the brothel run by Mrs Jolley in Suffolk Street, where she was decoyed under the pretence of being taken into service, though she did not become an official member of Mrs Jolley's establishment. After she had seen Charteris a number of times – only Charteris, no other men – she became pregnant, was abandoned and had to apply for poor relief to the parish of St Margaret's, Westminster, in 1729.

Charteris's house in Scotland was little more than a brothel, run by a full-time matron, Mary Clapham, whom he treated violently and eventually dismissed after years of service. One Scots rape victim described him as 'the huge raw Beast that in guid faith got me with Bairn. I know him by his nasty Legg for he has rapt it around my Arse mony a guid time.'[45] So, here is Charteris viewing the latest arrivals and eagerly anticipating sampling the new goods. But nemesis awaits. That tumbling pile of pots on the left of the picture represents a tower of destruction, but not only for Moll. As to her immediate future, she is about to be sold to Charteris, with all the horror that implies.

Moll's literary counterpart, Fanny Hill, can expect a more enjoyable introduction to the flesh markets. She is, after all, a 'Woman of Pleasure', and her initiation into erotic ecstasy is at the hands of another young woman, Phoebe, at the brothel to which she has been decoyed. Fanny is so naive that when Phoebe begins to seduce her, she reflects, 'this was new, this was odd' but puts it down to 'pure kindness, which, for aught I knew, it might be the London way to express in that manner'. It is not long before Fanny is moved from tame and passive endurance of Phoebe's advances to discovering that 'her lascivious touches had lighted up a new fire that wantoned through all my veins', to appreciating that Phoebe, 'the hackneyed, thoroughbred Phoebe', had found in her vocation of breaking in young girls 'the gratification of one of those arbitrary tastes for which there is no accounting'. Following these Sapphic delights, Fanny is sold to a repellent elderly gentleman, over sixty years old, with a cadaverous hue, goggling eyes and 'breath like a jakes'. Horrified, Fanny fights him off (to her bawd's discomfort) and later surrenders her virginity in fine romantic style to a handsome young man, the love of her life. So far, so very different from the reality of life in the Garden and the grim world of Hogarth.

By Plate 2 of *The Harlot's Progress*, Moll is at the top of her trade. As the mistress of a wealthy London Jew, she lives in a beautiful town house, complete with a black slave, mahogany furniture and a silver tea service, all symbols of the colonial wealth enjoyed by the mercantile class which Hogarth despised. But Moll's protector has returned unexpectedly from the Exchange, almost catching Moll in bed with her aristocratic lover, and Moll has created a diversion, kicking over the table and snapping her fingers, so that her lover can creep out undetected. Moll's protector is no fool, however: the viewer can judge from his expression that he is not taken in by this performance, and Moll's days as his mistress are numbered. As are the days of her beauty: visible on her head and breast are two pox marks, indicating that she has already succumbed to venereal disease.

Although there is more than a touch of anti-Semitism in Hogarth's Jewish merchant, Jewish punters were well regarded by prostitutes. The Sephardic Jews whose predecessors had arrived in England under Oliver Cromwell in 1653 were a familiar sight in the purlieus of Drury Lane and Covent Garden. By 1736, they were frequenting the whorehouses at the Garden three or four times a week, particularly on Sundays, with 'upright gait, morose speech and pretty smooth Counternance'. Completely Anglicized, they were every bit as good as their gentile counterparts at foppery and lechery, except on Shabbos. But by sundown on Saturday night they were out there spending their money on drinking and loose living. Jews were generally popular among the whores, as they were good spenders and enthusiastic lechers but rarely heavy drinkers. They were also kind and courteous to women and not given to drunken brutality.

As one might expect, there were also Jewish bawds, such as Rose Marks, who, in a textbook example of *chutzpah*, pleaded poverty when charged with keeping a magnificently successful disorderly house at Duke's Place, St James's, and a Mrs Gould, who opened a bagnio in Bow Street in 1742, moving up to much better premises at Russell Street in 1745 which became a well-appointed seraglio with a quiet but distinguished clientele, mainly Jewish, consisting of merchants, bankers and brokers, who would come to her house on Saturday evenings and stay over until Monday mornings.[46] In this quiet, well-disciplined, well-appointed brothel, 'respectable gentlemen' could escape from 'the Noise and Stresses of the Exchange'. Even the girls were well behaved. There was no employment here for any girl who was 'addicted to intoxication or who used any bad language'.[47] A reference to Mrs Gould as 'waddling' suggests that success agreed with her, and by 1779 she seems to have retired with a handsome fortune. Fanny Hill, meanwhile, briefly becomes a Marylebone mistress, having been taken in by the arrogant but handsome Mr H, a middle-aged gentleman.

By Plate 3, Moll has gone downmarket. Having deceived her wealthy Jewish patron, she has been demoted to the position of a common prostitute and is living in a dingy garret in the Garden. Tankards on the floor show that she is drinking heavily, and the medicine bottles and black patches on her face indicate that her syphilis has grown more advanced; her maid's nose is eaten up with lesions. Moll's 'sign', a witch's hat and a broom, appear on the wall above her bed, as does a picture of MacHeath, the popular anti-hero from *The Beggar's Opera*, a symbol of lawlessness. But Moll still

The doomed Moll Hackabout, from Hogarth's The Harlot's Progress, *about to be arrested by a magistrate (1732).*

smiles on, staring out at us, unaware of the fact that she is about to be disturbed by a visitation from the forces of law and order in the form of Sir John Gonson, a Justice of the Peace and scourge of prostitutes, who has arrived with a deputation of men to arrest her.

Meanwhile, her literary counterpart, Fanny Hill, is in trouble, too. But not for long. Flung off by her lover after he found her having sex with a servant boy (Fanny's response to finding Mr H *en flagrante* with the maid), she is taken in by the kindly Mrs Cole, a sympathetic bawd who runs a successful operation fronted by a dress shop. When the house is eventually raided, Fanny escapes into the night, unlike poor Moll, who is next seen, in Plate 4, as a prisoner at Bridewell, beating hemp. The change in Moll's circumstances is illustrated by the discrepancy between her appearance, in her fine silks, and the cheerless prison. Meanwhile, Moll's maid, nothing if not resourceful, is attempting to capture the attention of their jailer with a sly wink and a tweak of her garter.

By Plate 5, Moll is back in her garret in the Garden, and dying of syphilis, indicated by the shroud-like blankets which swathe her body to 'sweat' her. Two doctors are arguing about the effectiveness of their cures, while ignoring her evident distress, and her landlady is going through Moll's trunk stealing her clothes, her witch's hat, her mask and her high heels. By the fire sits a hapless victim of all this: Moll's son, who seems doomed to enter the world of vice and crime.

Children were the innocent victims of prostitution, as is evident from this account of Mary David, born in Hertfordshire. Mary's father died when she was a child, and her mother remarried a poor man. Mary was sent to London as a servant, and worked for two years for a family in Berkeley Square. The footman, although he was already married, seduced her under promise of marriage. She lost her place when she became pregnant. The footman helped her with the child at first, but then she took a place as a wet-nurse and put her own child out to nurse with a woman in Tottenham Court Road. The child she nursed was weaned, her milk dried up and she went to live in the house in Tottenham Court Road. The landlady was very civil, and allowed her to get into debt. Then, one night between eleven and twelve, her landlady came upstairs, 'with manners totally changed, and swore with the grossest abuse, that she would turn her into the street, child and all, unless she brought her some pay'. When Mary asked how she could possibly do that, the landlady replied that 'girls with worse faces than she often picked up a great deal'.

Mary now discovered that one other young lodger there was a kept mistress, and the house was, in fact, 'though in a very private way, a bad house'. Mary took to prostitution, 'driven out in bitter anguish', and eventually found poor friends who took her in. She gave up her child to the parish workhouse, and returned to her mother, in the country. But then she found, 'to her inescapable grief', that she was pregnant again, 'from the sad effects of the

135

prostitution'. Her first child was now dead; the parish had refused to take it from the parish nurse and it had died with a black eye, a broken collarbone and whooping-cough. Mary managed to persuade the Foundling Hospital to take her second child, and from this her story emerges. And, since that story was not known in the country, she planned to return there after she had sold her milk in London.[48] Mary's subsequent fate is unknown, but, given her circumstances, likely to have been an unhappy one.

By Plate 6, the final, black frame of Hogarth's sad story, Moll Hackabout is dead, and her fellow prostitutes are crowding around her coffin. The cautionary tale of Moll's short life is unheeded by the girls taking the opportunity to ply their trade. The parson, staring into space, is slipping his hand beneath the skirt of Moll's friend, while spilling his drink – a symbol of premature ejaculation – watched with resignation by Moll's former maid. Moll's friend gazes out of the picture with half-closed eyes and a faint smile on her lips, an expression reminiscent of Moll's in Plate 3. The cycle of innocence corrupted, sex, decay and death will continue unabated.[49]

Fanny, meanwhile, survives to inherit a house in the country and is reunited with her first love. *Fanny Hill* is the Harlot as Heroine, an Enlightenment fantasy, with Fanny inhabiting a benevolent universe free of drunkenness and crime, almost entirely run by women, and where sex takes place in safe, indoor environments, and is a vice, more or less, of the middle and upper ranks of society.[50]

Comparing Hogarth and Cleland, it is obvious which version of fallen women was more accurate, and yet *Fanny Hill* is a wonderful piece of escapism, a classic of erotic fiction written by an author who appreciated the possibility of sexual enjoyment for women, although his graphic depictions of young men and detailed descriptions of their organs of generation suggest, at least to this reader, that his interests lay elsewhere.

Moll's life ended unhappily; so did that of Mother Needham, who was arrested in March 1731 on Sir John Gonson's orders, and sentenced to the pillory for her complicity in the rape by Colonel

Charteris of the servant Anne Bond, having 'frightened her into Compliance with his filthy Desires' by holding a pistol to her head.[51]

Thanks to her friends in high places, Needham was permitted to lie face down on the pillory, which would protect her face. According to the *Daily Courant*, 'at first she received little Resentment from the Populace, by reason of the great Guard of Constables that surrounded her; but near the latter End of her Time she was pelted in an unmerciful manner'. According to the *Daily Advertiser*, 'notwithstanding the diligence of the Beadles and a number of Persons who had been paid to protect her she was so severely pelted by the Mob that her life was despaired of'. Several sources claim that she died of her injuries at the scene. But she appears to have been taken down, and committed to Newgate, where she died shortly afterwards.

As for Charteris, he stood trial for rape. The court was told that Anne Bond, who was unemployed, was sitting at the door of her lodgings one day when a woman appeared and offered her a job working for Charteris. The moment she took up her position, he laid siege to her. At seven o'clock one morning, 'the Colonel rang a Bell and bid the Clerk of the Kitchen call the Lancashire Bitch into the Dining Room'. Charteris locked the door, threw her on the couch, gagged her with his nightcap and raped her. When she threatened to tell her friends, he horse-whipped her and took away her clothes and money.

Charteris's rich and powerful friends filled the court to hear him sentenced to death for rape – but he spent less than a month in Newgate and received a royal pardon. Charteris had made himself immune to prosecution by cultivating friendships with some of the most powerful men in the land, including the Duke of Wharton (his own cousin) and the Prime Minister, Robert Walpole.[52] But he was not immune to mob justice. After he was released from Newgate, a crowd set upon him, and, after yet another girl had been rescued from his house, in this instance by her sister, the neighbours stormed his house, bearing 'Stones, Brickbats, and other such vulgar

Ammunition'.[53] When Charteris died of venereal disease in 1731, a jeering mob wrenched the lid off his coffin, threw dead dogs and cats into it and attempted to mutilate his body.

Covent Garden Piazza was indeed 'that great square of Venus', with a floating population of prostitutes offering a plethora of sexual possibilities to the voracious punters. While this chapter has concentrated on the mainstream erotic tastes, let us turn now to the more recondite, even bizarre activities that were on offer in eighteenth-century London.

7

PERVERSE PLEASURES AND UNNATURAL LUSTS

'When Sodomites were so impudent to ply on
th'Exchange
And by Daylight the Piazza of Covent Garden
to range . . .'

When the actor David Garrick asked Samuel Johnson what he considered to be the two most important things in life, Johnson replied: 'Drinking and fucking!' Many Londoners would have agreed with him. Sexuality takes many different forms, however, and London in the eighteenth century had much to offer those with more recherché tastes. In this chapter, we'll investigate such phenomena as the 'Sodomitical clubs', the flagellation brothels, lesbianism, auto-erotic asphyxiation and last but not least the notorious Hellfire Club. Let us turn first to the 'molly houses', sex clubs for homosexuals from all social backgrounds, but particularly popular with effeminate men or 'mollies'.

In May 1726 the *London Journal* carried an account of twenty

'Sodomitical clubs' in which patrons made their assignations 'and then withdrew into some dark Corners to perpetrate their odious Wickedness',[1] including molly houses such as the Talbot Inn in the Strand, the Fountain in the Strand and the Three Potters in Cripplegate Without. Meanwhile, the male proprietor of the male brothel in Camomile Street, Bishopsgate, went under the splendidly camp pseudonym of 'Countess of Camomile'.

The most famous molly house was undoubtedly 'Mother Clap's' in Holborn, which had beds in every room and catered for 'thirty to forty Chaps every night' and even more on Sundays, the most popular night of the week for homosexual assignations. Mother Clap (her name appears to be a reference to the pox) was a tolerant old bawd, quite prepared to overhear her patrons 'talk all manner of gross and vile obscenity and be wonderfully pleased with it'.[2]

When Mother Clap's was raided, in 1726, and its patrons put on trial, one eyewitness described seeing between forty and fifty men making love to one another, 'calling one another "my dear" and hugging, kissing and tickling each other as if they were a mixture of wanton males and females, and assuming effeminate voices and airs'; they indulged in dancing and making curtsies and

> telling each other that they ought to be whipped for not coming to school more frequently. Some were completely rigged in gowns, petticoats, headcloths, fine laced shoes, furbelowed scarves, and masks; some had riding hoods; some were dressed like milkmaids, others like shepherdesses with green hats, waistcoats, and petticoats; and others had their faces patched and painted and wore very extensive hoop petticoats, which had been very lately introduced.

The patrons sat on one another's laps, kissing in a lewd manner and using their hands indecently; after an interval of toying and playing,[3] they would repair to a back room or 'chapel' for sex or 'marriage'. When they emerged, they would regale their friends with full details of their 'wedding night', and 'brag, in plain terms, of what they had been doing'.[4]

At the Fountain in Russell Square, cross-dressers even enacted childbirth scenes, where one molly would deliver a doll. According to Ned Ward, a chronicler of London low life, said doll would be 'Christened and the Holy Sacrament of Baptism impudently Prophan'd'. Ward, a tabloid moralist, disapproved of the mollies, condemning them as so totally destitute of all masculine attributes that they preferred to behave as women. They adopted all the small vanities natural to the feminine sex to such an extent that 'they will try to speak, walk, chatter, shriek and scold as women do, aping them as well in other respects'.[5] On occasion, the mollies, or rent boys, lost out: one young man, Edward Courtney, told a magistrates' court that he had been prevailed upon to have sex with a country gentleman at the Royal Oak in Pall Mall, and was told that he would be paid 'handsomely', only to discover that 'he stayed all night but in the morning he gave me no more than a sixpence!'[6]

Female prostitutes faced a sliding scale of punishments when apprehended, determined by their class and the social standing of their punters, ranging from a fine to a prison sentence. The stakes were considerably higher for homosexuals, punters and renters alike, and the punishments more severe. Young male prostitutes, or 'catamites', might have cruised the Royal Exchange, picking up rich merchants, but the consequences of arrest and prosecution were far worse than they were for women. Buggery was still illegal, a capital offence which theoretically carried a death sentence if penetration could be proved. While most judges were reluctant to hang 'sodomites', convicted homosexuals faced heavy prison sentences, with the act itself being classified as a form of common assault, and being 'outed' could ruin a man's reputation.

In 1707, there was a great scandal when a 'Sodomites' Club' in the City was raided. Forty men who frequented the alleys around the Royal Exchange were arrested, including Jacob Ecclestone, a merchant, who later committed suicide in Newgate; a draper,

William Grant, who hanged himself in the same prison; a Mr Jermain, curate of St Dunstan's-in-the-East, who slashed his throat with a razor, and a Mr Bearden who killed himself in the same fashion.[7] In 1726, the Societies for the Reformation of Manners closed down over twenty molly houses, including Mother Clap's. The enlightened patroness found herself in the pillory, and later died of her injuries, just like her fellow bawd Mother Needham. Several of her clients were executed.

Public tolerance of 'sodomites' did not improve over the years. In October 1764, the *Public Advertiser* reported that 'A bugger aged sixty was put in the Cheapside Pillory. The Mob tore off his clothes, pelted him with Filth, whipt him almost to Death. He was naked and covered with Dung. When the Hour was up he was carried almost unconscious back to Newgate.'[8]

Class and wealth proved no defence against homophobia as is illustrated by the sad fate of Sir Richard Payne Knight (1751–1824),

Richard Payne Knight c. 1793. His 'Discourse on the Worship of Priapus' caused a scandal.

MP for Leominster, connoisseur and antiquarian. From being a backbench MP in a sleepy rural constituency, Knight was reviled as a dangerous subversive when his book on classical antiquities appeared in 1786; hatred and disdain were heaped upon him and some of his best friends, including Horace Walpole, disowned him.

Knight's early life gave no indication of this sensational destiny. He was born in Herefordshire, a sickly child who attended neither public school nor university. Knight's family were philistine Tory landowners who distrusted his bookish tendencies, and, years later, Knight admitted that his unhappy childhood and feelings of abandonment might have been the cause of the 'ungovern'd passions' which led him astray. Although Knight never confided the exact nature of these passions, his choice of subject matter and that he never married provide a clue. This, and the fact that he devoted his twenties to an extended Grand Tour, spending months in Italy in the company of other young men, excavating the Roman remains at Herculaneum which had yielded up a treasure of erotic imagery. Accompanying Knight was his closest friend, John Robert Cozens, a gifted young artist. Cozens, like Knight, was a delicate young man, with a history of mental and physical illness, but the two appeared firm friends until, in the course of one trip, they reached Naples. There, for reasons that have never been disclosed, Knight and Cozens parted for ever, and Cozens suffered a mental breakdown. Supported by the writer William Beckford, Cozens returned to England and was diagnosed with incurable madness by Dr Thomas Monro, medical director of Bedlam. Knight never saw his friend again, but, until Cozens's death in 1799, he paid for his medical care.

Knight, meanwhile, returned to London and fell under the spell of Pierre François Hugues, the *soi-disant* Baron d'Hancarville (1719–1805). A decadent drifter, always in debt, often in prison, d'Hancarville charmed everyone who came in contact with him, winning reluctant admiration from all with his deft combination of the forbidden and the exotic.[9] The shrewd and manipulative

143

d'Hancarville swiftly made himself the object of Knight's 'ungovern'd passions', paving the way for a scandal which would destroy Knight's career. D'Hancarville was a pornographer who somehow managed to obtain over 700 vases for the envoy Sir William Hamilton, but he could be a deadly ally. One colleague, Winckelmann, was murdered in Vienna. D'Hancarville himself was expelled from Naples for publishing pornographic pictures; in 1769 he managed to make a killing by producing cheaper versions.

D'Hancarville published his own book in 1785. This purported to be a study of the arts of Ancient Greece but was in effect a volume of pornography devoted to the worship of Priapus, depicting couples in a variety of sexual positions under the benevolent gaze of the said deity. In one illustration the happy couple are even depicted 'harvesting' Priapus's seed.[10] This inspired Knight to go into print on his own account, and in 1786 he published his *Account of the Remains of the Worship of Priapus*, a scholarly account of his findings in Italy, which also included a dissertation, 'Discourse on the Worship of Priapus'. At first glance, this seems little more than the usual exercise in dilettantism by a learned gentleman who has been on his Grand Tour and seeks recognition in print. The publication's ostensible purpose was to serve as a back-up to a colleague's *Account of the Remains of the Worship of Priapus lately existing at Isernia, in the Kingdom of Naples*, which also sounds deadly dull. However, it was the illustrations which really gave the game away: two dozen sexually explicit black and white images among the 217 quarto pages, culminating in a scene where a satyr is depicted having sex with a goat. As if this was not enough, Knight's innocent tone of 'enlightened paganism', in the course of which he argued that sex was a legitimate form of worship and that the crucifix itself, as worshipped by Christians, was a phallic symbol, was taken as evidence of profound anti-clericalism. Although Knight attempted to limit any damage to his reputation by making his book a subscription-only publication, limited to learned gentlemen, news of this sensational tome soon leaked out. Unlike d'Hancarville, a professional pornographer who had absolutely nothing to lose, Knight suffered utter vilification. At one stroke this gentle, learned backbencher was transformed into a monster of depravity. Knight retreated to his country pile a dejected figure, and never lived down the shame. He was not to know that his book, republished in the nineteenth century, would become one of the most popular works of Victorian homosexual pornography. Whether this information would have been of any consolation to him is a matter for conjecture.[11]

While Knight was condemned for his learned treatise on male sexuality, a greater degree of tolerance was extended towards one of the most celebrated and curious cases of male to female cross-dressing, that of Chevalier d'Eon de Beaumont (1728–1810). The Chevalier came to England in 1752 in connection with preliminary talks leading to the Treaty of Versailles. He first attracted attention owing to a number of plots attempting to return him forcibly to France. The Chevalier received sympathetic press coverage, which reflected favourably on the relative freedom of England compared with France. At some point during the 1760s, the Chevalier began to appear in public in women's clothes. The rumour was circulated that 'he' had been brought up as a boy, and for political reasons could only now return to his true gender. Reasons for his decision to adopt female dress were legion: some even suggested that he was ordered to do so by Louis XVI, and that he had completed several spying missions for France while disguised as a woman. He did keep press cuttings about cross-dressing, hermaphrodites and related issues, so the topic was obviously very important to him.

The Chevalier's decision to dress as a woman prompted a frenzy of press speculation as to his true gender. The *Morning Post* pledged £200,000 to whoever could settle the argument and the debate raged as to whether he was 'a man, an hermaphrodite or any other animal'. Legal disputes over gambling on the issue led to a court case, Hayes *v*. Jaques (1777), in which two doctors testified that the Chevalier was a woman. One claimed that he had treated her for 'women's disorders', while the other stated that she had made amorous suggestions to him. The court ruled that he was a woman, and the Chevalier signed an affidavit swearing that he had no inter-est in the bets taken out on him. Press speculation did not however subside: an article appeared in the *Morning Herald and Daily Advertiser* stating that he had always been a woman and concluding that 'the visitation of M. D'Eon to this country in the attire of the feminine, it is hoped will operate so forcibly as to induce such ladies who have usurped a right to wearing breeches, to leave them off'.

Between 1794 and 1796, the Chevalier drew large crowds to his public fencing displays – whilst dressed as a woman. Despite being referred to in the *Public Ledger* as 'an impertinent French female' most press coverage was favourable. The Chevalier was regarded as a woman who had been forced to disguise herself as a man but who had now reassigned herself to her true gender. His reticence towards women when he himself was in breeches was taken as fur-ther evidence of his female identity, while his status as an aristocrat also offered protection.

The Chevalier died in 1810, and when his body was examined, he was discovered to have been a man. But, while he was indis-putably male, it was noted that 'the throat was by no means a man's; the shoulders were square, the breast remarkably full, the arms, hands and fingers those of a stout female; and the legs and feet cor-responding with the arms'.[12]

Lesbians (the term was used in its modern meaning from 1732) had a lower profile, partly because sexual acts between women have never been illegal, and partly because lesbianism has rarely been perceived as a threat to the status quo. Lesbian displays would have been on the menu of any self-respecting seraglio: a standard service for male punters keen to watch some girl-on-girl action, as in the seduction of Fanny Hill by an older woman at the outset of her sexual career. Genuine lesbian relationships were common among prostitutes; many women developed close emotional and physical bonds as a means of survival and as a response to male abuse.

Punters or 'cullies' were not surprised to encounter lesbians in the course of their sexual adventures. *Harris's List of Covent Garden Ladies* tells us about a Miss Wilson of Green Street, Cavendish Square, who is of above average height and lacking in conventional female graces: 'her hands and arms, her limbs, indeed, in general, are more calculated for the milk-carrier, than the soft delights of love'. Miss Wilson frequently declared that 'a female bed-fellow can give more real joys than ever she experienced with the male part of the sex' and that 'many of the pranks she has played with her own sex in bed (where she is as lascivious as a goat) have come to our knowledge'.[13]

'Mother Courage' of Suffolk Street and Frances Bradshaw of Bow Street catered for the lesbian trade, while Sisters Anne and Elanor [*sic*] Redshawe ran 'an extremely secretive discreet House of Intrigue in Tavistock Street, catering for Ladies in the Highest Keeping' and wealthy married women who came in disguise to amuse themselves.[14]

Lesbians were tolerated if they appeared reassuringly feminine, or if they were, like Queen Anne, of such exalted station that they were immune to the law. The Fleet Registers give three examples of women marrying each other, without any action being taken against them.[15] While heterosexual women who dressed as men to enlist in the military, such as Hannah Snell, the Female Marine (1723–92), were tolerated, visibly butch women received very different treatment, since passing for a man endowed them with greater social and economic status. Catherine Vizzani, an Italian courtesan caught trying to elope with another woman whilst dressed as a man, was shot dead in 1755.[16]

There were more visible lesbians down in the East End, where a balladeer immortalized this couple in 1728:

'Two Kissing Girls of Spitalfields'

That one's a Man is false, they've both been felt,
Tho' Jolly swears, Bess is, or sh' has been gelt [castrated]

She bullies, whistles, sings, and rants and swears
Beyond the Plyers at St. Katern's Stairs [St Katharine's
    Docks];
She kisses all, but Jenny is her dear,
She feels her Bubbies, and she bites her ear:
They to the Garret or the Cellar sneak.
Play tricks, and put each other to the Squeak.
What Pity 'tis, in such a case as this,
One does not pass a Metamorphosis,
Then they'd not stop the flowing Breach of Dagnum
With *Digitus vel instrumentum magnum*.[17]

Dagenham Breach was a thousand-acre lake next to the Thames resulting from a repair to its walls from 1714 to eliminate a 400-foot mud bank that was a danger to shipping. It was near St Katharine's Docks, where men plied for work as porters unloading ships. The last line says that these women will have to plug up the hole with a finger ('digit') in the absence of any larger instrument, alluding to their lack of a penis. So this Latin tag appears to have been a variant on the old gag about the boy sticking his finger in the dyke.

Penis or no, lesbians were a common feature of medical textbooks, many of which served as a source of titillation, notably in descriptions of the clitoris. This magnificent organ, first officially discovered by anatomists in the sixteenth century, was regarded as a form of mini-penis. The larger the clitoris, writers argued, the greater the propensity to 'tribadism' or 'frottage' (rubbing) and women having sex with each other like men. According to one author, 'Women well furnished in these Parts may divert themselves with their Companions to whom for the most part they can give as much Pleasure as Men do but cannot receive in any proportion the Pleasure themselves, for want of Ejaculation, the Crisis of Enjoyment to the Male in the Intrigues of *Venus*. I am informed that Diversions of this nature are frequently practis'd by robust and lustful Females who cannot with any prospect of safety to their Reputations venture upon the Embraces of a Man, though they are never so strongly inclin'd'.[18]

Despite the fact that the average clitoris is about the length of half a finger, a bawdy literature developed in which women from certain racial backgrounds were more generously endowed, and therefore more libidinous, particularly the Italians (stereotyped as sex-mad, yet again), Turkish, Arab and black women, who were reputed to have clitorises as large and as effective as a penis. The collective attitude of (male) authors to lesbianism was, as is so often the case with men, erotic fascination, tinged with the occasional reminder that such conduct was, of course, immoral. The anonymous scribe of *Satan's Harvest Home* issued a rebuke to 'Sapphists' who 'not content with our Sex, begins *Amours* with her own, and teaches the Female World a new Sort of Sin, call'd the *Flats,* practis'd at Twickenham at this day'.[19]

The mention of an innocuous south-west London suburb is a reference to Lady Mary Wortley Montagu, an aristocratic English traveller who eventually retired to Twickenham. Lady Mary was so inspired by the beauty and solidarity of the Turkish women she met during her travels that she was suspected of having indulged in the pleasures of the harem, which, according to the author of *Satan's Harvest Home*, was a veritable cornucopia of girl-on-girl action, steam baths and cucumbers, which he refers to as 'the Game of Flats'. This is a reference to games with playing cards, which were called 'flats', and an allusion to the rubbing together of two 'flat' female pudenda. For example, sex between women was described in 1698–9 as 'a New Game / Call'd Flats with a Swinging Clitoris'. The lesbian usage, though it can be traced back to at least 1663, is not recorded in the *Oxford English Dictionary*.[20]

'Flats' was said to be particularly popular among the Turks:

ordinarily the Women bathe by themselves, bond and free together; so that you shall many Times see young Maids, exceeding beautiful, gathered from all Parts of the World, exposed naked to the View of other Women, who thereupon fall in Love with them . . . By this you may guess, what the strict Watch over Females comes to, and that it is not enough to avoid the Company of an adulterous Man, for the *Females* burn in Love one towards another; and the Pandaresses [female pimps] to such refined Lovers are the Bards [bawds]; and, therefore, some *Turks* will deny their Wives the Use of their public Baths, but they cannot do it altogether, because their Law allows them.[21]

In keeping with the theory that foreign girls were better endowed, and more libidinous, women had to travel abroad to experience the wilder shores of love. This attitude is apparent in *A Sapphic Epistle to Mrs D* (1782), in which the anonymous Mrs D pursues lesbian amours in Italy, 'where many lascivious females divert themselves one with another'. Men should beware, warns another poet, lest their sweethearts be seduced by other women when their backs are turned:

> Know, whilst you idle thus away your time,
> Women in secret joys consume their prime,
> Some fav'urite maid, or handy young coquette
> Steals the rich prize you vainly strive to get;
> Of them be cautious, but the artful prude
> Watch most, for she will thoughtless girls delude . . .
> Your lovely nymph, in private quench'd her flame
> With some experienc'd, well-known crafty dame.[22]

Those lesbians, and straight women, for whom clitoral orgasm was not sufficient could console themselves with a dildo, which had become a must-have accessory for any self-respecting woman or man about town by the early eighteenth century. One Georges-Louis Lesage (1676–1759), visiting England in 1713, noted that there were always some women in St James's Park carrying baskets full of dolls which seemed to be in great demand with the young ladies. Instead of legs, the dolls supported a cylinder, covered with cloth, which was about six inches long and one inch wide. According to Lesage, one young woman complained that hers was too big and she wanted to exchange it for a smaller one, but the vendor refused to do so, arguing that it would be impossible to resell it.[23]

'Signor Dildo' as Rochester referred to this 'cylinder' in his poem of 1678 was much in demand, and an entire tradition of bawdy verse developed lauding the properties of this essential item. One poem describes the exploits of a dildo when it arrives in London. Nicknamed 'Monsieur Thing', the poem follows it from Covent Garden to Fleet Street and to the homes of several ladies in dire need of its services:

> The Engine does come up so near to Nature,
> Can spout so pleasing, betwixt Wind and Water,
> Warm mild, or any other Liquid softer,
> Slow as they please, or, if they please, much faster.

Monsieur Thing then meets another merchant's wife, who immediately takes a shine to him:

> She boldly work'd him up into an Oil,
> So did she make the Creature slave and toil;
> She wrought him till he was just out of breath,
> And harrast Seignior almost unto Death.

His troubles are not over, however, as he is called upon to satisfy an old maid and a couple of lesbians, one of whom ties him to her middle:

> She acted Man, being in a merry Mood,
> Striving to please her Partner as she cou'd;
> And thus they took it in their turns to please
> Their Lustful Inclinations to appease.[24]

Sold at sixpence a copy, 'Monsieur Thing's Origin' did not please everybody: one female bookseller who caught a pair of hawkers selling the poem outside her shop set the constables on them.[25]

Another source of amusement was the sex doll, which could be ordered by eighteenth-century males with sufficient means for their private amusement.[26] Published in 1748, *Adollizing: or, a lively picture of a doll-worship* assures the reader that this extraordinary episode is based on a true story. Clodius, a person of high distinction, failing to seduce the beautiful young Clarabella, takes himself off to a 'Latin artist' (Italians once again being synonymous with sex in eighteenth-century London) who makes a doll, 'as big as life' and with perfect craftsmanship, right down to 'the arch'd mount, just o'er the cloven part', upon which 'a tuft of hair he fixes with nice art'.[27] This doll is not for display only:

> A seven-inch bore, proportion'd to his mind,
> With oval entrance, all with spunge [*sic*] he lin'd,
> Which warmly mollify'd, is fit for use,
> And will the sought-for consequence produce.[28]

Eventually, Clodius becomes bored with his doll, and, despite experimenting with different heads, abandons it in favour of Clarabella, who eventually thaws sufficiently to reciprocate his advances.

Eighteenth-century Londoners were intrigued by, and not always tolerant of, sexual diversity, whilst being fascinated by freak show aspects of human sexuality such as hermaphrodites and 'castrati' or eunuchs, who, it was believed, were capable of sexual intercourse but sexually sterile. An entire body of pornographic literature developed devoted to the premise that a sexually frustrated woman could find relief with a eunuch as there was no danger of getting pregnant. 'Castrati' are 'very tractable; it gratifies their pride to be taken notice of by a woman and they toil like horses'.[29] In one tale, Lady

Lucian decides to try out Signor Squalini, a singer, who proves most satisfactory and is hired as her music tutor. One day, however, the happy musicians are disturbed by Lady Lucian's husband, who passed by her door and:

> heard his lady cry out in an extatic [sic] tone of voice, 'Give what thou can'st, and let me dream the rest.' His lordship was too well read in Pope, not to know where that line was, and the occasion of speaking it; he laid his hand immediately upon the lock of the door, and giving it a push, open, for the lady had omitted to bolt it, he beheld my lady and her master – not playing the harpsi-chord, but playing upon it: her ladyship couchant upon the instrument, which served her for a sopha [sic], and the master recumbent on the lady, while every now and then he touched the keys of the harpsichord with his feet.

Three days later, husband and wife parted by mutual consent, allowing Lady Lucian the opportunity to enjoy the society of her dear castrato without molestation.[30]

Flagellation had always been popular, particularly among the nobility – and with women as well as men. Queen Catherine de' Medici was said to enjoy placing her maids of honour over her knee and whipping them like little children, and pages often found them-selves upon the whipping block as well. Flagellation, as we know, constituted one of the standard services of brothels. In *The Virtuoso* (1678) Thomas Shadwell portrayed an elderly gentleman who 'loves castigation mightily'[31] whilst the *Treatise on the Use of Flogging* (1718) established this fetish firmly in the public consciousness, and led to a flogging boom, with specialist brothels opening all over London. Mother Burgess, one of many bawds who specialized in flagellation, was immortalized in 'The Paphian Grove' (1738):

> With Breeches down, there let some lusty Ladd,
> (to desp'rate Sickness desperate Cures are had!)

> With honest Birch excoriate your Hide
> And flog the Cupid from your scourged Bankside!

'Paphian', derived from Aphrodite, the goddess of love, referred to any act of illicit love.[32]

One of the best-known flogging brothels was Mary Wilson's, originally opened around 1777 in New Road, St Pancras, then moving to larger premises at nearby Tonbridge Place. Wilson published *The Exhibition of Female Flagellants*, praising the benefits of being whipped by women, before moving to fashionable Bond Street, then St John's Wood. An erudite woman, who translated and published European erotic novels, she noted that there were three types of client who enjoyed flagellation:

1. Those who like to receive a fustigation, more or less severe from the hands of a fine woman, who is sufficiently robust to wield the rod with vigour and effect.
2. Those who desire to administer birch discipline on the white and plump buttocks of a female.
3. Those who neither wish to be passive recipients nor active administrators of birch discipline, but derive sufficient excitement as mere spectators of the sport.[33]

She also recognized that flagellation had considerable appeal:

It is very true that there are innumerable old generals, admirals, colonels and captains, as well as bishops, judges, barristers, lords, commoners and physicians, who periodically go to be whipped, merely because it warms their blood, and keeps up a little agreeable excitement in their systems long after the power of enjoying the opposite sex has failed them; but it is equally true, that hundreds of young men through having been educated at institutions where the masters are fond of administering birch discipline, and recollecting certain sensations produced by it, have imbibed a passion for it, and have longed to receive the same chastisement from the hands of a fine woman . . .[34]

When Wilson moved on for good to Paris, her brothel went to Theresa Berkeley, one of the most famous experts in flagellation. In 1787, Berkeley took control of a house of assignation known as the 'White House' at 21 Soho Square. This was a grand mansion with opulent decor, and featured the Gold Room, the Silver Room and the Bronze Room – all equipped with mirrors, so that the girls and their clients could view their performances. There was also a Painted Chamber, a Grotto and a Coal Hole, but the *pièce de résistance* was the 'Skeleton Room', fitted with a cupboard from which a human skeleton emerged, a subtle *memento mori* for older punters.

Mrs Berkeley, or 'The Governess' as she came to be known, moved to new premises at 28 Charlotte Street in 1828. She made it a habit to find out 'every idea, every caprice, every wish of her clients', no matters how recherché, as long as she got paid.

Her instruments of torture were more numerous than those of any other governess. Her supply of birch was extensive, and kept in water, so that it was always green and pliant: she had shafts with a dozen whip thongs on each of them; a dozen different sizes of cat-o'-nine-tails, some with needle points worked into them; various kinds of thin bending canes; leather straps like coach traces; battle-doors [*sic*], made of thick sole-leather, with inch nails run through to docket, and currycomb tough hides rendered callous by many years flagellation. Holly brushes, furze brushes; a prickly evergreen, called butcher's brush and during the summer, a glass and China vases, filled with a constant supply of green nettles, with which she often restored the dead to life. Thus, at her shop, whoever went with plenty of money, could be birched, whipped, fustigated, scourged, needle-pricked, half-hung, holly-brushed, furze-brushed, butcher-brushed, stinging-nettled, curry-combed, phlebotomized, and tortured till he had a belly full.[35]

On the second floor, clients who so wished could be strung up via a hook and pulley attached to the ceiling, by which she could draw a man up by his hands. 'For those whose lech it was to flog a woman, she would herself submit to a certain extent; but if they were gluttons at it, she had women in attendance who would take any number of lashes the flogger pleased, provided he forked out an ad valorem duty. Among these were Miss Ring, Hannah Jones, Sally Taylor, One-eyed Peg, Bauld-cunted Poll, and a black girl, called Ebony Bet.'

'The Governess' also invented the 'Berkeley Horse' in the spring of 1828. According to the pornography expert Henry Spencer Ashbee, this contraption was

> a notorious machine for Mrs Berkley [*sic*] to flog gentlemen upon . . . It is capable of being opened to a considerable extent, so as to bring the body to any angle that might be desirable. There is a print in Mrs Berkley's memoirs, representing a man upon it quite naked. A woman is sitting in a chair exactly under it, with her bosom, belly, and bush exposed: she is manualizing his embolon [plug], whilst Mrs Berkley is birching his posteriors. When the new flogging machine was invented, the designer told her it would bring her into notice, and go by her name after her death; and it did cause her to be talked of, and brought her a great deal of business.[36]

It certainly did. 'The Governess' made £10,000 at her Charlotte Street establishment between 1828 and her death in 1836. Her fortune went to her brother-in-law, a missionary, who rejected it because he disapproved of the manner in which it had been made.[37]

A Mrs Collet ran a similar establishment in Covent Garden, known to have been patronized by the Prince of Wales (later George IV), although 'it is not known whether the Royal Wrist wielded the whip, or the Royal Buttocks submitted to it'.[38] The craze for flagellation was so great at this period that one old roué,

The notorious Berkeley Horse invented by Theresa Berkeley.
Enthusiasts were bound to this apparatus and whipped.

Chace Pine, devised a machine which could whip forty persons at a time although many enthusiasts would argue that this approach lacks the human touch.[39]

The public appetite for books about flagellation fuelled the emerging pornography industry, which was to take off during the nineteenth century with the development of mass-production printing. Eighteenth-century readers were catered for with titles such as Jacques Boileau's *Histoire des flagellants* (Amsterdam, 1701), which inspired many sequels and parodies. The pornographer Edmund Curll translated the 1718 edition of John Henry Melbonius's *De usu flagorum* (first published 1639) or *A Treatise of the Use of Flogging* and defended his publication with spurious medical claims, arguing that 'the rods' represented a cure for impotence and venereal disease, and reading about such topics offered comfort for men and women unable to obtain sexual satisfaction by more conventional means. 'There are Persons who are stimulated to *Venery by Strokes of Rods, and worked up into a Flame of Lust by Blows,*' he reminds us, 'and that the Part, which distinguishes us to be Men, should be raised by the Charm of invigorating Lashes.' He supports his argument with classical quotations and the observation that old lechers use flogging to 're-inflame the cold parts'.[40]

Flogging appealed particularly to the nobility, perhaps because, as Mary Wilson suggested, they had been aroused by early experiences of flagellation at their public schools. One popular anecdote concerned an elderly aristocrat who rented a house in St James's Place and hired an attractive elderly woman as his housekeeper. One day each week, she had been instructed to lay out scrubbing brushes, mops, and every other item necessary to clean a room, and to engage two women to meet him there on that day. One of these women was to 'role play' a housekeeper and the other a chambermaid. The nobleman would then dress himself up as a parish girl and begin scrubbing the room. Afterwards, either one or both of the women would scold him for doing a poor job and then whip him, just as many parish girls were whipped by their mistresses.

'Amorous strangulation', or auto-erotic asphyxiation, was not unknown in eighteenth-century London, as illustrated by the peculiar case of Franz Kotzwara (1730–91), a Bohemian musician.[41] This celebrated double bass player and composer of 'The Battle of Prague' (which commemorates the Prussian victory in 1757 over the Austrians at Prague) had a taste for wine, women and kinky sex. On 2 September 1791 he visited the brothel at 5 Vine Street in St Martin's, where he met with the prostitute Susannah Hill. Following dinner, Kotzwara demanded that she cut off his testicles, a service which she refused to perform. Kotzwara then strangled himself on a rope hooked to the door, ostensibly while having sex with the girl. This led to a spectacular trial at the Old Bailey, where Hill was charged with murder. But once testimony was produced which documented Kotzwara's eclectic sexual tastes, Hill was -acquitted. Kotzwara's is the first documented case of auto-erotic asphyxiation.

The final player in this account of sexual perversity is Sir Francis Dashwood (1708–81), proprietor of the Hellfire Club, although it must be admitted that the most infamous behaviour associated with this establishment occurred outside London. The original Hellfire Club had been founded by Philip, Duke of Wharton in 1719, when Dashwood would have been too young to be a member. Lord Wharton was a prominent politician with two separate lives; the first as a man of letters, and the second as a drunkard, a rioter, an infidel and a rake. Members of the club were assumed to include Wharton's immediate friends, the Earl of Hillsborough, the Earl of Lichfield and Sir Edmund O'Brien. This Hellfire Club was a typical early eighteenth-century club in that it was formed for one specific purpose: in this case, to ridicule religion and conventional morality – hence its name. While its supposed president was the Devil, and members referred to themselves as 'devils', there was no actual devil worship in evidence. Instead, activities included mock religious ceremonies, and dinners to which members turned up dressed as characters from the Bible, and ate dishes such as Holy Ghost Pie and Devil's Loin, washed down with Hell-fire punch. The club met on Sundays at different locations around London, with one popular venue being the Greyhound Tavern. However, it was unusual in that it admitted women as members, and, since respectable ladies could not frequent taverns, meetings were also held at members' houses.

From these relatively innocuous origins, the Hellfire Club took a different turn under the presidency of Sir Francis Dashwood, a rake who had fornicated his way across Europe on his Grand Tour.[42] Dashwood was alternately fascinated and repelled by Roman Catholicism – it was said that at one moment Dashwood would be jeering at the rituals and vestments and at the next sobbing and praying on his knees – as well as Freemasonry and Satanism. On one occasion, he produced a whip in the Sistine Chapel and beat those kneeling in prayer. Dashwood returned to England and was elected MP for New Romney. His private life, meanwhile, was increasingly devoted to decadence and dissolution.

In 1746, Dashwood founded his Order of the Knights of St

Francis, which initially met at the George and Vulture tavern in the Cornhill. The Knights convened in a room dominated by 'an everlasting Rosicrucian lamp', a large crystal globe encircled by a gold serpent with its tail in its mouth. The globe was crowned with a pair of silver wings and was suspended in chains in the form of twisted serpents. The Hellfire Club proved so popular that the George and Vulture became too small for its devotions, so proceedings moved to Dashwood's extravagant country house at West Wycombe. This neo-Gothic fantasy included a west wing which was a replica of a temple to Bacchus. The first meeting of Dashwood's 'brotherhood' was held on Walpurgis Night 1752. Walpurgis Night is a pre-Christian festival, celebrated on 1 May, and reflected Sir Francis's obsession with paganism. But the event was not a success, perhaps because of objections raised by his long-suffering wife, the 'pious prude' Mary Ellis, and he did not hold parties at home again. Instead, in 1751, Dashwood leased Medmenham Abbey from a friend, Francis Duffield. On the Thames near Marlow, about six miles from West Wycombe, the house had originally been a Cistercian abbey before being rebuilt as a Tudor mansion. Dashwood had the abbey rebuilt in Gothic Revival style, and the motto *Fais ce que tu voudras* ('Do what thou wilt', an injunction later taken up by Aleister Crowley) was placed above a doorway in stained glass.

There had been a cave beneath the original abbey, with a low narrow entrance surrounded by yew trees. Believing this to be an old pagan site, Dashwood had a further network of caves excavated, where he and his followers could celebrate their rites. For some idea of what actually went on, one must turn to coffee-house gossips such as Horace Walpole, who described these events as 'rigorously pagan: Bacchus and Venus were the deities to whom they almost publicly sacrificed; and the nymphs and the hogsheads that were laid in against the festivals of this new church, sufficiently informed the neighbourhood of the complexion of those hermits.' The thirteen members addressed each other as 'brothers' and the leader, who changed regularly, as 'Abbot'. During meetings members supposedly wore ritual clothing: white trousers, jacket and cap, while the 'Abbot' wore a red ensemble of the same style.

The Hellfire Club was an open secret among the establishment, and its members and visitors included some of the most influential political figures of the day: Lord Bute, who was to become Prime Minister; Lord Sandwich, a sadistic rapist and First Lord of the Admiralty, described as 'completely depraved, as mischievous as a monkey and as lecherous as a goat'; and his rival, John Wilkes, the radical MP and journalist. Other devotees included Thomas Potter, son of the Archbishop of Canterbury, Paymaster General and a rumoured necrophiliac; and William Douglas, later 4th Duke of Queensberry, one of the richest and most rapacious men of his age. Benjamin Franklin, the Prince of Wales and even Horace Walpole himself were alleged members.

Dashwood's mistress, 'Hell-fire Stanhope', one of London's top bawds, ferried molls down from the city to participate in orgies, and also initiated upper-class ladies into the club. These women included Dashwood's half-sister, Mary Walcott; Frances, Viscountess Fane; and Lady Mary Wortley Montagu, who no doubt enjoyed the lesbian displays which were actively encouraged.[43] Inevitably, it was claimed that Dashwood's monks celebrated black mass, with satanic prayers offered in the flickering candlelight over the naked body of an aristocratic young woman, as masked participants gathered round to watch and then sipped wine from her navel, but to the modern eye, events as described seem no more sinister than an erotic party or a sex club.

Dashwood is remembered as a libertine *par excellence*, but even Dashwood did not believe that pleasure should be for everybody. Whatever went on at the Hellfire Club, he was still a member of the establishment. Enjoyment was not for the common man: Dashwood's first act on becoming Chancellor of the Exchequer in 1762 was to levy a tax on cider, an act which must have earned the condemnation of pagans and Christians alike.

*

Over the centuries, London's whores had proved capable of indulging every peccadillo imaginable. What these women and men could not have foreseen, however, was the next development in the city's sexual history. As London became the world's great capital of industry and commerce, a global workshop and a glittering metropolis, it also became the centre of the world's sex trade, as young girls arrived in their tens of thousands, desperate for a new life but soon drawn into the net of the world's oldest profession.

8

WEST END GIRLS

'The streets of London are an open book . . .'

In 1853, the Pre-Raphaelite artist Holman Hunt exhibited a painting entitled *The Awakening Conscience*. The art historian Peter Quennell described the scene, which depicts a young woman with dishevelled hair leaping from the grip of her foxy lover, touched to the heart by the associations of the music he has been 'strumming' on the piano in an 'incautious' moment. Holman Hunt intended to illustrate the 'manner in which the appeal of the spirit of heavenly love calls a soul to abandon a lower life'. His piano playing and her 'career of shame' are simultaneously interrupted as her conscience breaks like dawn across her clouded features.[1] The young woman's expression was regarded as so disturbing in the original version that the first owner of the painting asked Holman Hunt to tone it down.

And who is this young woman with the dishevelled hair and a rather startled expression, turning away from her life of luxury? She is, of course, a 'fallen woman', who depends for her livelihood on the charity of rich gentlemen such as the foxy lover upon whose lap she rests. Holman Hunt was so determined that his depiction should be accurate that he visited several houses in St John's Wood, the neighbourhood associated with 'kept women', to gain an accurate impression of such a creature and her way of life. As a result, the canvas presents an invaluable record of the home of a mid-Victorian *demi-mondaine*. Her sitting room is cheerful, opulent and overcrowded, with an upright rosewood piano, a busy carpet clashing with the florid wallpaper, a gilded clock beneath a glass bell and a gold-framed mirror which reflects a sunny back garden through the open window. All the furniture is new, expensive and, according to Pre-Raphaelite aesthetics, embarrassingly vulgar. This is a gilded cage, similar to many other gilded cages all over north London, where many a 'soiled dove' was kept in her love nest by a generous gallant.[2] Motivated by moral fervour, Holman Hunt drives home the message with clunkingly explicit imagery: the young woman's pet cat is toying with a bird; the fingers of a discarded glove, lying on the floor, point to her future: she too will be carelessly thrown aside, when the time comes. Hogarth would have blushed at the younger painter's earnestly doctrinaire approach.

But for all her awakening conscience, Holman Hunt is keen to remind us that this dove's flight will not be an easy one. Victorian morality dictated that once a young woman had turned her back on respectable society, rehabilitation would be a lengthy process, if it came at all. 'The doors of the wholly respectable world are closed against her,' wrote Quennell in his commentary on the painting. 'She must be content perhaps with a quiet country refuge, there under an assumed name to pass her remaining days in piety and good works.'[3]

The popular notion was that a fallen woman was always fallen. If she fluttered back to the domestic dovecote, it was as a crippled supplicant. While *The Awakening Conscience* represented the most upmarket form of prostitution, Dante Gabriel Rossetti's *Found* (begun in 1853 and never fully completed) was more brutal. Writing to Holman Hunt and anxious to explain that the concept of

Found preceded Holman Hunt's depiction of a fallen woman, Rossetti told his colleague that the picture represents a London street at dawn, with the lamps still lit along a bridge that forms the distant background.

> A drover has left his cart standing in the middle of the road, in which stands a bleating calf on its way to market, and has run a little way after a girl who has passed him, wandering in the streets. He had just come up with her and she, recognizing him, has sunk under her shame upon her knees, against the wall of a raised churchyard in the foreground, while he stands holding her hands as he seized them, half in bewilderment and half guarding her from doing herself a hurt. The calf, a white one, will be a beautiful and suggestive part of the thing.[4]

The girl is clearly that popular cliché, the lost innocent who has been decoyed up to London and fallen among thieves. The honest yeoman, filled with pity and repulsion by her plight, is either her father or her childhood sweetheart.

One of the most famous fictional depictions of the wages of sin occurs in *David Copperfield* by Charles Dickens, when old Mr Peggotty, who has wandered across Europe searching for his lost daughter, eventually tracks her down near Golden Square, in Soho, with the assistance of another prostitute, Martha. When David and Peggotty meet her, Martha is on the brink of suicide:

> As if she were a part of the refuse it had cast out, and left to corruption and decay, the girl we had followed strayed down to the river's brink, and stood in the midst of this night-picture, lonely and still, looking at the water . . . I think she was talking to herself. I am sure, although absorbed in gazing at the water, that her shawl was off her shoulders, and that she was muffling her hands in it, in an unsettled and bewildered way, more like the action of a sleepwalker than a waking person. I know, and never can

forget, that there was that in her wild manner which gave me no assurance but that she would sink before my eyes, until I had her arm within my grasp . . . We carried her away from the water to where there were some dry stones, and there laid her down, crying and moaning. In a little while she sat among the stones holding her wretched head with both her hands. 'Oh, the river!' she cried passionately. 'Oh, the river!'[5]

Martha is past saving; but David and Peggotty do at least trace 'Little Emily', who, having been 'ruined' (that is, seduced) by the rakish Steerforth, is considered unfit to return to her family but is instead bundled off in an emigrant ship bound for Australia to start a new life. Death by drowning was a common fate for London's prostitutes, and a popular theme for writers and artists. While *Found Drowned* by George Frederick Watts was exhibited in 1850, Thomas Hood explored the theme in 'The Bridge of Sighs', where the poet gazes voyeuristically upon the drowned body of a young woman, speculating as to the tragic cause of her death and lingering salaciously over the soaking garments which cling to her wet body, the looped auburn tresses dripping with water and 'those poor lips of her, oozing clammily'.[6]

On a lighter note, a cartoon appeared in *Punch* on 10 January 1857, depicting 'The Great Social Evil'. The time: midnight. The scene: 'not a hundred miles from the Haymarket'. It depicts two women: Fanny, who is resplendent in her finery but haggard, and Bella, whose shabby clothes denote her rustic origins. Fanny is propping up a theatre doorway where *La Traviata* (an opera about a doomed courtesan) is playing. She looks as miserable as sin and the punch line is glaringly obvious: 'Ah, Fanny!' exclaims Bella, looking at her friend. 'How long have you been gay!' ('Gay' at that period was street slang for 'prostitute'.) Thomas Hardy, creator of one of literature's most famous fallen women, Tess of the D'Urbervilles, was also attracted by the irony of the 'gay' woman in 'The Ruined Maid':

'O 'Melia, my dear, this does everything crown!
Who could have supposed I should meet you in Town?
And whence such fair garments, such prosperi-ty?'
'O didn't you know I'd been ruined?' said she.

'You left us in tatters, without shoes or socks,
Tired of digging potatoes, and spudding up docks;
And now you've gay bracelets and bright feathers three!'
'Yes: that's how we dress when we're ruined,' said she.

'Your hands were like paws then, your face blue and bleak
But now I'm bewitched by your delicate cheek,
And your little gloves fit as on any la-dy!'
'We never do work when we're ruined,' said she.

'You used to call home-life a hag-ridden dream,
And you'd sigh, and you'd sock [sulk]; but at present you seem
To know not of megrims or melancho-ly!'
'True. One's pretty lively when ruined,' said she.[7]

These representations of fallen women all appeared at the height of
a moral panic about prostitution, fanned into hysteria by social
reformers and the popular press. Dr Michael Ryan, an authority on
prostitution, claimed that, by 1857, there were 80,000 prostitutes
working in London, making over £8m a year.[8] The significance of
this turnover was not lost on the industrious Victorian establishment, with newspaper columnists reduced to spluttering moral
outrage by the prostitutes' earning power and the fact that none of
them paid taxes. In time-honoured fashion, whores were demonized as a menace to public health. 'Who are those fair creatures,
neither chaperone nor chaperoned, those somebodies nobody
knows, who elbow our wives and daughters in the parks and
promenades?' demanded Dr William Acton (1813–75), a noted
campaigner against prostitution. 'Who are those painted, dressy

women, flaunting along the streets and boldly accosting the passers-by?'[9]

Who were these women? They were the visible evidence of a flourishing night-time economy (and, it has to be said, a daytime economy too) which offered rich rewards and considerable incentives compared with twelve-hour days losing their eyesight sewing shirts in a sweatshop or scrubbing floors. The logic of their choice was lost upon misogynistic commentators who characterized prostitutes in vivid rhetoric as rolling along the road to ruin in hired carriages, looking out with shameless faces and despairing eyes, to the envy of their wretched sisters, who slouched along in faded finery and the mere rags of fashionable attire.[10]

Acton described an upmarket prostitute as the 'flaunting, extravagant quean', young and fair, dragging a besotted young lover like a lackey to parties, flower shows and the races, and night after night to select balls, plays or public saloons, and then dropping him once she has spent his allowance, taking up with another man, possibly his best friend, until she has run the gauntlet of men about town and is reduced to going downmarket, becoming a toast of the tavern by the age of thirty, 'the loudest of the loud, in the utmost blaze of finery, looked on as first-rate company by aspiring gents, surrounded by a knot of gentlemen who applaud her rampant nonsense, and wandering, hotel-sick, businessmen whose footsteps stray at night to where she keeps her foolish court'.[11]

At this point, Acton becomes positively venomous: 'She is a sort of whitewashed sepulchre, fair to the eye, but full of inner rottenness – a mercenary human tigress,' demanding respect but insufferably rude, proud and high-minded one moment, but not ashamed to beg for a shilling the next, spending her considerable earnings with romantic extravagance upon her own appearance and upon the sharks and parasites who feed off her and her world. These were the young women condemned by Acton because they 'flaunted it first rate' on the streets of London,[12] and they were vilified not only for exploiting sexuality (their own and that of their clients) and selling themselves for money, but as a result of that age-old stereotype, the Madonna and the Magdalene, the mother and the whore. According to prevailing Victorian morality, the role of the woman was to be 'the angel of the house', who set the moral tone of the family through sacrifice and self-denial and whose body was the exclusive property of her husband. Sex, as far as 'respectable' women were concerned, was a duty.

Dr William Acton, who was a consultant gynaecologist, maintained that the majority of 'respectable' women did not enjoy performing their conjugal rites and

> (happily for them) are not very much troubled with sexual feeling of any kind. What men are habitually, women are only exceptionally. The best mothers, wives, and managers of households, know little or nothing of sexual indulgences. Love of home, children, and domestic duties, are the only passion they feel . . . she submits to her husband but only to please him; and, but for the desire of maternity, would far rather be relieved from his attentions.[13]

While the aristocracy had always had their affairs, the lord taking a mistress while his lady pursued her intrigues after producing an heir and a spare, the effect of such social conditioning upon the middle classes was to create a vast market of punters. For where was a man to turn if his wife despised sex? 'Walter', the anonymous author of a notorious sexual memoir, struggled for years with fidelity; his is a rather extreme example of an unhappy marriage but provides some insight into the frustrated husband's mentality:

> I tried to like, to love her. It was impossible. Hateful in day, she was loathsome to me in bed. Long I strove to do my duty, and be faithful, yet to such a pitch did my disgust at length go, that laying by her side, I had wet dreams nightly, sooner than relieve myself in her. I have frigged myself in the streets before entering

my house, sooner than fuck her. I loving women . . . ready to be kind and loving to her, was driven to avoid her as I would a corpse. I have followed a woman for miles with my prick stiff, yet went to my wretched home pure, because I had vowed to be chaste. My heart was burning to have an affectionate kiss, a voluptuous sigh from some woman, yet I avoided obtaining it. My health began to give way; sleepless nights, weary days made me contemplate suicide.[14]

'Walter' was, of course, the punter *par excellence*, and we shall return to his anecdotes in due course, but his needs were familiar to thousands of London men, and an army of prostitutes inevitably sprang up to service them.

Those 'respectable' women who enjoyed sex to the extent of having an affair were subject to a vicious double standard, illustrated perfectly by a triptych of paintings by Augustus Egg entitled *Past and Present* (*c*. 1858), depicting the collapse of a middle-class marriage.

In the first, *The Infidelity Discovered*, a well-dressed wife lies headlong on the drawing-room floor. She is sobbing desperately at her husband's feet, as he crumples in his fist a letter he has intercepted from her lover. Their two young daughters look on with horror, and the scene drips with symbolism: the house of cards the little girls have been building has collapsed; a novel by Balzac (who frequently wrote about adultery) lies nearby; and on the table is an apple with a knife through its heart, representing Original Sin. The position of the woman's body is ambiguous: is she lying down because she is begging for forgiveness, or because her husband has knocked her to the floor?

In the second painting, *The Abandoned Daughters*, the action has moved on by five years. The daughters are in mourning for their father, who has just died, leaving them orphaned, and, because of their mother's adultery, unlikely to find appropriate suitors. There is a little cloud under the moon, which the daughters can see from their bedroom window, as they pray for their father and their mother. In the third painting, *Past and Present*, their mother can see the same little cloud, from her refuge behind a boat under a bridge on the banks of the river. Cast out by her lover, she cradles her illegitimate child beneath her cloak. Their fate is clear: if mother and child do not succumb to malnutrition and hypothermia, they may well consign themselves to the waters of the Thames.

The paintings caused predictable outrage, with publications such as the *Athenaeum* condemning the subject matter as 'an impure thing that seems out of place in a gallery of laughing brightness, where young happy faces come to chat and trifle' and observing that there 'must be a line drawn as to where the horrors that should be painted for public and innocent sight begin, and we think Mr Egg has put one foot at least beyond this line'. In sorrow rather than in anger the anonymous critic for *The Art-Journal* found the subject matter 'too poignant for a series of paintings', while Holman Hunt concluded that the paintings would not be popular with the public and assumed that Egg was drawn to the theme on moral grounds. Egg himself remained silent. But given the poignancy and impending tragedy of the last scene, one cannot help wondering whether his triptych was actually designed as a comment on the cruelty of Victorian marriage and the double standards which dictated that a cheating husband was entitled to his pleasure, but that a fallen 'angel of the house' was destined to be a social outcast, condemned to die destitute on the streets of London.

Pragmatic commentators such as Parent-Duchâtelet argued that 'prostitution exists, and will ever exist, in all great towns, because, like mendicancy and gambling, it is an industry and an expedient against hunger',[15] and that it should be legalized. His views were echoed by the campaigning journalist Henry Mayhew (1812–87) in his masterpiece *London Labour and the London Poor* (1851–62), one of the classic works of social investigation. Mayhew recognized prostitution as a social phenomenon going all the way back to ancient Rome. It was not merely an object for repulsion or false sentiment but a fact of life which had to be addressed and dealt with.

A product of his age, Mayhew was not without his own preju-
dices, but as the subsequent anecdotes reveal, he was fascinated by
prostitution and relatively tolerant towards the women who had
chosen 'the life'. While Acton's approach was bombastic and opin-
ionated, Mayhew presented his evidence to readers in the form of
dozens of interviews with the prostitutes themselves, and it is these
eyewitness accounts which provide an intriguing insight into the
underworld of Victorian sexuality.

Mayhew cast his net wide with his working definition of a prostitute as 'literally every woman who yields to her passions and loses
her virtue'. He then proceeded to classify London's working girls
into six categories:

1. Kept mistresses
   Prima donnas
2. Convives
   a. Independent
   b. Subject to mistress
   i. board lodgers (given board)
   ii. dress lodgers (given board & dress)
3 Low lodging houses' women
4. Sailors' and soldiers' women
5. Park women
6. Thieves' women.[16]

Although he recognized that 'the shades of London prostitution . . .
are as numberless as those of society at large', Mayhew's taxonomy
reflected Victorian society: upper-class 'kept women', middle-class
'prima donnas' and working-class streetwalkers.

The premier division of whores consisted of kept women or mistresses. These 'seclusives', as Mayhew referred to them, lived in
elegant suburban villas identical to the type represented in *The
Awakening Conscience*; they drove their carriages through Hyde
Park, took a box at the opera and even attended the most exclusive

balls, moving through the upper echelons of society unchallenged, thanks to the machinations of their lovers. These girls serviced 'the upper ten thousand' or ruling class, and were supported by their men of opulence and rank in the privacy of their own homes.[17] Mayhew does not name these women outright but instead, in journalistic tradition, bestows *noms de guerre* derived from the whores of classical antiquity, so we hear about 'Laïs', who was 'under the protection of a prince of the blood royal'; 'Aspasia', whose 'friend' was 'one of the most influential noblemen', and 'Phryne', the *'chère amie'* of a well-known Guards officer, or a banker, or a broker. Far from being ostracized or lonely, these ladies enjoyed a lavish lifestyle, calling on one another and leaving their cards at the fashionable hour, in a parody of conventional society women. In many cases, their relationships with their lovers proved as enduring and satisfactory as conventional marriages.

However, there was a perennial disadvantage in being the sole mistress of an older man; younger women hankered for the diverting company of a fit, young lover, the consequences of which could be disastrous. Mayhew tells of 'Lady Blank', who took the fancy of the great 'Lord X', when they met at a brothel in Bolton Row. Lord X set her up in a splendid house overlooking Regent's Park, with an allowance of £4000 a year. Soon Lady Blank was living the life, with a carriage and stud, a box at the opera, fashionable clothes and jewels. Lord X became possessive, however, and when she introduced an attractive young man as her cousin, he began to watch her more closely. Soon, Lady Blank was surrounded by spies; she was too naive to realize that everyone around her had been bribed. Eventually, she was 'surprised with her paramour in a position that placed doubt out of the question', and the next day, with a few sarcastic remarks, Lord X gave her £500 and her marching orders.[18]

Across the Channel, during the Second Empire, the top-drawer whores were regarded as national treasures. These women were the supermodels of their day, a manifestation of imperial wealth, and every detail of their lives – from their investments in property, the carriages they kept, the clothes they wore and the succession of opulent lovers they entertained – was the subject of eager discussion and national pride.[19] The Goncourt brothers, a pair of French novelists, bribed the maid of a famous courtesan to show them the magnificent Valenciennes lace lingerie, designed at considerable expense, which her mistress planned to wear while receiving specially favoured visitors. There were no discreet pseudonyms in their writing. The names of Hortense Schneider (1833–1920), esteemed opera star and mistress of Edward VIII, and 'La Païva', the Russian Jewess Esther Lachman, who became one of the most famous courtesans of the 1870s, in one generation, and of Liane de Pougy and Cléo de Mérode in the next, were repeated not only in Paris but in every European capital. Beyond praise or blame, these women drew crowds of admiring onlookers when they appeared in their carriages in the Bois de Boulogne.

English *cocottes*, as a rule, did not achieve quite the same high status, but there was a brief interval when the London *demi-monde* produced a number of celebrated characters. Harriette Wilson (1786–1832) was an early example. Born Harriette Doubechet in Shepherd Market, she was one of fifteen children of a Swiss watchmaker. The family were poor and had to shift for themselves, but they were also enterprising, with the girls quick to see the advantages of entering 'the life'. Harriette and two of her sisters, Amy and Fanny, became renowned courtesans, known as 'The Three Graces', while the most successful member of the family was their sister Sophia, who married into the aristocracy. Harriette was not beautiful but made up for it in terms of vivacity and sex appeal. Her first lover was the Earl of Craven, and as the courtesan of the Marquess of Argyll, she had a considerable amount of power and could move in the highest social circles, able to take a box at the opera and appear in her trademark white muslin. Harriette showed a touching readiness to compensate for her lack of education by reading up on the great thinkers of the day, such as Rousseau, Racine and Boswell, the better to entertain her intellectual lovers, but she was also something of an entrepreneur. Once she had officially 'retired' at the age of thirty-two and was safely married to 'Colonel' William Rochfort (his title appears to have been bogus), Harriette wrote her memoirs and sent copies of the manuscript to all her exes with a demand for £200 in return for silence. Given that Harriette's exes had included two past prime ministers, two future ones, numerous aristocrats and Members of Parliament, she had no shortage of scandalous material. Cabinet ministers and diplomats went rushing across Europe to silence her, while the King, George IV, moaned that the 'Wilson business' had nearly destroyed him. Harriette had not, however, foreseen the robust response of one of her most famous lovers, the Duke of Wellington, to her attempts at blackmail: four words scrawled across the title page of her manuscript, 'Publish and be Damned!' So Harriette did. And she was. Harriette's portrait of the Iron Duke was not flattering: she described him as 'most unentertaining', commented that when he came round to see her in the evenings he dressed 'like a ratcatcher' and was bad in bed.[20]

On publication day, Harriette's publisher, Stockdale, had to erect barriers outside his shop in the Haymarket to hold back the crowds. This original 'kiss 'n' tell' memoir earned publisher and author £10,000 each, but they both paid a high price. Stockdale was overwhelmed with lawsuits and Harriette was ostracized. When Harriette later appeared in the papers charged with beating her French maid, the press went to town on her ruined looks and her scoundrel of a husband. She is thought to have died around 1832. Wellington, and the rest of the establishment, had their revenge.[21]

Then there was Cora Pearl, the 'undisputed Queen of Beauty', who nevertheless had to move to Paris to become the toast of the town, and, most famous of all, the redoubtable 'Skittles', Catherine Walters, a courtesan in the grand tradition, companion as well as concubine, friend to poets, artists and musicians and one of the last great courtesans.

These were the girls Mayhew referred to as the 'prima donnas',

The Victorian courtesan Catherine Walters or 'Skittles',
a celebrated 'horsebreaker', in her riding habit c. 1870.

or leading ladies. These were the stars of the *demi-monde*; they reigned supreme in the West End.[22] With their distinctive 'yellow chignons' (bleached blonde hair) they were to be seen in the parks in ravishing hats, drawing up their elegant carriages or horses close to the rails and chatting with the gentlemen. It was not difficult, according to one writer in the *Pall Mall Gazette*, to guess the occupation of the dashing equestrienne who saluted half a dozen men at a time with her whip or with a wink, or who varied the monotony of a safe seat by holding her hands behind her back, while gracefully swerving over to listen to the compliments of a walking admirer.[23]

Skittles in particular was an excellent horsewoman and her exploits in Hyde Park drew crowds of admirers, eagerly wondering whether her skills in the bedroom were commensurate with her technique in the saddle. In 1862, Skittles' antics proved such a draw that she effectively stopped the traffic in Hyde Park, jeopardizing access to the Great Exhibition in nearby South Kensington.[24] Prima donnas such as Skittles went on display everywhere: in boxes at the theatre, at concerts, wherever fashionable people congregated. Theoretically barred from events where royalty was present, these women were visible anywhere which was open to paying customers and where one did not have to rely on breeding or family connections to get in.

Skittles proved to be the most celebrated courtesan of the period. So called because her first job was working at a bowling alley in Park Lane, and because she rolled over easily, Skittles started life in Liverpool as plain Catherine Walters, born the daughter of an Irish customs officer in Toxteth in 1839. In 1856, at the age of seventeen, Catherine arrived in London to seek her fortune. After five years working the Haymarket, she met the Marquess of Hartington (later the 8th Duke of Devonshire), an aspiring Liberal MP, who fell madly in love with her and set her up in a house in Mayfair complete with servants, carriages and an annuity of £2000 a year.

Skittles swiftly became the darling of the London scene: Sir Edwin Landseer painted her portrait, and hung it in the Royal Academy; the future poet laureate Alfred Austen and Wilfred Scrawen Blunt dedicated poems to her; even the formidable Prime Minister, William Gladstone, who had a soft spot for prostitutes, invited her to tea. Skittles was smart enough to understand that her quirky character was a major factor of her charm. She romanticized her origins, hammed up her Scouse accent and entranced her admirers with a winning combination of classical beauty and a mouth like a docker. She also took the opportunity to improve herself. Intelligent, witty and well read, she was interested in art, music and religion. One of Skittles' greatest assets was her discretion: she was reputed to have had affairs with half the crowned heads of Europe, but never confirmed or denied these rumours. She really was one of the greatest *grandes horizontales*, in a direct line of descent from Nell Gwyn, and as such it was only fitting that eventually she became the mistress of her greatest conquest, the Prince of Wales, the future King Edward VII.

If Skittles was the last true courtesan, Edward was the last of our promiscuous monarchs, having had affairs throughout his married life, with the acquiescence of his long-suffering wife, Princess Alexandra of Denmark. Edward's name was linked with all the great beauties of the day, including the actress Lily Langtry, Alice Keppel (great-grandmother of Camilla Parker Bowles) and Lady Randolph Churchill, mother of Sir Winston. Skittles retired in 1890, a wealthy woman, and clearly a healthy one too, as she lived on until 1920 in her splendid Mayfair home, a survivor of another age.

Mayhew regarded high-class courtesans such as Skittles as a bad influence, railing that these girls set a poor example to the lower orders with their dazzling extravagance and were nothing more than 'tubercules on the social system'.[25] But these were the top whores. Whatever Mayhew's moral outrage, these women operated without fear of criminal prosecution. The Metropolitan police left them alone: it would have been impossible to do otherwise, considering that their clients included aristocrats, MPs, barristers and military commanders. So, as in previous generations, the kept women were almost immune to prosecution and were most likely to quit the life through a prestigious marriage or comfortable retirement.

Houses of assignation, which have been considered in earlier chapters, remained a popular feature of London's sexual life. It was in these establishments, wrote Mayhew, that 'ladies of intrigue' found their pleasure. Ladies of intrigue, he wrote, were 'married women who have connection with other men than their husbands, and unmarried women who gratify their passion secretly',[26] and who 'merely to satisfy their animal instincts, intrigue with men whom they do not truly love'.[27] Mayhew had heard of a house of assignation in Regent Street, but dealt with it in a cursory fashion, since 'this sort of clandestine prostitution is not nearly so common in England as in France and other parts of the continent, where chastity and faithfulness among married women are remarkable for their absence'.[28] He did pause to relate one anecdote which revealed how these houses operated.

The story concerns a high-society woman, let us call her Lady Susan, who, married to a man of considerable wealth, nevertheless found that she was unhappy with him, and eventually came to the conclusion that she was trapped in a marriage with a man who made her miserable. Lady Susan was naturally passionate, and, desperate for an affair, decided to visit a house in Mayfair that one of her female friends had mentioned some time before. Ordering a cab, she was driven to the house and knocked at the door. When it opened, there was no need for her to explain herself; the nature of her visit was understood. Lady Susan was shown upstairs into a handsomely appointed sitting room, there to await the arrival of her unknown paramour.

After a little time, the door opened and a gentleman appeared. The curtains were drawn and the blinds turned down, so that the entire room was pervaded with a dim, soft light which prevented her from seeing him clearly. The man approached Lady Susan and began to speak softly on some indifferent subject. Lady Susan listened for a moment and then gave a cry of astonishment as she realized that the voice was that of her husband. He, equally confused, realized that he had accidentally met his own wife in a house of ill fame – his wife, whom he had treated unkindly and cruelly, leaving her to languish at home while he roamed about London. This tryst with a twist had a successful outcome, however, as it concluded with a reconciliation when both husband and wife admitted that they were equally to blame.

Every evening, any stranger to London could not fail to be struck by the extraordinary scenes as the dense throng of people crowded along London Bridge, Fleet Street, Cheapside, Holborn, Oxford Street and the Strand. But nothing made more of a vivid impression than the gaiety of Regent Street and the Haymarket, with the architectural splendour of its aristocratic streets, the brilliant illumination of the shops, cafés and concert rooms, and the troops of elegantly dressed courtesans rustling in silks and satins, and waving to everyone, from

*Prostitutes offer their services in the Haymarket in London's
West End c. 1860.*

the ragged crossing-sweeper and the tattered shoe-black to the high-
bred gentlemen of fashion and sons of the nobility.

It was to this part of the West End that London's prostitutes were
drawn like moths to a flame. Every form of prostitute was to be found
in the Haymarket: beautiful girls with blooming cheeks, newly up
from the country; pale, elegant milliners; French girls, notable for
their dark silk coats and white or dark silk bonnets, trimmed with
brightly coloured ribbons or flowers, who patrolled a beat on Pall
Mall so that they could hover outside the gentlemen's clubs; and, of
course, the bloated old women who had grown grey in the service of
prostitution, or been invalided out through venereal disease.

The Haymarket was the heart of the theatre district, so there
were always rich pickings to be had as the crowds spilled out onto
the pavements, aroused by the dramatic spectacle witnessed on
stage and eager for more excitement. By the 1850s, the Haymarket
was also the heart of London's nightlife, offering food, drink and

entertainment to every level of society, from expensive supper clubs such as Kate Hamilton's, the Turkish divans (similar to today's cigar bars), where men gathered to smoke tobacco and pick up women, and the night houses, where patrons paid over the odds for dinner while the girls worked the room. Even the kept women emerged briefly to visit the supper rooms, where their fashionable carriages might be seen drawn up outside, or to attend the Alhambra Music Hall.

'The Halls' as they were known were the Victorian equivalent of the notorious Restoration playhouses, bawdy, smoky, genial dens of iniquity popular with all social classes, who flocked to watch a succession of daring variety acts, consisting of coarse popular songs and saucy comedians. The Alhambra was inevitably popular with prostitutes, both for work and recreation. It was a great lofty building, ablaze with light, gorgeous with colour and gilding. Wine, spirits and ale flowed, and everybody appeared well dressed, the gaslight making even tawdry finery look like elegant costumes. The quality lounged on the balcony and in the boxes, watching the performances, which according to one commentator were designed to outrage moral decency for the amusement of those patrons who were so depraved that they required constant stimulation.

In the haze of tobacco smoke, the heat and glare of gas, the excitement of strong drink and the unrestrained licence of many of the most prominent visitors, a 'ballet' would be performed by a throng of bold women, two-score half-naked girls and middle-aged women, all painted and raddled, brassy smiles plastered across their weary faces as they skipped and pranced in response to the applause that greeted an indecent gesture or an obscene leer; these were the dancers who were willing to divest themselves of the last remaining shreds of modesty – and most of their clothes as well.

These acts drummed up trade for the working girls who trawled the halls, just as their orange girl predecessors had done in previous generations. Here, flaunting, talking, laughing, not merely tolerated but actively encouraged, they were treated to rich food and fine wines at their admirers' expense. These were the 'gay' ladies, and the West End was their world.

For all his reforming zeal, even Mayhew was quite taken with the vivid scenes in the Haymarket and recorded the beautiful young women in their feathers and lace with the enthusiasm of a tourist. Other commentators were less forgiving, such as the columnist in *Household Words* who regarded the same part of London as 'blackguard, ruffianly and deeply dangerous':

> If Piccadilly may be termed an artery of the metropolis, most assuredly that strip of pavement between the top of the Haymarket and the Regent Circus is one of its ulcers. It is always an offensive place to pass, even in the daytime; but at night it is absolutely hideous, with its sparring snobs, and flashing satins, and sporting gents ['sporting' was a euphemism for 'on the pull'], and painted cheeks, and brandy-sparkling eyes, and bad tobacco, and hoarse horse-laughs, and loud indecency. From an extensive continental experience of cities, I can take personally an example from three quarters of the globe; but I have never anywhere witnessed such open ruffianism and wretched profligacy as rings along those Piccadilly flagstones any time after the gas is lighted.[29]

Meanwhile, the sexual compulsive 'Walter', who seems to have been a difficult man to shock, professed himself astonished by the sight of women relieving themselves openly on a street near the Strand which was

> dark of a night and a favourite place for doxies to go to relieve their bladders. The police took no notice of such trifles, provided it was not done in the greater thoroughfare (although I have seen at night women do it openly in the gutters in the Strand); in the particular street I have seen them pissing almost in rows; yet they mostly went in twos to do that job, for a woman likes a screen, one

usually standing up till the other has finished, and then taking her turn. Indeed the pissing in all bye-streets of the Strand was continuous, for although the population of London was only half of what it is now, the number of gay ladies seemed double there.[30]

Mayhew disapproved of the kept women, the pampered soiled doves of St John's Wood, but he was rather more sympathetic towards the West End girls or 'Cyprians'. Prone to sentimentality, he cast them as ephemeral butterflies with an uncertain future. He classified the girls into two distinct categories, the 'Better Educated' and the 'More Genteel'. Mayhew found himself drawn to the 'Better Educated' girls, who were plainly dressed, came from middle-class homes and had 'a lady's education'. The 'More Genteel' prostitutes dressed in high fashion. One thing both categories of girls had in common was their abandoned state. They were former milliners or dressmakers from the West End who had fallen into prostitution after being seduced and abandoned by clerks or shop assistants or gentlemen of the town. Others were former servants who had lost their jobs after being seduced, or worse, by the gentlemen of the house or fellow servants.

A considerable number had come up to London from the provinces with young men who subsequently abandoned them, or were decoyed to London by pimps in the age-old fashion. Again, as in previous generations, some girls had arrived in London looking for work and resorted to prostitution when the going got rough, while others were on the run from unhappy families and sexual abuse. There were also 'seclusives' down on their luck, having been abandoned by their former lovers, and a number of French, Belgian and German girls. Mayhew admitted that:

They present a stunning spectacle, walking the streets in black silk cloaks or light grey mantles, many with silk paletots [coats] and wide skirts, extended by an ample crinoline, looking almost like a pyramid, with the apex terminating at the black or white satin bonnet, trimmed with waving ribbons and gay flowers. Some have cheeks red with rouge, and here and there are women radiant with health. Many look cold and heartless; others have 'an interesting appearance'.[31]

London's most splendid shopping mall, the Burlington Arcade, was a favourite beat. This elegant arcade, running between Piccadilly and Bond Street, is still celebrated for its array of exotic luxury goods, from glittering jewellery to soft cashmere and exquisite chocolates; but in Victorian London, sex was for sale here too. Between the hours of three and five in the afternoon the 'Cyprian corps', consisting of the massed ranks of the Prima Donnas, the Better Educated and the More Genteel, could tout for business and bag an entire range of clients, from a dashing young blade to a ruddy-faced gentleman farmer up from the country or a silver-haired old charmer.

Far from protesting about having their mall overrun by prostitutes, many of the proprietors recognized that they were good for business and resorted to 'Paphian intricacies' (another reference to Aphrodite), renting out rooms above their shops in return for a share of the takings. Once a woman had approached her prey, it was an easy matter to steer him inside a friendly bonnet shop or accommodating tobacconist's and upstairs to the bedroom.[32] 'Walter' and two of his friends amused themselves in one such establishment: 'it was not an unusual thing then for two [women] to have a cigar shop, with a big sofa in a back parlour, one keeping shop whilst the other fucked. Whilst the strumming was going on in the parlour, people bought cigars and tobacco – for it was really sold there, – little did they guess the fun going on behind that red curtain.'[33]

And of course, as always, there were the enthusiastic amateurs. Occasionally, one might see beautiful young shopgirls or milliners flitting along Regent Street or Pall Mall like bright birds of passage, to meet with some gentleman on the sly, and to earn a few shillings to top up their meagre salaries. Sometimes, one might see a fashionable young widow, or a beautiful young wife, wending her way in the evenings to meet with some rickety, white-haired old gentleman loitering about Pall Mall. And such scenes did not even merit a second glance: such things were not wondered at by those acquainted with high life in London.[34] Acton referred to these amateurs as 'dollymops', young women who prostituted themselves for their own pleasure, in return for a few trinkets. These girls tended to be servants, shopgirls or maids who met men during the course of business; instead of heading for the casinos and taverns, they flirted with their customers from behind the shop counter, or were accosted while returning to their lodgings, or walking their employers' children in the park. Nursemaids were particularly popular with soldiers, and the girls were flattered by the attention, succumbing easily to 'scarlet fever', attracted by their dashing red uniforms. 'A red coat is all powerful with this class, who prefer a soldier to a servant, or any other description of man they come in contact with.'[35]

Even when business was nominally over for the day, the Cyprian corps remained in the West End. Mayhew and his friends watched them walking up and down Regent Street and the Haymarket, some by themselves, some in pairs, some with a gallant they had picked up, calling at the wine-vaults or restaurants, or sitting down in the brilliant coffee rooms, adorned with large mirrors, to a cup of coffee or China tea. They patrolled the theatre district of Leicester Square and Haymarket as crowds of theatre-goers poured out into the streets after the performances, but they were also to be seen plying for trade at the crowded bars, 'these dreadful hotbeds of vice and immorality' as one commentator described them.

When a young man meets there with handsome fine-looking girls, well-dressed with genteel manners, he forgets the indecency of their appearance and the looseness and impropriety of their language and behaviour, if these do not attract him the more, and he gets interested and entangled with them, and is led astray; and this the more readily as he sees around him much older men of respectable appearance, without scruple talking and romping with them.[36]

This prostitute described a typical day in her life to the journalist Bracebridge Hemyng, Mayhew's researcher, in the 1850s:

> I get up about four o'clock, dress and dine: after that I may walk about the streets for an hour or two and pick up anyone I am fortunate enough to meet, that is if I want money; afterwards I go to Holborn, dance a little, and if anyone likes me I take him home with me. If not, I go to the Haymarket, and wander from one cafe to another, from Sally's at the Carlton, from Barns' to Sam's, and if I find no one there I go, if I feel inclined, to the divans. I like the Grand Turkish best, but you don't as a rule find good men at any of the divans.[37]

Many of the more faded prostitutes frequented the Pavilion to meet gentlemen and enjoy the singing and instrumental music over some liquor, while the younger and more affluent girls flocked to the music halls, or the Argyll Rooms, rustling in splendid dresses, to spend the time till midnight, when they accompanied the gentlemen they had picked up there to the expensive supper rooms and night houses. Acton described a visit to the Argyll Rooms where he sat in

> a spacious room, the fittings of which are of a most costly description, while brilliant gas illuminations, reflected by numerous mirrors, impart a fairy-like aspect to the scene. The company is mixed. The women are of course all prostitutes. They are for the most part pretty, and quietly, though expensively dressed, while delicate complexions, unaccompanied by the pallor of ill-health, are neither few nor far between. This appearance is doubtless due in many cases to the artistic manner of the make-up by

powder and cosmetics, on the employment of which extreme care is bestowed.[38]

The Argyll Rooms offered the perfect opportunity for 'sporting ladies', another euphemism for prostitutes, to consort with 'sporting' aristocrats, such as Lord Hastings, a famous playboy and prankster who once emptied a sack of rats onto the dance floor.[39] Meanwhile, at the Portland Rooms, where the most expensive courtesans worked the room between midnight and four in the morning, punters could see the Parisian 'can-can' danced, 'in every unrestricted form, the women behaving in a more Bacchanalian fashion than in other places'.[40] The chief attraction of the can-can was, of course, that the dancers were performing in voluminous skirts, and no knickers.

After a hard afternoon working the Burlington Arcade, the girls' favourite rendezvous was Kate Hamilton's supper club, where they could dissipate their ennui and restore themselves for another night of carousing at a private party or Mott's casino. Kate Hamilton's was actually the Cafe Royal, but such was Kate's influence in 1850s London that the club bore her name. Situated in Princess Street, near Leicester Square, Kate's club was approached by a long and securely guarded passage leading to a saloon where the mistress of the establishment sat enthroned among her favourites, a formidable figure weighing twenty stone, with the weather-beaten features of an ex-sailor. Seated on a raised platform, in a low-cut dress, Kate Hamilton sipped champagne steadily from midnight to daylight, keeping order with her powerful voice and shaking like a blancmange every time she laughed.[41]

Kate made a killing by selling food and drink at highly inflated prices. She had a bouncer on the door to keep out the riff-raff and only gentlemen prepared to spend over £5 were admitted. Mayhew noted that these supper rooms were 'frequented by a better set of men and women than perhaps any other in London'.[42] Kate could afford to bribe the authorities, but every now and again there was a raid. There was a well-rehearsed drill on such occasions: when the alarm went up that the police were on the way, carpets were rolled up in the twinkling of an eye, floorboards were raised and bottles and glasses thrust underneath, everyone assumed a virtuous, demure air and spoke in subdued tones, as if butter wouldn't melt, while a bevy of police officers headed by an inspector marched solemnly in and, having completed the farce, marched solemnly out again.[43]

Over the course of the evening, many of the girls were seen walking with young, middle-aged and sometimes frail old men to Oxenden Street, Panton Street and James Street, near the Haymarket. They were taking their clients to 'houses of accommodation', which was safer than going home with them. 'Walter' described one to which he had resorted in his youth: 'It was a gentleman's house, although the room cost but five shillings; red curtains, looking-glasses, wax lights, clean linen, a huge chair, a large bed, and a cheval- glass, large enough for the biggest couple to be reflected in, were all there.'[44]

For all their glamour, the off-duty lives of the Cyprian corps were grim. They might be treated to splendid suppers amidst lascivious smiles in the Haymarket, but they lived in seedy flats in Soho, Pimlico or Chelsea, and were so careless and extravagant that they were often reduced to pawning their dresses to buy food. Mayhew painted a disheartening picture of the girls at home, 'sprawled lazily in bed, in sad dishabille, with dishevelled hair and muddy eyes, their voices hoarse with bad temper and misery'.[45]

The girls who could not afford to rent their own flats shared lodging houses or 'convives' (shared in connivance with the landlord) just off Piccadilly. It was in these frowzy and horribly overpriced rooms that the girls demonstrated a degree of loyalty which genuinely impressed Mayhew. 'They may have dispensed with all womanly modesty,' he admitted, 'but they bond with each other fast, and within hours are referring to one another as "my dear"; they lend each other clothes and money, and even support one another with unparalleled generosity. They are forced to room together, as no respectable landlord would take them in.'[46]

This sense of solidarity sprang from the fact that, as Nickie Roberts reminds us, prostitution at this period was essentially female controlled. Brothels, lodging houses and accommodation houses were mostly run by women, all of whom had been through the experience of prostitution themselves. Madams or bawds took a cut from the girls who worked on their premises, but pimps were virtually unknown. One reformer, Mary Higgs, gained a glimpse of this solidarity when she visited a lodging house; although she disapproves, of course, of the girls' lifestyle, there is a trace of admiration in her description: 'round the fire was a group of girls far gone in dissipation, good-looking girls most of them, but shameless; smoking cigarettes, boasting of drinks or drinkers, using foul language, singing music-hall songs, or talking vileness. The room grew full and breakfasts were about. A girl called "Dot" danced the "cake-walk" in the middle of the room.'[47]

It was a precarious life. 'Strange things happen to us sometimes,' one told Mayhew. 'We may now and then die of consumption; but the other day a lady friend of mine met a gentleman at Sam's, and yesterday they were married at St George's, Hanover Square. The gentleman had lots of money, I believe, and he started off with her at once for the continent. It is a very strange and unusual case, but we often do marry, and well too; why shouldn't we, we are pretty, we dress well, we can talk and insinuate ourselves into the hearts of men by appealing to their passions and their senses.'[48]

The second class of prostitutes in the Haymarket, the third in Mayhew's whores' division, were the young working-class girls, daughters of domestic servants and labourers. Some of these girls were of a tender age, thirteen and upwards, and were to be seen wandering around Leicester Square and along the Haymarket and Regent Street. They dressed in girlish light cotton gowns, and crinolines that seemed too fancy for the daytime, with light grey or brown cloaks and funny little pork pie hats in white or red, some with a waving feather. Some walked timidly, others were brazen; some looked artless and ingenuous, others artful and pert. Some had fine features and good figures, while others were short and dumpy. These were girls who sold themselves for a lower price, and haunted the coffee shops around Leicester Square, where the blinds were drawn down, and there were notices over the door announcing that 'beds are to be had within'.[49] Many of these girls qualified as Mayhew's 'thieves' women'; they were often in league with pickpockets, who robbed their clients of their watches, purses, pins and fine silk or linen handkerchiefs (which they would sell after the embroidered initials had been unpicked) after the girls had duped them down a dark alley.

Many went into their occupation willingly, with a pragmatic rationale. 'Walter' picked up such a girl in the Strand, and, after the usual business had been transacted, had a long chat with the girl, named Kitty, who possessed 'a frankness, openness and freshness which delighted me',[50] as does her level of denial. When he asks: 'How long have you been gay?' Kitty retorts, 'I ain't gay!', astonished. When 'Walter' points out that 'you let men fuck you, don't you?', she insists, 'Yes, but I ain't gay!' The gay ladies, as far as she is concerned, are the ones who 'come out regular of a night, dressed up, and gets their livings by it'.[51] Further questioning elicits the information that both Kitty's parents are employed, her mother as a charwoman, and that she is supposed to be at home, looking after little brothers and sisters. Instead of which, she locks them in the kitchen and heads up West. 'Walter' is quite disturbed by this. '"They may set fire to themselves!" said I. "There ain't no fire; after we have had breakfast, I puts it out, and lights it at night if mother wants hot water."'[52] 'Walter' struck up something of a relationship with Kitty, and saw her several times. The most poignant element of his description is the reason Kitty sells herself: to buy food. They can't live on what her mother earns, and Kitty's takings go on sausages, pies and sausage rolls. 'That's what you went gay for?'

'Walter' says, incredulously. 'Sausage rolls?' 'Yes, meat-pies and pastry too.'[53]

Mayhew records a similar conversation with another girl, 'Dolly', who hated working the Haymarket, but loved dancing, and spent the money she earned on new clothes and a new bonnet every week. A former servant who had been sacked after being seduced by the master of the house, Dolly was making the best of things in a tough world.

Others, as in our next example, were victims of entrapment, decoyed into the life with a technique unchanged since the days of evil Mother Needham. Mayhew interviewed this young lady, 'Bella', who lived in a brothel in Langham Place. From the outside, with its handsome green curtains, this appears to be a substantial and highly respectable town house. And, once inside, the veil of respectability continued, as Mayhew and his colleague were shown into a comfortably furnished room with yielding sofas and glass chandeliers. Bella entered the room and, after some confusion when she asked the men what they would like and was surprised when they only wanted to talk, a bottle of wine was sent for which loosened her tongue.

Bella's tale was sadly familiar. A young girl from Stepney who had lost her mother in childhood, she had never been warned by her father, a joiner, about the dangers facing an attractive young girl at large in the East End. One afternoon, Bella was befriended by a kindly middle-aged lady who invited her round for tea. The next thing she knew was that she had been made drunk, signed some papers, and had 'her spirit broken'. In return for working as a prostitute, Bella was fed and clothed, and had become inured to her way of life. She couldn't imagine anything else, now. She never thought about it; she would go mad if she did; she lived in the present, and never went blubbering about as some did. She tried to be as jolly as she could; where was the fun in being miserable?[54] This, Mayhew recalled, was the prevailing philosophy among prostitutes. The girls got through it as best they could with a stoical attitude and plenty of White Satin, a popular brand of gin.

Alcoholism was rife. Mayhew interviewed another woman, in the Haymarket, a woman grown old and fallen upon hard times. 'Times is altered, sir, since I come on the town,' she confided. 'Nothing lasts forever and I've stood my share of wear and tear.'[55] This woman demonstrates the same weary stoicism: 'I don't think much of my way of life. You folks as has honour, and character, and feelings, and such, can't understand how all that's been beaten out of people like me. I don't feel. *I'm used to it*.' Although she admitted that when she heard of her mother's death, she did cry and she was genuinely heartbroken, 'but Lor', where's the good of fretting? It's the drink mostly that keeps me going. You've no idea how I look forward to my drop of gin. It's everything to me.'[56]

Drink helped to dull the pain of violent beatings from punters and lovers alike. Mayhew met another young girl, just twenty-one, and down on her luck after parting from her gentleman. The said gentleman had seen her flirting with a friend at the Assembly Rooms in Holborn and beaten her so violently that she had been confined to bed for three months. Eventually, she summoned up the courage to run away, taking £300 and most of her clothes and jewellery. But she had to sell the jewellery, and when the proceeds ran out, she had been reduced to 'walking in the Haymarket' and turning tricks at the cafés. Now she had been forced to sell the remainder of her dresses. 'Since then I have been more shabby in appearance, and not so much noticed.'[57]

This unfortunate seemed, even at such a tender age, destined to end up like those poor degraded creatures who constituted Mayhew's third category of Haymarket women, the worn-out wretches who skulked about, scrounging a living from the fashionable passers-by and the more affluent prostitutes who paid them to go away.

However, this picture of prostitutes as doomed and damned for all eternity represents only one side of the story. One of Mayhew's interviewees, a young lady at the top of her game, was deeply offended when he asked what she thought would become of her. 'What do I think will become of me? What an absurd question. I could marry to-morrow if I liked!' she responded pertly. Mayhew was repelled by this unrepentant attitude, describing the girl as a typical example of her class. 'They live entirely for the moment, and care little about the morrow until they are actually pressed in any way, and then they are fertile in expedients,' he noted, wearily.[58] But this young lady was not alone in her defiant attitude. On 24 February 1858, when moral panic about prostitution was at its height, a letter appeared in *The Times* actually written by 'Another Unfortunate', who described herself as 'one of those who, as Rousseau says, are born to be prostitutes', and made a spirited defence of her profession, demanding to be treated with the same courtesy as a 'respectable' woman. 'I earn my money and pay my way . . . I do not get drunk, nor fight, nor create uproar in the streets or out of them. I do not use bad language. I do not offend the public eye by open indecencies.' The prostitute then reminded her readers that she had not only paid her debt to society, but had contributed to the economy, paying the most fashionable West End milliners, silk makers and boot makers, who all knew who she was and how she earned her money, and solicited her business as earnestly and cringingly as if she were married to the chairman of the Society for the Suppression of Vice.

This letter inspired an editorial the very next day, in which the anonymous leader writer commented that

the great bulk of the London prostitutes are not Magdalens, nor specimens of humanity in agony, nor Clarissa Harlowes. They are not – the bulk of them – cowering under gateways, nor preparing to throw themselves from Waterloo Bridge, but are comfortably practising their trade, either as the entire or partial means of their subsistence. They have no remorse or misgivings about the nature of their pursuit; on the contrary, they consider the calling an advantageous one, and they look upon their success in it with satisfaction.[59]

Dr William Acton also believed that the phrase 'Once a harlot, always a harlot' was a myth. During the course of his extensive research, Acton had found plenty of evidence to show that prostitution was a transitory state. Otherwise, he argued, where on earth did all those women go? London's 80,000 prostitutes did not simply vanish into thin air. They were not all struck down in mid-career by suicide, alcoholism or venereal disease, nor did they fall by the wayside like autumn leaves, to be heaped up to rot, or crawl home to die of remorse. Instead, argued Acton, after a maximum of four years on the streets they were fully conversant with the hardships of the trade and ready to escape should the opportunity present itself. Anyone who had survived the life would by this stage have a healthy physique, an excellent constitution, good business sense and an unparalleled insight into human nature which could only be an asset in any career she chose. Any sensible woman by then would have made 'a dash at respectability by marriage' or sunk her savings into a milliner's shop or a lodging house. Emigration to the colonies, with the promise of a fresh start, was another popular choice.

The last word on a successful transition from prostitution comes from the writer Arthur Munby, who recorded the fascinating story of Sarah Tanner. Munby had first met Sarah in 1855, when she was 'a maid of all work to a tradesman in Oxford Street: a lively honest rosy-faced girl, virtuous & self-possessed', a brunette with fine hazel eyes. Munby ran into her a year or so later, on Regent Street, 'arrayed in gorgeous apparel'. It appeared that Sarah had got tired of being in service, wanted to see life and be independent, and so had *chosen* to become a prostitute, of her own accord. Sarah had taken it up as a profession, even reading and taking writing lessons so that she would be a fit companion to gentlemen. She saw no harm in it, enjoyed it very much, thought it might raise her and perhaps be profitable. After taking her for a glass of beer, which Sarah did not ask for, Munby took his leave of her. He saw her a few times subsequently, on duty (although there is no indication that he availed himself of her professional services), until one day he ran into her dressed differently again, like a respectable upper servant, in quiet, tasteful clothes. "'I've left the streets and settled down," she said quietly. "I'd been on the streets three years, and saved up – I told you I should get on, you know – and so I thought I'd leave, and I've taken a coffeehouse with my earnings – the Hampshire Coffeehouse, over Waterloo Bridge." I laughed, incredulous. "Quite true," said she simply. "I manage it all myself, & I can give you chops & tea – & anything you like: you must come & see me.'"

Munby was surprised and impressed by Sarah's entrepreneurial spirit.

> Now here is a handsome young woman of twenty-six, who, having begun life as a servant of all work, and then spent three years in *voluntary* prostitution amongst men of a class much above her own, retires with a little competence, and invests the earnings of her infamous trade in a respectable coffeehouse, where she settles down in homely usefulness and virtuous comfort! Surely then this story is a singular contribution to the statistics of the 'Social Evil' and of female character and society in the lower classes.[60]

Sarah's story is a satisfying corrective to the repellent depiction of 'flaunting queans' and mercenary human tigresses served up in the popular press. However, in an overcrowded city riddled with poverty and social injustice, there was inevitably a more sinister side. To experience this, let us accompany Mayhew and Acton on their expedition into darkest London.

SLAVES OF THE LONDON PAVEMENT

'Render up your body or die'

While the dashing courtesans of the Haymarket ruled the West End, life in the East End was one long battle for survival. Poverty and hunger, rather than an excessive desire for extravagant clothing and a proclivity to sin, drove young women onto the streets. During the course of his research, Henry Mayhew was shocked to hear from one seamstress who sewed shirts from five o'clock in the morning until midnight, but still did not earn enough money to feed herself and her child.[1] Struggling to survive on derisory wages, young women often faced a stark choice: 'render up your body or die'. Prostitution, for all its drawbacks, was a welcome alternative to starvation. It was also a welcome alternative to a wretched, poverty-stricken marriage.

For all the glamour of the West End, a million Londoners lived in slums where the streets were frequently so narrow that you could step from the window of one house into that of its opposite neighbour, while the houses were piled so high, storey upon storey, that the light could scarcely penetrate into the court or alley that lay between. Far from the theatres and cafés of the Haymarket, this was a world where there were no sewers or privies or drains and the houses were filthy and overcrowded. Most families lived in a single room, sleeping together on a heap of straw and rags, men and women, brothers and sisters, old and young. The only water source was a parish pump, and this water was so difficult to obtain that the majority of families lived in unsanitary conditions.[2] In 1883, in *The Bitter Cry of Outcast London*, W. C. Preston recalled visiting a tenement house in which one cellar was occupied by a father, mother, three children and four pigs; in another room, a man lay ill with smallpox, while his wife was recovering from the birth of her eighth child and the other children ran around naked and dirty; an underground kitchen turned out to be occupied by seven people and the corpse of a child that nobody could afford to bury.[3] Intimacy, comfort and recreational sex were impossible in such inhumane conditions; instead, any sex that did take place was nasty, brutish and short. The possibility of further pregnancies and childbirth rendered women frigid with anxiety, while contraception (in the form of condoms and pessaries) was prohibitively expensive for women who could not even afford to buy food. Beer and gin, at least, offered parents a brief spate of oblivion from the struggle to feed and clothe their families. Men took their pleasure, if they could afford it, with the cheapest whores available in the nearby taverns, while domestic violence was an inevitable consequence of mental and physical exhaustion and despair.

In *Liza of Lambeth* the author Somerset Maugham drew on his experience as a medical student at St Thomas's Hospital, where he had witnessed the aftermath of countless 'domestics'. A friend of Liza's confides that she was beaten up by her new husband: 'I 'ad ter go ter the 'orspital – it bled all dahn my fice, and went streamin' like a bust water-pipe.' But, after threatening to have her husband arrested, the woman relents. 'I wouldn't charge 'im. I know 'e don't mean it; 'e's as gentle as a lamb when 'e's sober.'[4] A classic victim, this young woman espoused the sentimental view that a fist was as good as a kiss in such straitened times.

Insanitary conditions meant that the infant mortality rate was high in the East End, but many women were so desperate that they found themselves unable to face the prospect of another birth. These were the women who, for a fee of ten shillings, put themselves in the hands of an abortionist. There was an abortionist in every working-class district of London. Some were wise women, noted for their infallible folk remedies, treating their patients with herbs and tinctures; others were struck-off doctors, or half-trained nurses skilled in the application of hot baths, pints of gin and long knitting needles. In most cases, these latter procedures resulted in severe, sometimes fatal injury to the mother, left to haemorrhage to death or succumb to peritonitis. If she survived, the mother was still liable to be prosecuted for infanticide, as, to all intents and purposes, abortion remained illegal until the passing of the Abortion Act in 1967.

If a child still succeeded in being born, its parents had one final option: infanticide. Some mothers, faced with another mouth to feed, suffocated their babies or left them to die of malnutrition and neglect; some babies were sent to 'baby-farms', where newborns were taken in and raised for a small fee, frequently growing up to become prostitutes in their turn. In a more macabre development, many 'baby farmers' disposed of their tiny charges in the river. Every year, the Thames would yield up its grisly catch of infant corpses;[5] the sight of drowned babies floating in the Thames became such a regular occurrence that it scarcely occasioned comment.

Little wonder then that when glamorous young women returned to the slums to visit their families, loaded with gifts and cash, younger girls flocked to follow their example. Our *Times* correspondent, 'Another Unfortunate', recalls just such an incident when she was thirteen years old and a cousin arrived, lavishly dressed and bearing trinkets and ribbons. 'Another Unfortunate' was captivated and her ambition was stirred. This, she realized, was the way out, this was the way to escape from sharing one room with her brick-layer father and several siblings and watching her parents' wages going on beer and gin. This was infinitely preferable to her mother's life, her figure wrecked by childbirth and working in the brickfield. 'Another Unfortunate', like many a pragmatic backstreet girl, had no illusions regarding surrendering her 'honour' to obtain this lifestyle.

> I was a fine, robust, healthy girl, 13 years of age. I had larked with the boys of my own age. I had huddled with them, boys and girls together, all night long in our common haunts. I had seen much and heard abundantly of the mysteries of the sexes. To me such things had been matters of common sight and common talk. For some time I had coquetted on the verge of a strong curiosity, and a natural desire, and without a particle of affection, scarce a partiality, I lost – what? not my virtue, for I never had any. According to my own ideas at the time I only extended my rightful enjoyments.

'Another Unfortunate' did not have to wait long before she received the opportunity to put her knowledge to profitable use. 'In the com-mencement of my fifteenth year one of our be-ribboned visitors took me off, and introduced me to the great world, and thus commenced my career as what you better classes call a prostitute.' 'Another Unfortunate' was fortunate enough to find her own Professor Higgins in the form of a kindly older gentleman who educated her and taught her the social graces, enabling her to gain the skills to write letters to *The Times* arguing the case for prostitutes.[6]

During a 'pilgrimage' to the East End, accompanied for his own safety by the Assistant Commissioner of the Metropolitan Police, Dr William Acton was dismayed to see 'respectable' women rubbing shoulders with prostitutes like 'Another Unfortunate' in a music hall. The bar was crowded with well-dressed women, some of whom were prostitutes, but many of whom were married women, out with their husbands to enjoy a drink and a smoke and watch the turns on stage as a brief respite from their daily troubles. Acton was surprised by this 'elbowing of vice and virtue' although he had witnessed similar scenes in the West End. What also surprised him was the reverence shown by locals to girls who had evidently done well from prostitution, and the attitude of tolerance towards the 'gay' women. 'Any persons connected with them whom they see well-dressed, and with money in their pockets, command a kind of respect, although the source from whence the means are obtained may be a disreputable one.' Acton found these reunions disturbing and his attitude was one of disgust at witnessing 'the vicious and profligate sisterhood flaunting it gaily, or "first-rate", in their language – accepting all the attentions of men, freely plied with liquor, sitting in the best places, dressed far above their station, with plenty of money to spend, and denying themselves no amusement or enjoyment, encumbered with no domestic ties, and burdened with no children'.[7] Acton fretted about the effect this would have upon respectable women. 'This actual superiority of a loose life could not have escaped the attention of the quick-witted sex,' he worried, as though the sight of Victorian women enjoying themselves was completely unacceptable!

But life on the streets, or in a brothel, was preferable to life at home with drunken parents, no food and no clothes. As Mother Willit of Gerrard Street, Soho, put it: 'So help her kidneys, she *alu'us* turned her gals out with a clean arse and a good tog [dress]; and as she turned 'em out, she didn't care who turned 'em up, 'cause 'em vos as clean as a smelt [fish] and as fresh as a daisy – she vouldn't have a speck'd [diseased] un if she know'd it.'[8]

Other women, of course, were not so fortunate. These are the lower categories of Henry Mayhew's classes of prostitutes, the street-walkers, the dress lodgers, the sailors' women who worked the docks, and the lowly park women. The streetwalkers fared particularly harshly. In 'A Night on Waterloo Bridge', American journalist James Greenwood describes a typical night on the 'Bridge of Sighs'.

It is a freezing cold night, with a small rain falling, and he finds himself speculating as to how many 'unfortunates' came to this scene, to stand on the centre parapet and brood on the prospect of that final terrible leap into the dark, and how many changed their minds, brought to their senses by the contemplation of the black and awful depth and the bleak wind that blew off the icy water. Greenwood interviews a policeman, who has become experienced in dealing with maudlin prostitutes who always seemed to find the bridge awkward to get over on their way home to Blackfriars. 'I ain't equal to explainin' it' the policeman admits, 'but it's a dark and solitary bit after the gas of the public-houses and that, and it strikes 'em as such, I suppose, and sets 'em thinking of the lots that have made a jump of it when they got as far as the middle arch, and then they get the 'blues,' and there's no doing anything with 'em. It would do good to some of them fast young fellows who go in for 'seeing life,'

Death by drowning was a common fate for London's prostitutes and a popular theme for writers and artists. Cover illustration for Charles Selby's London by Night *(1886).*

as they call it, if they could see some of them miserable gals shivering home over the bridge here, in the dark and rain, sometimes at one or two in the morning.[9]

Greenwood waits around, and sees for himself an amazing number of wretched girls and women come hurrying from the Strand side of the bridge, and, 'with an aspect exactly as opposite to "gay" as black is to white, making haste, through the rain which had saturated their flimsy skirts and covered the pavement with a thick paste of mud, cruelly cold to ill-shod feet, towards the miserable lodgings in the poorer neighbourhoods of Lambeth and Blackfriars which were dignified with the name of home'.[10]

The only whores who seemed cheerful were the ones still the worse for drink, who were distinguished by their cheerful singing, keeping their courage up, Greenwood reflects, like small boys whistling in the dark. As for the rest, 'they looked so wretchedly wet, cold, and utterly comfortless, that it would have been a mercy rather than a sin to have conferred a glass of brandy on them'. One of the youngest whores begs him to buy her a cup of coffee, and he relents, regarding her as a sorry child 'for really she was little better', and she jokes that the man on the coffee stall is as good as a father to her, before falling into such a severe coughing fit that it is obvious she is not long for this world. The stall is a snug little cabin, built of boards and canvas, with the cheerful glow of a charcoal fire within, and the stallholder himself dispensing the smoking beverage and bread and butter to seven or eight female outcasts who huddle together in the friendly shelter, two or three being seated on a form and dozing by the fire, their drenched clothes steaming in the heat. By the light of the fire, Greenwood observes the ghastly contrast between their pinched and haggard faces, pale except for the paint patches that glare like plague spots and their dishevelled finery, the drooping feathers and festoons of rainbow ribbon with which their hats are trimmed.

On his way back, Greenwood spots another low-life scene in one of the recesses of Waterloo Bridge. There are two women, one young and well but flashily dressed, the other miserable, shabby and middle aged, wearing an old black cloak with which she is trying to protect the younger woman from the rain. With them is an unprepossessing individual of the male sex, whose cadaverous features are a combination of the lowest of the low: he looks like a dog-stealer, a police informer and a street-fighter. The older woman is trying to persuade the younger one to go 'back', wherever that might be, or face getting into a row. 'Lor! you needn't fret about that,' declares the cadaverous gentleman, with a growl that sounds like a preliminary to a bite. 'She'll come to her senses. She's a pretty one to cut the high caper – without a rag to call her own.' This sneer appears to cut the young woman to the quick. Casting off the protective wing of the older woman's cloak, she bursts out: 'Curse you both! Curse you both! Who was it that robbed me of my good clothes? Who cheated and plundered me but you, you thief, till I hadn't a skirt to call my own!'

'Never mind who cheated you,' responds the bully. 'That's nothing to do with them clothes what's only lent you. If yer don't know how to behave in 'em, come on home and get out of 'em.' Then, seeing Greenwood for the first time, he nudges the older woman, and addresses the girl in a softer voice, remarking that it's no good her sitting there 'ketching cold', and the trio move away towards the Surrey side [the South Bank] of the bridge, the young woman still insisting that she won't go back, she would rather be dead and buried. As Greenwood watches them walk away, a female voice comments: 'That's the way with them marms; they gets a silk gown on, and then a Duchess ain't good enough to be their sister. Serve her right, whatever she gets.' The voice comes from a ragged, starved-looking wretch, the bones showing sharp under her white skin, who is so drunk that she can scarcely stand and has to hold on to the stone-work for support. This apparition tells Greenwood that the young woman is a 'dress woman, one of them that they tog out so that they may show off at their best and make the most of their faces'. But they can't trust the girls, adds the awful creature, venturing to take the steadying grasp from the stone coping that she might clap both her skinny hands in malicious glee. 'They never trust 'em further than they can see 'em. You might tell that by the shadder.' The 'shadder' or shadow was tasked with sticking close to the 'dress woman', or 'dress whore' (a prostitute who hired her clothes from a procuress), and never leaving her, not even for a minute. The dress women are 'no more their own mistresses than galley-slaves are,' she concludes. 'And serve 'em right!' As for the man who accompanied them, well, he was worse than a dog. 'For dogs don't eat each other!' she screams. 'He'd steal his mother's crutches if she was a cripple, and get drunk with the money he sold them for, and go home and beat her.' And with that, the poor shameful creature staggers away.[11]

This 'dress woman', or 'dress lodger', had probably tried to run away from Catherine Street, off the Strand, which was a popular locale with this type of prostitute. During the day and the early part of the evening, the dress women would stop almost every man they met, but with reasonable decorum. Under the influence of drink, they plied their trade with increasing rudeness and freedom as the night wore on, while their 'shadders' followed at a respectful distance. Unlike other categories of prostitute, dress women led a particularly miserable life, sent out 'rouged and whitewashed, with painted lips and eyebrows, and false hair', to parade in Catherine Street, Langham Place, the Haymarket Theatre, the City Road and the Lyceum, and restricted to specific beats on the same side of one particular street within a few hundred yards or less of one particular spot. If they failed to pick up a punter, their shadows would sally forth and canvass on their behalf, or swear at the girls, and even beat them.

In *The Night Side of London*, J. Ewing Ritchie echoed the sentiments of the mad woman on Waterloo Bridge, commenting that these gay ladies were worse off than the American slaves. Dress women started in the business at eighteen and were easily burned out, particularly by the effects of alcohol. Catherine Street might have appeared festive, while the gas burned brightly by night, and there was dancing, and wine, and songs, but these girls paid the price. In the small hours, you might hear the hollow laughter, sadder than tears, of a drunken dress lodger, freshly ejected from a pub, and too far gone to have any decency left. 'Drink and sadness combined have tortured her brain to madness. Her curses fill the air; a crowd collects; the police come up; she is borne on a stretcher to Bow-street, and in the morning is dismissed with a reprimand, or sentenced to a month's imprisonment, as the sitting magistrate is in a good temper or the reverse.' This was a common sight on Catherine Street, says our correspondent. 'I have known life lost here in these midnight brawls; yet by day it has a dull and decent appearance, and little would the passing stranger guess all its revelations of sorrow and of crime.'[12]

Alcoholism was an occupational hazard for prostitutes. 'When I'm sad, I drink,' one told Henry Mayhew. 'And I'm very often sad.'[13] While the courtesans of the West End tippled champagne or White Satin gin, their less fortunate sisters drank themselves to death. One such was 'Lucy', or 'Lushing Loo', whose fondness for the bottle has given her that suggestive name. Mayhew interviewed Loo in an East End pub. At first, her appearance seemed to be at odds with her name. She looks lady-like, if somewhat haggard. Tastefully, if cheaply, dressed, she seems quiet and dejected. Mayhew suspects she needs a drink, and offers her half a crown. Her eyes light up, and, instead of the usual fare served in gin palaces, her tastes are sufficiently aristocratic for her to order 'a drain of pale', a glass of fine brandy. Loo proceeds to order glass after glass, and becomes maudlin. When Mayhew enquires as to what the matter could be, she lays her hand to her head and cries that she wishes she were dead, and laid in her coffin, 'and it won't be long now until she is'. And then with a typical alcoholic mood swing, she brightens up and starts singing. Once she's settled down a bit, Mayhew enquires as to her former occupation. 'Oh, I'm a seduced milliner,' she says, impatiently, ready to please a potential client. 'Anything you like!'[14] Mayhew urges Loo to enter a refuge, wean herself off the drink and learn an honest trade, but Loo is indifferent to her fate. 'I don't wish to live,' she replies. 'I shall soon get D. T. [*delirium tremens*, a symptom of advanced alcoholism] and then I'll kill myself in a fit of madness.'[15] Soon after, a young Frenchman enters the bar, singing '*Vive l'amour, le vin, et le tabac*' (long live love, wine and tobacco) and Mayhew leaves him in conversation with Loo.

But Loo is a paragon of abstinence compared with 'China Emma', so called because her lover was a Chinese sailor called Appoo. Appoo regularly sent money home to Emma, and obviously had some feeling for her as he made regular and drastic attempts to cure her alcoholism. When Emma got drunk, Appoo tied up her arms and legs, dragged her outside into the gutter and threw buckets of water over her, but even this didn't succeed. 'I'd die for the drink,' Emma told Mayhew, 'I don't care what I does to get it.' Emma had even tried to kill herself on several occasions by jumping in the Thames, but her efforts were always frustrated. Once she even jumped out of a first-floor window in Jamaica Place straight into the river, but a passing boatman hooked her out and she ended up in court, sentenced to a month in jail for attempted suicide.[16]

Emma was a sailor's woman, a category of prostitutes towards whom Mayhew was reasonably sympathetic. He deplored (as ever) their extravagance but was impressed by the way the sailors treated their women. Sailors were a vital source of revenue in the East End; tens of thousands of men descended on the London docks from all over the world, arriving in the world's busiest port, ready for shore leave and with their pay burning a hole in their pockets. And the sailors' women or 'leggers' motts'[17] were there to help them spend it. With high-rolling sailors looking for a good time, brothel keeping inevitably flourished in the East End. One aspect of the sailors' behaviour intrigued Mayhew; rather than having several women, many sailors would take up with one girl, who effectively became their wife for the duration. Another curiosity was that very few

English girls became sailors' women; they were generally German or Irish. Mayhew noted many 'tall, brazen-faced' German women, dressed in gaudy colours, dancing and pirouetting in a dance hall off the Ratcliffe Highway.

Just as in the West End, the red-light district was concentrated on a certain number of streets consisting of the Ratcliffe Highway, Frederick Street, Brunswick Street and Shadwell High Street.[18] This quarter burst into life every night when the whores paraded up and down in short nightgowns and night-jackets, outside notorious pubs such as the Half Moon and Seven Stars, the Ship and Shears and the Duke of York in Shadwell High Street, and the Shakespeare's Head in Shadwell Walk,[19] 'flaunting about bare-headed, in dirty-white muslin and greasy, cheap blue silk, with originally ugly faces horribly seamed with small-pox, and disfigured by vice'.[20]

Many of the girls had distinctive names: 'Cocoa Bet'; 'Salmony-faced Mary Anne'; and the legendary 'Black Sall', described by one writer like a ship: 'a Dutch-built piratical schooner carrying on a free trade under the black flag . . . many a stout and lusty lugger has borne down upon, and hoisted the British standard over, our sable privateer, Black Sall'.[21]

Towards the latter half of the nineteenth century, sailors' spending patterns altered dramatically, due to the setting up of savings banks. Sailors were encouraged to bank the greater part of their pay, much to the relief of their families, but to the detriment of those whores and publicans who relied on their custom.

For investigators such as Mayhew and Acton, the East End was another country, and a dangerous one at that: Mayhew perceived Whitechapel as a suspicious, unhealthy locality, its population a strange amalgamation of Jews, English, French, Germans and other 'antagonistic elements that must clash and jar'. But the social reformer had the grace to concede that the theatres and music halls were first rate, with their awesome firework displays, blue demons, red demons, Satans who vanished through a trapdoor and gauzy nymphs sitting astride sunbeams halfway between the stage and the flies. Outside the theatres, fights frequently added to the sense of high drama, as in this incident:

> Three times in ten minutes I saw crowds collect round doorways, attracted by fights, especially by fights between women. One of them, her face covered with blood, tears in her eyes, drunk, was trying to fly at a man while the mob watched and laughed. And as if the uproar were a signal, the population of the neighbouring 'lanes' came pouring into the street, children in rags, paupers, street women, as if a human sewer were suddenly clearing itself.[22]

During his inspection of the many brothels which 'infested' the East End, Mayhew noted miserable establishments with faded chintz curtains and four-poster beds, and clapped-out old women sitting around sharing a can of beer. He also witnessed a development which he found almost too horrible to describe, comparing it with the work of a sensational novelist. On this occasion, he visited a shabby house, a 'wretched tumble down hovel' with no front door, in Victoria Place, Bluegate. Upon entering, he found a pitiful old woman and a young girl huddling for warmth around a miserable coke fire. The old woman told Mayhew that she paid five shillings a week rent, and charged the prostitutes who used her rooms four shillings a week, but that trade was slack as the shipping on the river was slow. Mayhew went upstairs and began his tour of inspection.

> The first room we entered contained a Lascar [a sailor with the East India company], who had come over in some vessel, and his woman. There was a sickly smell in the chamber, that I discovered proceeded from the opium he had been smoking. There was not a chair to be seen; nothing but a table, upon which were placed a few odds-and-ends. The Lascar was lying on a paliasse [mattress] placed upon the floor (there was no bedstead), apparently

stupefied from the effects of the opium he had been taking. A couple of old tattered blankets sufficed to cover him. By his bed-side sat his woman, who was half idiotically endeavouring to derive some stupefaction from the ashes he had left in his pipe. Her face was grimy and unwashed, and her hands so black and filthy that mustard-and-cress might have been sown successfully upon them. As she was huddled up with her back against the wall she appeared an animated bundle of rags. She was apparently a powerfully made woman, and although her face was wrinkled and careworn, she did not look exactly decrepit, but more like one thoroughly broken down in spirit than in body. In all probability she was diseased.[23]

This is a grimly prescient picture of prostitution and addiction, the Victorian equivalent of a crack house. While alcohol had always played its part in the history of prostitution, drug use was a new and disturbing development.

As if this level of degradation was not enough, Mayhew paints an even more desperate picture of low life in his portrayal of a 'park woman'. These poor creatures were even lower in the food chain than the worn-out unfortunates who skulked about the West End, scrounging a living from fashionable passers-by and the more afflu-ent prostitutes who paid them to go away. According to Mayhew, the park women were utterly lost to all sense of shame; they wan-dered about London's parks after nightfall, and consented to any species of humiliation in return for a few shillings. Park women could be met in Hyde Park, between the hours of five and ten (until the gates were closed) in winter. In Green Park, and the Mall, which was a nocturnal thoroughfare, you could spot these low wretches walking about sometimes with men, more generally alone, often early in the morning. They were to be seen reclining on the benches placed under the trees, originally intended, no doubt, for a different purpose, occasionally with the head of a drunken man reposing in their lap. Far from being the slender beauties and willing whores encountered by James Boswell, these women were so brutalized and scarred by alcohol and disease that the parks were the only venues left to them; they operated in the shadows, away from the gaslight which would have exposed the ravages of time, the defects of their personal appearance and the shabbiness of their ancient and dilapidated attire.

Mayhew describes these women as engaging in disgusting practices that were gratifying only to men of morbid and diseased imaginations (a prudish reference to fellatio) but whatever services they offered, one thing was obvious: in the West End, Hyde Park had become the Victorian equivalent of Gropecunt Lane, the knackers' yard for ageing whores. Mayhew interviewed one woman who always wore a long thick veil concealing her features, which made her interesting to the unsuspicious and unwise. This park woman had started her career as one of Mayhew's 'better educated' prostitutes. A former governess, she had lived on the continent with her lover until he blew his brains out with a pistol in a fit of desperation, having lost a fortune at the casino. Eventually returning to England, she had drifted gradually downmarket due to alcoholism and poor health.

> 'I was infected with a disease, of which I did not know the evil effects if neglected,' she told Mayhew. 'The disastrous consequence of that neglect is only too apparent now. You will be disgusted, when I tell you that it attacked my face, and ruined my features to such an extent that I am hideous to look upon, and should be noticed by no one if I frequented those places where women of my class most congregate; indeed, I should be driven away with curses and execrations.'[24]

Mayhew was genuinely moved by the plight of this woman, endowed with a fair amount of education, speaking in a superior manner, making use of words that very few in her position would know how to employ, reduced by a variety of circumstances to the very bottom of a prostitute's career. She refused to enter a work-house, but she could not get a job. Although she could sew and paint in watercolours, nobody would hire her, because they didn't like to look at her face, which presented so dreadful an appearance that it frightened people. She had her moments, generally hours, of oblivion, when she was intoxicated, and spent all her money on drink. And she knew that she would not live long. She had injured her constitution greatly, and suffered from a disease which a hospital surgeon had told her would kill her in time. Mayhew paid her for the interview, and told her to spend the money on getting into a refuge, whilst knowing that she would use it to buy alcohol. She would not live long, she repeated, and she wanted to die as she was, where she was.

And it is here that Mayhew makes one of his mission statements: 'One only gets at the depravity of mankind by searching below the surface of society; and for certain purposes such knowledge and information are useful and beneficial to the community. Therefore the philanthropist must overcome his repugnance to the task, and draw back the veil that is thinly spread over the skeleton.'

Spurred on by these accounts of the depravity of mankind, militant Christians, feminists and other social reformers campaigned against prostitution as the century progressed. While the vast armies of peripatetic whores had roamed Haymarket in the 1850s and 1860s, and the sailors' women of the East End had catered to thousands, the following decade saw a concerted campaign to wipe out prostitution and impose middle-class morality on all Londoners, regardless of their economic circumstances. The onslaught on prostitution took a number of forms, sanitary and moral. In public health terms, the first Contagious Diseases Act of 1864, designed to protect the health of the military in ports and garrison towns, specified that all prostitutes servicing troops and sailors must undergo a compulsory medical examination. The Act, which derived from earlier legislation dealing with the health of cattle, summed up official Victorian attitudes towards whores. 'Prostitutes should be treated as foul sewers are treated, as physical facts and not as moral agents.'[25]

Under the terms of the Act, women convicted of being 'a common prostitute' were summonsed to undergo a medical inspection. If they refused, they were sent to a 'Lock hospital'. Lock hospitals, so named after the original establishment in London, ostensibly specialized in venereal medicine but were little more than prisons for whores, from which many women emerged to find their children in the workhouse and their few possessions auctioned off to pay their debts.[26]

Prostitutes were demonized by Victorian moralists for spreading venereal disease, despite the fact that mortality rates from syphilis were considerably lower than those from tuberculosis and childbirth. Being at the front line of the war against venereal disease, many whores were more expert in treatment than doctors, and their preventive measures included examining clients and refusing to have sex with infected men. They also resorted to herbal remedies or cleansing medications which were considerably more effective than the mercury recommended by doctors.[27]

Prostitutes also faced tougher policing measures. The Metropolitan Police Act in 1850 made loitering an offence, while from 1858, any house which 'harboured' more than one whore was deemed to be a 'disorderly house' and the landlady could be prosecuted. Publicans, who had once relied on a co-dependent relationship with whores to bring in the trade, were banned from allowing prostitutes to 'assemble and continue' on their premises.[28]

In addition to these medical and legal constraints, a sanctimonious layer of morality was descending on Victorian London like a fog, with famous campaigners such as William Gladstone reaching out to prostitutes as if they were brands to be snatched from the burning.

William Gladstone, four times British prime minister, had already taken the lead in the 1850s, when he began to visit the Argyll Rooms and develop friendships with prostitutes whom he wished to reform. Gladstone's motivations, however, appear some-what obscure. While his ostensible motive was to pluck fallen women from their depraved state and train them to be useful members of society, he also enjoyed putting himself in the way of temptation and wrote up the charms of the most attractive whores in his diary, in Italian. While it is doubtful that, unlike other politicians, he ever compromised himself or betrayed his marital vows, the premier was not immune to the attractions of the women he interviewed. Returning home from these visits, he would inevitably retire to his chambers and flagellate himself with a whip as punishment for what he considered to be his shameful desires.

'Refuges', such as the ones Gladstone visited, were opened where former prostitutes could retrain as factory workers or servants, although few women found the prospect appealing compared with the money they could earn 'on the game'. Another solution, advocated by Victorian doctors, police and the military, was to legalize prostitution, in line with Britain's continental neighbours. But such a pragmatic response met with outrage from middle-class feminists such as Josephine Butler, who had declared in 1871 that it was 'the old, the inveterate, the deeply rooted evil of prostitution itself against which we are destined to make war'.[29]

Butler's mission was to wipe prostitution off the face of the earth, or at least off the face of Great Britain, and so she founded the Social Purity Alliance in 1873, which required young men to abstain from all sexual activity. This organization inspired other such fellowships as the National Vigilance Association, intended to guard the nation's morals, and the White Cross Army, whose members were exhorted to 'endeavour to put down all indecent language and coarse jests' and 'to use every possible means to fulfil the commandment "keep THYSELF pure"'.[30] Butler and her supporters relied on moral outrage to focus public opinion on their campaigns. To this end, she exploited two sensational developments: the so-called 'white slave trade' or supposed international trafficking in women, and the phenomenon of child prostitution.

In a spirited piece of revisionism, prostitution historian Nickie Roberts maintains that 'white slavery' was an urban myth, but it was certainly one which exercised a powerful grip over the Victorian imagination. In such circumstances, the typical victim would have been an innocent white adolescent girl who was drugged and abducted by a sinister immigrant, and who would wake to find herself held captive in some infernal foreign brothel, where she would be subject to the pornographic lusts and whims of sadistic non-white pimps and handlers.[31] Moralists were convinced that such traffic in women existed, operated by established underground networks, and succeeded in whipping up hysteria about this imaginary outrage. A pamphlet by Alfred Dyer, 'The European Slave Trade in English Girls' (1880), claimed that English girls were being abducted by the score and forced to work in the brothels of Brussels. A parliamentary commission of inquiry subsequently revealed that there was already an existing traffic in established British prostitutes being recruited to continental brothels, of whom about 200 eventually returned home again, having discovered that they did not enjoy working under the strict regulations operating in French and Belgian establishments.

According to Roberts, evidence for the 'white slave trade' rests upon the international migration of whores which had developed towards the end of the nineteenth century. With the expansion of trade routes to the outposts of the British Empire, millions were on the move, not least enterprising prostitutes who felt they might fare better in America and the Colonies. These women willingly travelled thousands of miles to escape oppression in their own country and work in the USA, Latin America, Egypt, South Africa and Asia. Men often travelled with them, acting as their chaperones and agents, and providing valuable introductions in the overseas sex trade.

One such young woman was Fanny Epstein, a Jewish immigrant in Whitechapel, who left home with a man called Alexander Kahn in 1891 and set off for India. When she went missing, Fanny's father appealed to the Foreign Office and she was traced to the red-light district of Bombay. Officers from the Bombay police were duly dispatched to ask Fanny if she required help in getting home to England, only to be told that she had come to India of her own free will and intended to stay. She had no regret or embarrassment about her work and impressed the commissioner of the Bombay police as 'singularly calm and self-possessed, a somewhat determined young woman and well able to look after herself'.[32] Kahn had been arrested, but when Fanny testified that she had left home of her own free will and that Kahn had provided her with money to set herself up in Bombay, the case against him collapsed.

A further outburst of moral outrage developed with the campaign to raise the age of consent from twelve to sixteen years, and concern about the 'trade in virgins'. As we know from previous chapters, there had always been a trade in virgins from London's earliest days, with bawds reserving their latest recruits to be auctioned off to the highest bidder. It is also evident that despite the sentimental Victorian ideal of the innocent little girl as portrayed by Charles Dickens or Lewis Carroll, creator of *Alice in Wonderland*, in reality millions of children endured a short life of miserable exploitation in factories, coal mines and sweatshops. Given these conditions, it is scarcely surprising that they also faced sexual exploitation. Back in 1835, the London Society for the Protection of Young Females found 400 individuals making a living by procuring girls between the ages of eleven and fifteen 'for the purposes of prostitution',[33] while the same society recorded 2,700 cases of syphilis in girls between the ages of eleven and sixteen over an eight-year period.

'Walter' described one encounter with 'a small girl' who invited him into her 'miserable house'. Enticed by her 'smallness and freshness' ('Walter' imagined the girl to be about fifteen years but she appears to have been younger), he began to undress her, but was incapacitated by fear of disease, and asked for a condom. At this point of the narrative, the girl's mother entered the scene, breastfeeding a baby. She provided money for the girl to go off and buy a French letter, and sat and talked to 'Walter' as they awaited her daughter's return. 'She must live,' says the mother, philosophically, 'and she's better at home doing that, than doing it away from me.' The girl then returned, but 'Walter' had lost interest. 'The affair was not enticing,' he concluded, laconically.[34] 'Walter's' experience is shocking but not remarkable in a culture where children and young people were regularly exploited.

Waterloo was notorious for child prostitutes and beggars who plucked at the sleeves of passers-by, whining for pennies and making obscene suggestions in the hope of fleecing a potential client.[35] Judges reported that children had appeared before them aged less than fourteen who could not remember the circumstances of their first intercourse. As in previous centuries, the backstreets and rookeries of London teemed with vagabonds and tiny desperadoes who survived on their wits and scratched a living by begging, stealing and selling their bodies.

According to one investigator, old roués with a desire for 'green fruit'[36] frequented the child brothels or employed procuresses to track down virgins, as in this description of a 'fashionable villa' where virgins were regularly sacrificed. The proprietress welcomes our narrator in, and shows him

> a room where you can be perfectly secure. The walls are thick, there is a double carpet on the floor. The window, which fronts on the back garden, is doubly secured, first with shutters, then with heavy curtains. You lock the door and then you do as you please. The girl may scream blue murder, but not a sound will be heard. The servants will be far away at the other end of the house. I will only be about seeing that all is snug.[37]

Attempts to raise the age of consent were making little impression on Parliament until the campaigner Josephine Butler turned for help to the editor of the *Pall Mall Gazette*, W. T. Stead. Butler's mission was to stamp out prostitution in general and the trade in virgins in particular. As a committed Christian, Stead was sympathetic to Butler's views. He was also eager to make a name for himself as a journalist. In 1885, he undertook his own investigation into the sex trade. The result was 'The Maiden Tribute of Modern Babylon', one of the first examples of muck-racking sensationalism.[38]

While journalists such as Mayhew and his assistant Bracebridge Hemyng had interviewed and recorded the voices of working prostitutes, Stead set up his own sting operation by manipulating a young and impressionable girl as adroitly as any old bawd. One of Stead's contacts, a Member of Parliament, had told him over a glass of champagne that it was possible to buy a virgin for £5.[39] With the help of Bramwell Booth (son of the founder of the Salvation Army), Stead set out to prove this theory. Stead recruited a retired prostitute, Rebecca Jarrett, as his agent and she procured a girl for him.[40] The girl in question turned out to be thirteen-year-old Eliza Armstrong, who arrived with her mother, the latter sporting a split lip, evidence of the fact that Mr Armstrong, Eliza's father, had not approved of the enterprise. Eliza was wearing a long dark travelling dress with a yellow collar, a black hat and a hairstyle known as a 'Piccadilly bang' which Stead regarded as rather common. ('Bangs' or fringes, lying over the forehead and often curled with irons, were considered to be vulgar.)

Eliza was taken to a Madame Mourez, an underground midwife who certified her *virgo intacta*, and then Stead took her to a low boarding house in Poland Street where Rebecca Jarrett had obtained rooms. Stead ordered drinks, while Rebecca chloroformed Eliza and put her to bed. Stead, decked out in grotesque make-up that made him look like an old rake, insisted on entering Eliza's bedroom to carry out the charade as far as possible. But Eliza woke up screaming: Rebecca had forgotten how to chloroform her victim efficiently, and Stead retired in confusion.[41]

After being subjected to another examination, this time so that a proper physician could certify her unharmed for Stead and Booth's ultimate protection, Bramwell Booth packed the miserable girl off to the Salvation Army in France.[42]

Stead took great pride in this episode. 'Even at this day,' he wrote, 'I stand amazed at the audacity with which I carried the thing through.'[43] It did not occur to him that Eliza might have found the experience disturbing. 'Beyond the momentary surprise of the midwife's examination, which was necessary to prove that a little harlot had not been palmed off upon us, she experienced not the slightest inconvenience.'[44]

Despite the fact that Stead and Booth had exploited the girl much as any old rake would have done – for their own purposes and without her consent – Stead became an overnight sensation and, most importantly for any journalist, saw a massive boost in his paper's circulation figures. 'The Maiden Tribute' hit the headlines like a bombshell, promising readers *'shuddering horror . . . the violation of virgins'*, *'confessions of a brothel keeper'* and even *'strapping girls down'*.[45] The language of pornography had been pressed into the service of journalism in order to expose a social evil and boost the circulation of the *Pall Mall Gazette*. There were riots outside the offices of the *Gazette* as eager readers tried to get their hands on a copy, which was banned by W H Smith on moral grounds. Copies changed hands at twelve times the cover price and the articles were syndicated in the USA and published across Europe from France to Russia.[46]

As a result of the scandal, a massive demonstration, 250,000 strong, took place in Hyde Park, demanding the raising of the age of consent to sixteen. Feminists, socialists and Christians converged to express their horror at 'Modern Babylon': wearing white roses for purity, ten columns of marchers descended upon the park, accompanied by the sound of tambourines, drums and flutes, and carrying banners appealing to men to 'Protect the Girls of England' while inviting women to 'Join the War on Vice' and steer the nation away from 'Shame, Shame, Horror!' There were wagonloads of young virgins dressed in white, flying a flag which read 'The Innocents, Will They Be Slaughtered?' and then, borne aloft like a god, came the conquering hero, accompanied by shouts of 'Long live Stead!'[47]

While Stead succumbed to grandiose self-satisfaction, other more urbane commentators questioned his motives. The MP for Whitehaven suggested that Stead might be liable to criminal prosecution himself for buying a young girl, while the playwright George Bernard Shaw described the Eliza Armstrong case as 'a put-up job' and doubted his journalistic credentials. 'After that, it was clear that he was a man who could not work with anybody, and nobody could work with him.'[48] However, it was a Mrs Lynn Linton who seems to have got Stead pegged and hinted at his true motivation. This reactionary campaigner (she made it her life's work to deride the feminist 'new woman' beloved of the progressives) made a shrewd assessment of Stead as a dirty old man when she wrote that 'he exudes semen through the skin'.[49]

Meanwhile, Eliza Armstrong's mother read the *Pall Mall Gazette* and recognized her own daughter in the account of the young virgin, 'Lily', acquired by Stead. Mrs Armstrong had been told that Eliza had gone into service. Horrified to find out that the girl had been sent to France, Mrs Armstrong went to the papers, and received a sympathetic hearing from *Lloyd's Newspaper*, a rival scandal sheet. A reporter from *Lloyd's*, accompanied by another journalist from *St James's Gazette*, tracked down Madame Mourez, while Eliza's father, Mr Armstrong, headed to Paris to find his daughter, and got lost in the brothels (or at least that was his explanation).[50] Eliza, meanwhile, had been sent back to England, and was discovered with Stead, in his garden in Wimbledon. Stead, to his evident delight, found himself under arrest for fraudulently procuring Eliza; he felt he had proved his point by drawing attention to the so-called white slave trade. 'To the legal minds the substantial question was whether or not Eliza had been taken "fraudulently" out of possession of the parents, the axiom being that all fraud annuls all consent.'[51]

There was only one answer. Madame Mourez and Rebecca Jarrett got six months each, and Stead received three months, which he embraced enthusiastically because he felt vindicated and enjoyed the publicity. Incarcerated in Holloway (now a women's prison), Stead received sympathetic treatment: his 'cell' consisted of a room with an armchair, a blazing fire, a comfortable bed, a writing desk and a tea-table. The months in 'Happy Holloway' flew by; years later Stead was to reflect that he had never been happier.[52] Once he had completed his jail term, the *Pall Mall Gazette* took him back, 'provided there were no more virgins',[53] but his career faltered thereafter, and his behaviour became increasingly erratic. Every 10 November, Stead dressed up in his prison uniform, boarded his commuter train in Wimbledon, and walked across Waterloo Bridge in the style of a convict, reliving the glory days of his trial.

After a number of failed ventures, including a spiritualist newspaper, *Borderland*, aimed at the twilight world of mediums and table-tappers, Stead met his appropriately sensational end in 1912, during a transatlantic voyage, when 'the man of most importance now alive' went down with the ship that could not sink: the *Titanic*.[54]

For girls at risk of sexual exploitation, Stead's publicity stunt had one positive outcome. The Criminal Law Amendment Act of 1885 raised the age of consent from twelve to sixteen, made procurement a criminal offence and stated that the penalty for assaulting a girl under thirteen was whipping or penal servitude. The Act gave the police extensive powers against procurers and brothel keepers, but also had the effect of outlawing consensual male homosexuality, with disastrous consequences. The consequences were also severe for prostitutes. A new wave of repression followed, as lodging houses and brothels were closed down. In 1887 the brewery heir turned purity campaigner Frederick Charrington rampaged through the streets of the East End with his supporters, closing down brothels, assaulting prostitutes and in one case kicking a brothel attendant so hard in the stomach that Charrington was subsequently sued.[55] So many street prostitutes were arrested that open soliciting was replaced by a 'stealthy glance or mumbled word'.

The social purity movement proved catastrophic for whores.

With the closure of lodging houses and houses of assignation, women were forced to book into seedy hotels or to rent furnished rooms. In both instances, this entailed the risk of being alone with clients who might rob and/or assault them, a constant source of anxiety for any woman involved in the sex trade. But in this case the dangers were more acute: there was no vengeful madam to scold a penniless client or kick him out if he got rough; no fellow whore next door to storm in and knock him over the head with a frying pan if he became abusive. The only other option was to ply their trade on the streets, but down dark alleys where the police could not find them.

Conditions were more dangerous for London's whores than they had ever been. And it was at this point, at the height of the purity campaign, that they faced their most deadly enemy: the serial killer known as 'Jack the Ripper', who terrorized the East End in 1888 with the murders of five prostitutes, and who may also have been responsible for killing another six. From the first terrible discovery of a woman's body, to the killer's game of cat and mouse with the Metropolitan Police, Jack the Ripper's bloody campaign constituted a reign of terror in the foggy backstreets of the East End.

The first body was discovered on the morning of 31 August 1888, when a driver from Pickford's removals spotted a woman lying in an alleyway called Buck's Row, just off Whitechapel Road and yards from the London Hospital. Thinking the woman to be drunk, or dead, he and a colleague went to investigate, and found that the woman's head had been severed from her body, leaving a gash over an inch wide. When the body was taken to the mortuary one officer, an Inspector Spratley, casually turned up the victim's clothes and saw that the lower part of her abdomen had been ripped open. According to one investigator, the injuries were such that 'they could only have been inflicted by a madman'. The police surgeon, Dr Ralph Llewellyn, observed that he had never seen a more horrible case. 'She was ripped open just as you see a dead calf at a butcher's shop. The murder was done by someone very handy with the knife.'[56] Bystander apathy was a notable feature of this crime: one local resident heard five cries of 'Murder! Police!', but knowing Buck's Row to be a haunt of street prostitutes, she did not bother to find out what the fuss was about and was quite satisfied when the shouts for help died away.[57] The victim's name was Mary Ann Nichols, and the police had no idea of a motive, apart from a theory that Mary Ann might have been the victim of a blackmail gang. With the local division out of their depth, Chief Inspector Frederick Abberline, a detective with previous experience in Whitechapel, was brought in to head up the case.

A week later, on 8 September, the corpse of Annie Chapman was found in a passage leading to a lodging house at 29 Hanbury Street, Spitalfields. Annie lived with 'Sievey' who, as his name suggests, was a sieve-maker, in Dorset Street, and had left him in bed while she went out at 1.45 a.m. to earn the rent. Annie's body was discovered at 6 a.m. by a fellow lodger, John Davies, who lived on the top floor. He called across to some workmen, saying that a woman had clearly been murdered. 'Her clothes were thrown back, but her face was visible,' said James Kent, another eyewitness. 'Her apron seemed to be thrown back over her clothes. I could see from the feet up to the knees. She had a handkerchief of some kind round her throat, which seemed sucked into her throat . . . it seemed as if her inside had been pulled from her, and thrown at her. It was lying over her left shoulder.'[58]

At this point, rumours began to circulate to the effect that a man with a leather apron and a knife had been seen in the area. And there was indeed a 'Leather Apron' in the form of John Pizer, a Jewish tradesman, who was arrested and released when he convinced the police that he had nothing to do with the killings. Given the mood developing in the neighbourhood, 'Leather Apron' was lucky he did not get lynched, but the theory that the murders had been committed by a man in a leather apron gained credibility as the plot thickened.[59]

On 27 September 1888, the Central News Agency received a

letter which was subsequently forwarded to the Metropolitan Police on 29 September. Written in lurid prose, it purported to be from the murderer: 'Dear Boss . . .' the letter began. 'That joke about Leather Apron gave me real fits . . . I am down on whores and I shant quit ripping them till I do get buckled . . .' The letter continued in this vein and was signed 'Jack the Ripper', a name which naturally caught the popular imagination as soon as the police went public with it.

A day later, the body of Elizabeth Stride, nicknamed 'Long Liz', was discovered about 1 a.m., lying on the ground in Dutfield's Yard, off Berner Street (now Henriques Street) in Whitechapel. There was one clear-cut incision on the neck; the cause of death was massive blood loss from the nearly severed main artery on the left side. That there also were no mutilations to the abdomen has left some uncertainty about the identity of Elizabeth's murderer, along with the suggestion that her killer was disturbed during the attack. Three-quarters of an hour later, the body of Catherine Eddowes was found in Mitre Square in the City of London: her throat had been cut and a major part of her uterus, and her left kidney, had been removed. On 1 October, a postcard written in red ink was sent to the police. In this, the writer called himself 'saucy Jack' and referred to 'the double event' before signing off as Jack the Ripper.[60]

The press seized on the gruesome potential of 'The Double Event' and the murders became a source of public fascination, lurid, spine-chilling but sufficiently remote from most readers' cosy suburban world to pose a threat. *Reynold's Newspaper* ran with a piece of dog-gerel to the effect that 'Murder is stalking red handed 'mid the homes of the weary poor' while newsboys ran up and down the streets crying 'Latest Hawful Horror. A woman cut in pieces! Speshul!'[61] Chief Inspector Abberline noted the similarity between the victims and speculated as to the killer's motivation. All the victims were prostitutes, all middle-aged, all of medium height, and all with missing teeth, though the latter characteristic was not uncommon among working-class women of the period. Prostitutes interviewed by the press remained characteristically stoical. One, who had been on the game for twenty years, concluded: 'Well, suppose I do get killed, it will be a good thing for me, for the winter is coming on and the life is awful. I can't leave it; nobody would employ me.'[62]

In their search for a culprit, vigilante gangs targeted Jewish immigrants. As obvious aliens with distinctive cultural features and religious beliefs, they were inevitably a focus for violent anti-Semitism. Jewish boys were chased through the streets with cries of 'It was a Jew what did it!' and 'No Englishman did it!'[63] Immediately after the Eddowes murder, a piece of her bloodstained apron was found in a doorway in Goulston Street, Whitechapel. Above the piece of cloth, on the brick fascia in the doorway, was the legend, in chalk, 'The Juwes are The men that Will not be Blamed for nothing.' To this day, expert opinion is divided as to whether this was a message from the murderer, a piece of anti-Semitic graffiti, or an enigmatic reference to a piece of regalia, the 'juwes', which features in the ritual of the Freemasons.

The discovery of a female torso in the cellars of the new police building under construction at Whitehall added to the air of horror on 2 October 1888, while a deluge of copycat 'Jack the Ripper' letters added to the problems of the overstretched police. Then the Chairman of the Whitechapel Vigilance Committee, builder George Lusk, suffered an extremely unpleasant shock. On 16 October 1888, he received half a human kidney in a cardboard box through the post. With this gruesome object was a letter scrawled in a spidery hand, addressed 'From Hell' and concluding: 'Catch me when you can Mishter Lusk.' The writer claimed to have fried and eaten the other half of the 'kidne' [sic], which was 'very nise'. The shaken Lusk took both kidney and letter to the police. While the police and the police surgeon felt it was probably a hoax by a medical student, others believed it was part of Eddowes' missing organ.[64]

The Whitechapel murders were becoming notorious, with newspapers from Europe to the Americas speculating on the identity of the killer. Alleged culprits included doctors, slaughterers, sailors and lunatics of every description. The image of the killer as a 'shabby genteel' man dressed in black, wearing a slouch hat and carrying a shiny black doctor's bag began to take hold. The tabloids had seen nothing like this since the 'Maiden Tribute' and they had a field day. Though there were no Whitechapel murders in October there was still plenty to write about, including dozens of arrests on suspicion, usually followed by a quick release.

Among those questioned were Aaron Kosminski, a poor Polish Jew resident in Whitechapel; Montague John Druitt, a thirty-one-year-old barrister and school teacher who committed suicide in December 1888; Michael Ostrog, a Russian-born multi-pseudonymous thief and confidence trickster, believed to be fifty-five years old in 1888, and detained in asylums on several occasions; and Dr Francis J. Tumblety, fifty-six years old, an American 'quack', who was arrested in November 1888 for offences of gross indecency, and fled the country later the same month, having obtained bail at a very high price.

Friday, 9 November should have been a day of great celebration for Londoners, with the investiture of a new Lord Mayor. However, at 10.45 a.m., the body of Mary Jane Kelly was discovered in her room at 13 Miller's Court, off Dorset Street, Spitalfields. Mary Jane, who had taken to calling herself 'Marie' following a trip to Paris but who was commonly known as 'Ginger', was lying on the bed in her single room. She had been murdered with such ferocity that it beggared description. Her throat had been severed down to the spine, and her abdomen virtually emptied of its organs. Her heart was missing. The Ripper's latest atrocity completely overshadowed the Lord Mayor's celebrations, and led to the resignation of the Metropolitan Commissioner of Police, Sir Charles Warren.[65]

After the Kelly murder, and many more abortive arrests, the panic started to die down a little and a more quiescent atmosphere began to reign. In early 1889 Inspector Abberline left to take on other cases, and the inquiry was handed over to Inspector Henry Moore. His last extant report on the murders is dated 1896, when another 'Jack the Ripper' letter was received. There were brief flurries of press activity and wild suggestions that the 'Ripper' had returned on the occasions of subsequent murders. The last serious suspect was Tom Sadler, a sailor who was arrested in 1891 for the murder of the prostitute Frances Coles. When they tracked Sadler down to the Phoenix public house in Smithfield, the police were convinced that they had got their man. Sadler, a violent drunk with a history of assaulting women, fitted their profile. But when he went on trial for murder, the jury remained unconvinced of his guilt and Sadler walked free.

An entire genre of 'Ripperology' has developed over the years, with historians, psychologists and retired police officers bringing their considerable acumen to try to identify the perpetrator or perpetrators of these horrors. The *British Medical Journal* suggested that the atrocities might have been committed by a ruthless but enterprising gang eager to sell wombs to medical students,[66] while other theories as to the Ripper's identity laid the blame at the feet of Freemasons and even the Duke of Clarence, a younger son of Queen Victoria and thought to be mentally disturbed. In recent years, the American crime novelist Patricia Cornwell has put forward an ingenious case attributing the murders to the north London artist Walter Sickert, a theory as intriguing as any other in the dark realm of 'Ripperology'. Sickert had a ghastly fascination with prostitution and cruelty, as one of his most famous paintings indicates. Based on 'The Camden Town Murder', it shows the body of a prostitute lying on a bed, while her husband sits beside her, wringing his hands. A grim piece of social realism, it echoes the sentiment which must have run through the minds of those men whose women were murdered by the Ripper: as the man sits in his despair, one question is uppermost in his mind: 'What Shall We Do For The Rent?'

Whoever the Ripper may have been, the consequences of his bloody swathe through the East End were lethal for prostitutes. While the flitting shade of Jack the Ripper took his place alongside

Sweeney Todd as one of the grisly legends of Victorian London, his potential victims were forced to turn for protection to male pimps. Over the subsequent century, prostitution was to undergo a transition from a female-dominated industry into a lucrative division of organized crime.

10

'IT'S A SIN'

The perverse pleasures of pornography

The last rites of many a Victorian gentleman involved a discreet
fire at the bottom of the garden. As the smoke and ashes floated
far above the rose bushes and the scent of burning paper filled
the air, an observer might have wondered whether this was
some obscure religious observance, or a pagan custom retained
into the nineteenth century. They would have been wrong. The
fuel for these bonfires consisted of pornography, systematically
destroyed to protect the reputations of the recently deceased and
their families; under the Obscene Publications Act 1857, mere
possession of these smutty tomes merited a hefty fine or even a
spell in jail.

Those books which survived the attentions of the collectors'
nearest and dearest are contained in the British Museum's private
cases, accompanied by notes from the gentlemen's executors who, to
a man, considered the British Museum to be the best place for them,
away from the eyes of women and servants. The pornography

which has been preserved offers an extraordinary insight into Victorian sexuality; books and magazines devoted to every facet of erotic behaviour, some familiar, some shocking and some decidedly perverse. As Pearsall has noted in *The Worm in the Bud*, pornography constituted another element of the mysterious, submerged world of Victorian sexuality.

Victorian pornography offered vicarious thrills for those who preferred their pleasures at second hand. The repressed and masochistic William Gladstone read pornography as a means of testing his resistance to sexual temptation, before he progressed to the greater challenge of keeping company with prostitutes. For the majority of Victorian gentlemen, pornography had a more obvious appeal in the form of escapism, forbidden pleasure and release from sexual tension. The genre has, after all, been described as literature to be read with one hand. Collecting 'erotica' or 'curiosa' was decidedly a gentleman's pursuit, a fact reflected in the price of the books and magazines, which appeared in limited editions (around 300 copies was the average print run) and at a cost which put them well above the reach of the working man or the grimy fingers of leering schoolboys. Erotica was generally restricted to the upper classes and men of the Church, as it had been since the Renaissance. And it is at this point, perhaps, that a brief history of pornography will serve to put the genre in context.

Early erotica was printed in Latin, meaning that ordinary people could not read it. This way, 'curiosa' as it became known, was kept from the uneducated. The other consequence, of course, was that the greatest consumers of 'curiosa' consisted of those well versed in Latin: the priesthood.

One of the first pornographers was Pietro Aretino (1492–1556), an Italian author, affectionately referred to as '*il flagello de principi*' ('the scourge of princes') for his satires against royalty and the Church. A cheerful individual, Aretino actually died laughing: he fell backwards off a chair and struck his head after hearing his sister tell a dirty joke. In 1524, Aretino wrote a series of sonnets to accompany the drawings of sixteen sexual positions by Giuliano Romano, a twenty-five-year-old pupil of Raphael. Together, they produced one of the most notorious works of erotica, the *Sonnetti Lussuriosi*, or 'Sonnets of Pleasure'. The publication caused such outrage that Aretino had to flee Rome and was lucky to escape a prison sentence. The Church burned as many copies of the book as they could get their hands on, and no complete surviving copy is known to exist.

The first pornography in English became available during the sixteenth century, with English translations of classical texts such as Adlington's 1566 translation of Apuleius's *The Golden Ass*. This picaresque novel was originally written in Latin around the second century AD. In 1567 Arthur Golding translated Ovid's *Metamorphoses*, which portrayed a dizzying array of classical deities engaged in a variety of sexual activities while disguised as animals. Christopher Marlowe, meanwhile, translated Ovid's *Ars Amatoria* ('art of love', or more precisely in this context a celebration of extra-marital sex), the original version of which resulted in the poet being banished from Rome.

While a restricted quantity of pornography circulated during the seventeenth and eighteenth centuries, the genre really took off with developments in printing in the nineteenth century. Collectors tended to be wealthy businessmen or Anglican clergy who filed their pornography under the heading of 'anthropology'. As one genuine scholar at the British Museum remarked, in 1885, 'Of late the demand for bawdy books has become startlingly large. If the study of "Anthropology" goes on at this rate, heaven only knows what we shall reach in the next generation.'[1]

From the 1820s onwards, the heart of London's pornography industry was Holywell Street, off the Strand. Now long gone, it was demolished in 1901 to make way for the Aldwych and Kingsway. Holywell Street was otherwise known as Bookseller's Row, because it was full of print and book shops. By 1834, there were fifty-seven pornography shops in this one street, all with a display designed to attract the attention of passers-by. Pornographic novels, erotic prints, etchings and catalogues for prostitutes that contained their specialities were all sold here. Also on sale was *The Yokel's Preceptor*, an early guide to 'gay London', advising the best places to pick up homosexuals, disguised as a rantingly disapproving tract. As these shops sat alongside 'respectable' stores, Holywell Street drew a curiously mixed demographic of browsers looking for legitimate texts: lawyers from the nearby Inns of Court; professors from King's College, on the Strand; medical students searching out textbooks – all rubbing shoulders and jostling alongside prostitutes, homosexuals and curious young women, pressing their faces up against the glass. The *Daily Telegraph* deplored the fact that the young of either sex were to be seen there, 'furtively peering in at these sin-crammed shop windows, timorously gloating over suggestive title pages conning [reading] insidious placards, guiltily bending over engravings as vile in execution as they are in subject'.[2]

It was here that the cognoscenti might find publications devoted to every form of sexual pleasure, from representations of conventional copulation in numerous reprints and imitations of *Fanny Hill* to dirty comic verse such as:

> I don't like to see, though it's really a lark,
> A clergyman poking a girl in the park;
> Nor a young lady, wishing to be thought discreet,
> Looking at printshops in Holywell-street
> I don't like to see, coming out of Cremorne,
> A girl with her muslin much crumpled and torn,
> Arm in arm with a fellow who's had the mishap,
> To forget, when he shagged her, to button his flap.[3]

Holywell Street also offered literary and artistic representations of the more recherché delights of homosexual and lesbian sex, and flagellation, which has never gone out of favour in the British Isles and was particularly popular with the Victorians. Translations from French masterpieces and oriental sex manuals were also popular, some of which had been brought in from abroad with an ingenuity and resourcefulness which would put modern drug couriers to shame.

A typical example from the 1840s was the list of Henry Smith of 37 Holywell Street. This included early sex manuals and tales of sexual initiation such as: *Onanism Unveiled, or the Private Pleasures and Practices of the youth of both Sexes exposed, The Connubial Guide, or Married People's Best Friend* (price 6d); *The Royal Wedding Jester or all the Fun and Facetiae of the Wedding Night with all the good things said, sung, or done on that joyous occasion* (reduced price 2/6); *The Wedding Night or the Battles of Venus*,[4] while *Venus in the Cloisters, or the Jesuit and the Nun* revisited that old erotic standard, clerics behaving badly. *The Jolly Companion, Woman Disrobed* ('a most capital tale') offers similar content to a top-shelf magazine, while *Adventures of a Bedstead*, meanwhile, promises a variety of saucy escapades, as does *Tales of Twilight: or the Amorous Adventures of a company of Ladies before Marriage* (10/6, 8 fine coloured plates). *The Spreeish Spouter or Flash Cove's Slap-Up Reciter* is more perplexing, with its encoded title of Victorian sexual slang, but it appears to be popular verse, intended to be recited, about the adventure of a pleasure-loving young man (the 'flash cove') the specific nature of whose enjoyments or 'sprees' involve ejaculation (or 'spouting'). Something of the original charm is no doubt lost in translation.

'Confessions' were always a popular genre, and so our Victorian gentlemen could expect to sit back and find pleasure in tales such as *Adventures and Amours of a Barmaid*, a serial in a pornographic magazine entitled *The Boudoir*, in which our heroine picks up an elderly earl in Kensington Gardens, takes him home and enjoys watching 'the variations of his face as picking up a decidedly naughty book he eagerly scanned its contents'.[5]

One of the most successful pornographers was John Camden Hotten (1832–73), a founder of Chatto and Windus. Hotten succeeded in maintaining a toehold in the respectable world of mainstream publishing, operating out of a shop in Piccadilly, while bringing out clandestine texts such as *The Romance of Chastisement*, a sado-masochistic classic which inevitably attracted the attention of one of Hotten's most popular authors, the poet Algernon Charles Swinburne (1837–1909), who was a devotee of flagellation. It was suspected that Hotten blackmailed his author into producing pornographic verse alongside his more mainstream contributions, but such allegations did not prevent Hotten from gaining that final accolade, burial in Highgate Cemetery, marked by 'a modest tombstone, erected in his memory by the London booksellers'.[6]

Hotten was considerably more respectable than William Dugdale, 'one of the most prolific publishers of filthy books '7, who, in the 1860s, traded under several aliases, including Henry Smith, Turner, Young and Brown. Dugdale was one of the first publishers to provide eye-catching blurbs, snagging jaded rack browsers with copy such as: 'Nunnery Tales or Cruising Under False Colours – every stretch of voluptuous imagination is here fully depicted, rogering, ramming, one unbounded scene of lust, lechery and licentiousness.' And all for two guineas. Dugdale was a twisted, unpleasant character, whose CV included forgery and plagiarism; one trick of his was to take existing texts and reissue them with new names or take sections or chapters from existing texts and reissue them as new. He even published books with racy titles, such as Confessions of a Ballet Girl, which turned out to be completely innocent.8 Dugdale's publications included Raped on the Railway, in which a woman is raped and then flagellated on the so-called 'Scotch Express'.9 By the 1870s, more specialist material was available, such as The Romance of Lust (1873), which features a man who has sex with his own sister, who also turns out to be his daughter; The Story of a Dildo (1880); Kate Handcock or A Young Girl's Introduction to Fast Life (1882) and Laura Middleton, Her Brother and Her Lover (1890). Dugdale also republished The Lustful Turk, one of the original sources for the myth of 'white slavery', in which a young woman is kidnapped and taken to a brothel where she develops an infatuation with her abductor.

The pornography trade invariably attracted some eccentric and desperate characters. There was Edward Sellon, author of *The Ups and Downs of Life* (1867), who dabbled in Hindu literature and erotology, and wrote a treatise on snake worship. After losing his memory, Sellon became a fencing teacher, drove a mail coach between London and Cambridge and blew his brains out in Webb's Hotel, Piccadilly, at the age of forty-eight.[10]

Gifted authors, desperate for money, also turned to writing pornography. They included young Arthur Machen, who was to become a celebrated writer of horror and science fiction, and the poet Ernest Dowson. Rejected from medical school but with some literary talent, the resourceful Machen earned a crust by spending his days in the reading room of the British Museum translating Casanova's *Memoirs* and then *Le Moyen de Parvenir (Table Talk)* by Béroalde de Verville, the poor man's Rabelais. This last was considered so obscene that the printers refused to go on typesetting it after eighty pages. Meanwhile, Dowson translated French erotica to eke out his modest income as a writer and critic. Sadly, the financial rewards were not sufficient to prevent Dowson, a tubercular alcoholic, from dying in poverty at the age of thirty-two, but not before he had bequeathed the quotations 'days of wine and roses' and 'gone with the wind' to the English language.

One of the most popular genres in Holywell Street was devoted to flagellation. According to the publisher John Cannon, this was 'a letch which has existed from time immemorial',[11] and the trade certainly reflected the continuing fascination with *le vice anglais*. As our celebrated bawds have observed in previous chapters, a taste for flagellation appears to have been the inevitable legacy of a public school education. In the battle to maintain discipline over the future empire builders, few boys escaped the lash. Indeed, as Pearsall suggests, corporal punishment constituted one of the tribal rituals of the upper classes: one elderly correspondent to *The Morning Post* declared that, after being soundly beaten by Dr Keate, the headmaster of Eton, 'I am all the better for it, and am, therefore – ONE

WHO HAS BEEN WELL SWISHED.'[12] The Old Etonian Algernon Swinburne was a devotee, his enjoyment of the vice having begun after one particularly savage flogging at school, from which he bore the marks for over a month. This formative experience led, in adulthood, to his patronizing a brothel in St John's Wood where he could be chastised by rouged, golden-haired ladies who wielded the whip upon their gentlemen 'guests'.[13]

Flagellant literature falls into a number of categories: from the accounts of elderly roués who require sexual stimulation from a briskly administered whipping, as documented by Cleland in *Fanny Hill*, to the well-connected and influential men who enjoy a sex game during which they are 'punished' by a dominatrix, while other parties look on, and even join in. This is a form of role play, with each participant assigned the character of 'naughty child' or birch-wielding disciplinarian, as in the following extract. This depicts a flogging enthusiast pretending to be an impudent young boy who has insulted his mother and is now being punished for it by the redoubtable 'Mrs Trimmer' while his 'nurse' or governess looks on. The *mise-en-scène* is highly dramatic, with appropriately blood-curdling language, but while there cannot be any doubt about the measure of pain inflicted upon the individual concerned, we are also left in no doubt that this is how he obtains his pleasure

'Is it possible,' said Mrs Trimmer, pulling [the victim's] breeches down to his heels, 'that your mistress suffered this tyrannical gentleman to insult her in the manner she has represented?' 'No indeed ma'am, I never insulted my mamma, upon my honour, I did not,' roared the youth. 'Indeed, Mrs Trimmer,' replied the nurse, 'there's not so bold a boy in the parish.'

'So, so, so I understand!' said the mistress, (making him caper as high as young Vestris at every stroke of the rod.) 'Yes, yes, I can see you are a wicked young rascal!'

As the rascal begs his assailant to stop, the attack becomes more vigorous, with the dominatrix declaring that 'I'll whip this bold backside of his till I strip every bit of skin from it . . . You may roar, and cry, and kick, and plunge, and implore, my pretty gentleman, but all will not do; I'll whip you till the blood runs to your heels! You shall feel the tuition of this excellent rod!'[14]

Another popular sub-genre of flagellant literature added a lesbian twist by depicting the beating of young women by other young women, as in *The Merry Order of St Bridget*, which describes the erotic punishments within a closed order of nuns:

> She instantly, by desire, assumed the character of Flirtilla's Governess, and having stretched her, with some seeming reluctant struggles on the part of Flirtilla, on the bed, she uncovered to the waist the plumpest, fairest, and most beautiful posteriors that ever charmed mankind. Clarissa herself stood entranced at the lovely view, and suspended the rod, till Flirtilla, impatient for the delightful combat, cried out like a terrified child . . .[15]

While *The Englishwoman's Domestic Magazine* featured a long series on flogging, with hoax letters coming in from all quarters testifying to the benefits of flogging one's daughters, more extreme cases of sadism included the reflections of the brutal 'Colonel Spanker' (in reality one

The lesbian proprietor whips young Sabrina in Charles Lubbock's Madame Zuleika's Sapphic Academy *c. 1901.*

William Lazenby, 1825–88) whose *Experimental Lecture* revelled in the 'exciting and voluptuous pleasures to be derived from crushing and humiliating the spirit of a beautiful and modest young lady'.[16]

Henry Spencer Ashbee, a Victorian collector and self-appointed pornography expert, found flagellation so distasteful that he had to recruit a specialist to write about it in his catalogue of erotica. For Ashbee, the practice was 'the wild dream, or rather nightmare, of some vicious, used-up, old rake, who, positively worn out, and his hide tanned and whipped to insensibility by diurnal flogging, has gone mad on the subject of beastly flagellation'.[17]

According to the publisher John Cannon, flagellation was so popular 'and so extensively indulged in London at this day, that no less than twenty splendid establishments are supported entirely by this practice.'[18] London's dominatrices swished their way to a fortune: Mrs James, of 7 Carlisle Street, Soho, retired to a life of luxury in Notting Hill, while many had handsome addresses: Mrs Emma Lee, of 50 Margaret Street; Mrs Phillips, of 11 Upper Belgrave Place; and Mrs Shepherd, of 25 Gilbert Street.[19]

While much of the literature of flagellation is either coy or brutal, there is an account by 'Walter' which is so realistic as to have the ring of truth about it. The anonymous author of *My Secret Life* witnessed this incident during a trip to Belgium, when he and his mistress, a prostitute he refers to as 'Helen Marwood', visit a specialist brothel, as Helen's interest is piqued by the vice. It is a vivid but sordid description of a sexual encounter. Escorted by the 'Abbess', or dominatrix, who runs the brothel, Helen, wearing only her chemise, and 'Walter', in just his shirt and a mask, enter a room where they encounter a man kneeling on a large chair at the foot of the bed. The chair is draped with a towel to 'receive his spendings'. As if this was not enough, the 'patient', as 'Walter' refers to him

is wearing a woman's dress, tucked up to his waist, showing his naked rump and thighs, which strikes an incongruous note as he is still sporting men's socks and boots. A woman's bonnet is tied

237

carefully over his head and adjusted to conceal any beard or side-burns, and he has a mask over his eyes, leaving his mouth free. Behind him stands a young girl, dressed as a ballet dancer, but in a far from conventional fashion, as she has a very short skirt, bare legs and naked breasts. She is also holding a birch, displaying dark, hairy armpits. A second woman with yellow hair completes the tableau. As she is naked apart from boots and stockings it is quite obvious that her hair is dyed, as evidenced by the dark brown fringes on her armpits and pudenda.[20]

The 'patient' asks to see 'Walter's' penis – a request with which 'Walter' graciously complies, although he refuses to let the 'patient' touch him; the 'patient' also wants a look at Helen's cunt, but is refused. After some backchat, the abbess takes up her switch and begins to whip her 'patient', as the two other girls, 'Walter' and Helen look on.

'Walter' decides to walk round to the other side to see if the 'patient' is responding to this stimulation, and describes his prick as 'longish, pendant' but not sufficiently aroused, despite the fact that the abbess is swishing away with a will. 'Yellowhead', the woman with dyed hair, takes hold of the 'patient's' penis from behind, while the abbess winks at 'Walter'. Despite escalating cries of pain, the 'patient' still cannot obtain satisfaction, gripping the bedstead and crying as his backside becomes increasingly red. There is a rest, and some whispering between the abbess and her 'patient' and then Yellowhead takes up the birch, as 'Walter' and Helen move round the bed to watch, 'both of us excited, H's face flushed with lust, I felt her cunt, and she my pego, now stiff'. The 'patient' livens up at this display. 'Let me lick her cunt,' he whispers, and at first Helen refuses, but, short of money as usual, she eventually consents, demanding £5 for the pleasure. 'He'll pay, he's a gentleman,' the abbess reassures her, and Helen settles down on the bed, although it takes several pillows to manoeuvre her into a position where the 'patient's' tongue can reach the goal. But this is still not enough for the 'patient', who demands that 'Walter' 'frig' him. 'Walter' obliges, for a second, as the rod falls on the 'patient's' backside and he continues to lick Helen. Eventually, Yellowhead takes hold of the 'patient', gives him one or two gentle tugs, and a shower of semen spurts out. As he collapses, all passion spent, the only unsatisfied person in the room is Helen. 'Damn it,' she exclaims, 'I was just coming!' 'But the "patient" was lifeless,' 'Walter' tells us. 'All desire to lick her had gone.'[21]

'Walter's' anecdote is an absurd and pitiful take on human sexuality, in which the protagonists appear pathetic and comical, from the punter trussed up in a frock to the frustrated Helen, deprived of her orgasm, while the voyeuristic 'Walter' looks on and relishes every detail. It is far removed from the cheerful role play of the 'naughty boy' being 'swished' by the draconian 'Mrs Trimmer' in an earlier extract; and it is also, as Steven Marcus has noted, so graphic and so factual in its depiction of sexuality as to prefigure the Modernism of James Joyce or D. H. Lawrence.

As far as mainstream pornography was concerned, anything 'French' was considered titillating and there was an insatiable demand for Gallic erotica. 'My French Friend', a short story which appeared in *The Boudoir* magazine, dealt with the adventures of a 'pretty little morsel, ripe and melting as a plum, acquiescent and charming, ready to make the beast with two backs, to play the game of sixty-nine, to exercise the delicate manipulations of her soft fingers, or do the lolly-pop trick with her ripe lips at a moment's notice', who later proceeds to seduce her chambermaid.[22] To satisfy the demand for French pornography, booksellers smuggled contraband into England, with the help of contacts based in Paris. One such bookseller was Frederick Hankey, who had moved to Paris to give himself up, body and soul, to sexual fulfilment and decadence, although as his friend Henry Spencer Ashbee observed, he was 'a second Sade without the intellect'.[23] An unprepossessing young man, Hankey was short, with a head like an orange and a mouth like a slit. He was also a necrophiliac. Sir Richard Burton, the explorer and orientalist, had promised him the skin of an African woman, preferably torn off a live one, during a campaign in Dahomey (now Benin), although he was disappointed in his sick wish. 'I have been here three days and am grievously disappointed,' Burton wrote to a friend. 'Not a man killed, nor a fellow tortured. The canoe floating in blood is a myth of myths. Poor Hankey must wait for his *peau de femme*.'[24] When he heard that there was to be a public hanging in Paris, Hankey and a friend took a couple of young women along to the execution so that they could have sex during the event.

For all his considerable shortcomings, Hankey was a committed publisher and would do anything it took to get the job done. When his bookbinder became difficult, Hankey discovered his particular fetish and procured young girls for him; the books were bound, but the man's marriage was left in tatters. Hankey used couriers to smuggle the books into England, sometimes via the diplomatic bags of the British Embassy, thanks to his cousin's valet. On more than one occasion, a Mr Harris of Covent Garden smuggled books in and out of England 'in the bend of his back'.[25]

The need to smuggle texts in, combined with the prospect of fines and even imprisonment, had become a reality for pornographers thanks to the Society for the Suppression of Vice and the development of literary censorship. Up until the 1840s, censorship had been comparatively relaxed; a gentlemanly blind eye was turned to the excesses of pornography if it was distributed and enjoyed with discretion. The only law against sexually explicit material was King George III's 1787 Royal Proclamation 'For the Encouragement of Piety and Virtue, and for the Preventing and Punishing of Vice, Profaneness and Immorality', including the suppression of all 'loose and licentious Prints, Books, and Publications, dispersing Poison to the minds of the Young and Unwary and to Punish the Publishers and Vendors thereof'. This was policed by groups such as the Proclamation Society, which became the Society for the Suppression of Vice, instituted in 1802 to 'check the spread of open vice and immorality, and more especially to preserve the minds of the young from contamination by exposure to the corrupting influence of impure and licentious books, prints, and other publications', but this had little effect, because it had no power to destroy the material. However, purity crusaders were tightening their grip on the nation's morals and gaining widespread support for their campaign to clean up Britain. The society mustered sufficient establishment support to drive legislation through Parliament in the form of the Obscene Publications Act 1857, which gave magistrates the powers to order the destruction of 'any obscene publication held for sale or distribution on information laid before a court of summary jurisdiction'.[26]

According to the Society for the Suppression of Vice, anything 'obscene' was called 'pornography', literally, writings about or by prostitutes, or 'porni'; according to the *Oxford English Dictionary*, the first use of this word in the English language dates from 1850.

The Obscene Publications Act was introduced in September 1857 by Lord Campbell, the Lord Chief Justice. William Dugdale was one of the first to be arrested. When he appeared in court before Lord Campbell, Dugdale defended himself by protesting his innocence, pleading for the sake of his children, and then threatening the court with a knife. As one might expect, this final gesture was not well received and Dugdale was found guilty and sentenced to a long term of imprisonment. He died in the Clerkenwell House of Correction in 1869. Also arrested was Mary Elliot, one of the few female booksellers in Holywell Street. Elliot pleaded guilty and promised never to sell pornography again, but she was still sentenced to a year of hard labour, even though she was forty-nine years old.

One of the chief opponents of the Act was Lord Lyndhurst, who initiated the long-running debate as to the meaning of the term 'obscenity': 'but what is the interpretation which is to be put upon the word "obscene"?' he asked. 'I can easily conceive that two men will come to entirely different conclusions as to its meaning.'

Lyndhurst spelt out his objections by describing one famous painting thus: 'a woman stark naked, lying down, and a satyr standing by her with an expression on his face which shows most distinctly what his feelings are, and what is his object'. This sounded like just the sort of smut available in Holywell Street, until Lyndhurst revealed that he was actually describing Correggio's *Jupiter and Antiope* (1523), but his description also shows that one man's Renaissance masterpiece is another man's obscenity. And obscenity was to remain almost impossible to define far into the twentieth century, as attested by a number of controversial court cases.

Lord Campbell's definition of obscenity was 'intended to apply exclusively to works written for the single purpose of corrupting the morals of youth, and of a nature calculated to shock the common feelings of decency in any well-regulated mind'. His law was designed to eliminate the 'sale of poison more deadly than prussic acid, strychnine or arsenic', and would 'protect women, children, and the feeble-minded'.[27] The Act gave the police the power to search premises, but not people, where such publications were on sale, and permitted customs officers and Post Office officials to destroy consignments, and to prosecute offenders.

For all Lord Lyndhurst's efforts, the authorities refused to draw a distinction between high art and smut. In 1872 the publisher Henry Vizetelly was fined £100 and bound over for twelve months for publishing the English translation of Zola's *La Terre*. 'Nothing more diabolical has ever been written by the pen of man,' declared one Member of Parliament,[28] but this did not prevent Vizetelly bringing out the book again and being sent to prison for three months. In 1875 the Society for the Suppression of Vice campaigned against 'the book entitled Rabelais', a translation of the French genius. This objection provoked an inspired rant in the pages of *The Athenaeum* from Swinburne. Given that even established French scholars could scarcely understand what 'the book entitled Rabelais' was about, asked Swinburne, what right had the Society to object to it? What, pray, he demanded, was the Society going to do about 'the book entitled the Bible' or 'the book entitled Shakespeare?'[29] Were they intending to suppress these pillars of English culture as well? When the Society responded that they had no plans to ban the Bible or Shakespeare, Swinburne responded ironically. What! Were they really going to continue to let Shakespeare be sold in public? In W H Smith's stalls, on railway stations! What a shocking dereliction of duty.[30]

The Society for the Suppression of Vice did little to suppress the ingenuity and resourcefulness of Victorian pornographers. One method of avoiding prosecution under the Obscene Publications Act was to circulate books privately amongst the members of a society. This was the route taken by Sir Richard Burton, who created the Kama Shastra Society with Forster Fitzgerald Arbuthnot to print and circulate books which it would be illegal to publish in public. Burton's translation of *The Arabian Nights* was printed by the Kama Shastra Society and circulated in a subscribers-only edition of 1000 with a guarantee that there would never be a larger printing of the book in this form.

Burton had developed a fascination with the sex lives of the different cultures he encountered during his career as an army officer and spy. Fascinated by Islam, he became the first Western man to enter Mecca, disguised as an Arab. One of the first real sexologists, Burton even recorded the measurements of the penises of various inhabitants in his travel books. He also described sexual techniques common in the regions he visited, often hinting that he had participated, breaking both sexual and racial taboos. If not genuinely homosexual, Burton may have engaged in homosexual acts in the spirit of observer participation. He never directly acknowledges homosexuality in his writing but the rumours began in his army days, when he was allegedly asked by General Sir Charles James Napier to go undercover and investigate a male brothel reputedly frequented by British soldiers. His report was said to be so detailed that some believed he had been a punter, but as no report survives this may have been one of the many examples of the self-aggrandizing myth-making which Burton so enjoyed. According to the damning obituary by the French novelist Ouida in the *Fortnightly Review* in June 1906, 'he was ill fitted to run in official harness, and he had a Byronic love of shocking people, of telling tales against himself that had no foundation in fact'.

Burton's 1885 unexpurgated version of *The Arabian Nights* should not be confused with Andrew Lang's edition of 1898, designed for children. *The Arabian Nights* was one of the first English-language texts to address the practice of pederasty, which Burton claimed was prevalent in an area of the southern latitudes that he referred to as the 'Sotadic zone', a reference to Sotades, the Greek homoerotic poet. This increased the speculation and rumours about Burton's own sexuality that were already circulating. Typically, Burton took the credit for a translation of the *Kama Sutra* which appeared in 1883, although the majority of the work had been undertaken by Indian scholars.

While many of the illustrations in the Holywell Street genre were indeed as crude in execution as they were in subject matter, the field did produce one *bona fide* artistic genius in the form of Aubrey Beardsley (1872–98). Beardsley was a gifted and distinctive illustrator who became art editor of *The Yellow Book*, a literary magazine which showcased famous writers and artists such as Sir Frederick Leighton, John Singer Sargent, Max Beerbohm and Henry James. Although notionally 'decadent', the 'yellow' wrapper having been borrowed from the yellow dust-jackets which Parisian publishers used to signify the 'adult' content of their novels, *The Yellow Book* was a highly respected publication. When Beardsley was sacked for obscenity, he collaborated with Leonard Smithers on the short-lived but influential magazine *The Savoy*, where his talents flourished. This led to a new development in British publishing, that of beautifully produced 'erotica' such as Beardsley's illustrations for Pope's 'Rape of the Lock', his own romance entitled *Under the Hill* and an illustrated retelling of *Lysistrata*, Aristophanes' anti-war sex-strike comedy. These illustrations are fantastically delicate but sexually explicit renditions of naked young women reaching out to one another's pudenda, naked dwarves with giant penises reminiscent of Priapic Roman statuary, and mysterious pagan rituals featuring satyrs and the great god Pan. A vein of wit runs through these exquisite visions, as in the depiction of the grumpy middle-aged woman stumping upstairs after a night out who, it transpires, is *Messalina, Returning from the Bath*, off to pester her husband after being left unsatisfied by a night in the stews.

As a delicate, sensitive and artistic young man, Beardsley was inevitably interrogated about his sexual orientation. When the critic Haldane MacFall questioned his virility, classing him with Oscar Wilde as 'effeminate, sexless, and unclean', Beardsley responded tartly: 'As for my uncleanliness, I do my best for it in my morning bath, and if your critic has really any doubts as to my sex, he may come and see me take it.'[31] Despite this unfortunate start to their relationship, MacFall later became one of Beardsley's most devoted

An illustration by Aubrey Beardsley for Aristophanes'
anti-war comedy Lysistrata, *1896.*

245

supporters.[32] Beardsley was a consumptive; when the poet John Addington Symonds visited, he found the young artist 'lying out on a couch, horribly white' and wondered if he had arrived too late,[33] while the poet W. B. Yeats encountered him at a party thrown by Smithers, 'propped up on a chair in the middle of the room, grey and exhausted, and as I came in he left the chair and went into another room to spit blood'.[34] While Beardsley's friends and detractors wondered if he had even experienced any of the perverse erotic scenes which figured in his drawings, and speculated that his imagination exceeded his performance, Sir John Rothenstein denied that his 'morbid tendencies' were 'expressed in his art alone. I have the best authority for believing this to be wholly untrue, for asserting that during one short period of his life he was very dissolute.'[35] As well as the allegations that he was homosexual, rumours also circulated to the effect that he had an incestuous relationship with his sister, Mabel, which resulted in a miscarriage, one explanation for the disturbing images of foetus-like monsters which recur in his art.

Sadly, Beardsley did not live to fulfil his promise, but succumbed to tuberculosis in 1898, pleading with Smithers to destroy all his illustrations to *Lysistrata* 'by all that's holy',[36] after experiencing a deathbed conversion to Roman Catholicism. He was twenty-six years old. Fortunately for us, Smithers does not appear to have complied, and the illustrations remained in circulation.

Leonard Smithers (1861–1909), described by Oscar Wilde as 'the most learned erotomaniac in Europe', was a new breed of pornographer, a very different creature from the pathetic creep Hankey and the corrupt Dugdale. With his 'singularly clear cut aristocratic features', Smithers cut a dash in the shady world of dirty books; his authors included Oscar Wilde, Sir Richard Burton and Aleister Crowley, and Smithers did well out of them, acquiring a house in Bedford Square and a flat in Paris. He posted a slogan outside his Bond Street bookshop reading 'Smut is Cheap Today' and the money poured in. However, Smithers was not without his troubles. His wife became an alcoholic, and he himself dabbled in drink and drugs. In addition to this, he developed a taste for young girls. According to Oscar Wilde, 'he loves first editions, especially of women: little girls are his passion'.[37] He fell out with a colleague after being photographed having sex with his colleague's wife in the basement of their house, and went bankrupt in 1900. In 1909, he was found dead in his shabby lodgings in Cubitt Street, Islington, which contained nothing but the bed he died on, two empty hampers, and fifty empty bottles of Chlorodyne, a patent medicine containing laudanum, chloroform and cannabis.

Not every pornographer met such an ignoble fate. When Henry Spencer Ashbee died in 1900, it was revealed that he had bequeathed his entire collection of 15,299 pornographic books to the British Museum. At first, this august institution demonstrated reluctance in the face of such largesse, but when it was made plain that the museum would also receive Ashbee's outstanding collection of all the editions and translations of Cervantes' *Don Quixote* the bequest was finally accepted.[38] There was to be no bonfire at the bottom of the garden for Ashbee's collection. Wisely, he had blackmailed the British Museum into taking it, rather than have it destroyed or broken up into lots and auctioned off by dealers.

Henry Spencer Ashbee was the Victorian pornography collector *par excellence*, as the scale of his collection indicates. As a London merchant whose business often took him to mainland Europe, he amassed a handsome fortune which enabled him to devote his spare time to travel and collecting books, some legitimate, some less so.[39] In addition to accumulating the finest collection of Cervantes outside Spain and a selection of eighteenth- and nineteenth-century English watercolours, Ashbee had the most elaborate and extensive collection of pornography ever to have been assembled by a private individual. He also inherited a sizeable collection of sado-masochistic material from Frederick Hankey, after the latter's death in Paris in 1882. But Ashbee was not simply a collector. He was also an author, publishing the *Index Librorum Prohibitorum*: *Being Notes Bio-Biblio-Icono-graphical and Critical, on Curious and Uncommon*

Books under the pseudonym 'Pisanus Fraxi'. Even taking into account the scatological *nom de plume* ('Pisanus' means 'Piss anus' while 'Fraxi' is simply from the Latin *'fraxinus'* or ash tree) this tome does not at first sound promising, but when it appeared in March 1877 it transpired that this labour of love was an exhaustive survey of erotic literature, catalogued by the mysterious benefactor of Victorian pornography.

Ashbee's stated intention was to illustrate how widespread pornography actually was, and what a vast field of human and aesthetic experience it covered, and to preserve it for future generations. After all, Ashbee remarked,

> most of the books of this class are printed either privately or surreptitiously, in small issues, for special classes of readers or collectors ... they do not usually find their way into public libraries ... but are for the most part possessed by amateurs, at whose death they are not unfrequently burned; and they are always liable to destruction at the hands of the law ... their scarcity is very much in proportion to their age; and as society is constantly at war with them, the natural course is for them to die out altogether.[40]

Ashbee's cataloguing technique was systematic bordering on obsessive. Unlike other bibliophiles, he made it his rule 'never to criticise a work which I have not read, nor to describe a volume or an edition which I have not examined'[41] and was scrupulously methodical: 'In treating of obscene books, it is self evident that obscenities cannot be avoided. Nevertheless, although I do not hesitate to call things by their right names, and to employ technical terms when necessary, yet in my own text I never use an impure word when one less distasteful but equally expressive can be found.'[42] Ostensibly, Ashbee's attitude towards pornography was objective, and detached. Writing as though he had no personal interest in the acts depicted, but was describing the effects of toxic chemicals, Ashbee warned readers that these books 'should be used with caution even by the mature; they should be looked upon as poisons, and treated as such; should be distinctly labelled, and only confided to those who understand their potency, and are capable of rightly using them'.[43] Most important of all, the books should be kept out of the hands of the young and the impressionable. Ashbee even made a somewhat spurious claim that pornography possessed a moral purpose, and that 'immoral and amatory fiction' deserved study on the grounds that it contained 'a reflection of the manners and vices of the times, vices to be avoided, guarded against, reformed', which sounds like a typical example of Victorian hypocrisy when Ashbee's life and activities are considered in more detail.

One glaring omission was *My Secret Life* by 'Walter', published in Amsterdam around 1890, and therefore appearing too late to be included in the catalogue. It consists of eleven crown octavo volumes (a total of 4200 pages), rather poorly printed on handmade ribbed paper.[44] Errors in typography, spelling and grammar suggest that it was set by a French compositor, while the identity of the author is kept secret by the omission of names, locations and dates. Although each title page bears the imprint 'Amsterdam. Not for publication', the work was clearly designed to be circulated to a select number of readers; subsequent owners of the books included Aleister Crowley, Josef von Sternberg, Lord Mountbatten and Harold Lloyd.

My Secret Life consists of the sexual memoirs of a Victorian gentleman, recorded over a period of forty years. It is the distillation of a lifetime of dissipation during which he has probably 'fucked something like twelve hundred women, and have felt the cunts of certainly three hundred others of whom I have seen a hundred and fifty naked'. During the period he has had 'women of twenty-seven different Empires, Kingdoms or Countries, and eight or more different nationalities, including everyone in Europe except a Laplander'.[45] If not exactly well written, the book is an unflinching account of his sexual exploits, mostly with prostitutes. While 'Walter' does not emerge as an attractive man, his honesty and authenticity are refreshing, as are the occasional bouts of self-disgust, although his somewhat brutal approach is unlikely to appeal to female readers, as in the following example. After a three-way encounter with a prostitute and a drunken sailor, during which 'Walter' pays the couple to have sex while he watches (and then joins in), 'Walter' staggers home to find his wife is still awake: 'On entering my room there sat she reading, which was a very unusual thing. I sat down wishing she would leave the room, for I wanted to wash; and wondered what she would say if she saw me washing my prick at that time of night, or heard me splashing . . .'

After going for a wash, and being kept awake by 'fear of the pox', 'Walter' finds the memory of the previous escapade so exciting that 'my prick stood like steel. I could not dismiss it from my mind. I was so violently in rut. I thought of frigging, but an irrepressible desire for cunt, cunt and nothing but it made me forget my fear, my dislike to my wife, our quarrel, and everything else – and jumping out of bed I went into her room.

> 'I shan't let you, – what do you wake me for, and come to me in such a hurry after you have not been near me for a couple of months, – I shan't, – I dare say you know where to go.'
>
> But I jumped into bed, and forcing her on her back, drove my prick up her. It must have been stiff, and I violent, for she cried out that I hurt her. 'Don't do it so hard, – what are you about!' But I felt that I could murder her with my prick, and drove, and drove, and spent up her cursing. While I fucked her I hated her, – she was my spunk-emptier. 'Get off, you've done it, – and your language is most revolting.' Off I went to my bedroom for the night.[46]

And even this is not enough to keep 'Walter's' mind off the sailor.

> After I had got over my fears I had a very peculiar feeling about the evening's amusement. There was a certain amount of disgust,

yet a baudy [*sic*] titillation came shooting up my bullocks [*sic*] when I thought of his prick. I should have liked to have felt it longer, to have seen him fuck, to have frigged him till he spent. Then I felt annoyed with myself, and wondered at my thinking of that when I could not bear to be close to a man any-where, I who was drunk with the physical beauty of women. The affair gradually faded from my mind, but a few years after it revived. My imagination in such matters was then becoming more powerful, and giving me desire for variety in pleasures with the sex, and in a degree, with the sexes.[47]

'Walter' turns a cold, appraising gaze on Victorian sexual activities, and has an eye and an ear well tuned to the nuances of London low life which makes him an invaluable social commentator. Every detail of every sexual escapade is clear, 'the clothes they wore, the houses and rooms in which I had them . . . the way the bed and the furniture were placed, the side of the room that the windows were on, I remember perfectly'.[48] And there is also a marked emphasis on the commercial transaction of paying for sex; on one occasion, he is rendered almost impotent by the fact that he cannot reciprocate a young woman's advances after Derby Day because he has gambled away all his money at the races. Despite the girl's response: 'Never mind! Do me!' 'Walter' is almost unmanned until he finds a spare half a crown. The girl pockets the money and moments later, 'we stroked ourselves into Elysium'.[49]

Not for nothing was 'spending' his favourite term for ejaculation. 'Walter' was the ultimate Victorian punter, obsessed with 'cunt', and shows some grudging respect towards prostitutes but a rapacious attitude towards servants and young girls: as far as he was concerned, every woman had her price. The effect of reading 'Walter' for any length of time is one of monotony, as it is in the case of reading any obsessive author: the reader is almost bludgeoned into insensitivity, no matter how potentially arousing the subject matter, by the blunt instrument of the Anglo-Saxon sexual terms. Erotic prose is an art at which few English writers excel, as evidenced by the Pyrrhic victory of the 'bad sex awards' presented to British novelists in the late twentieth century. As Ashbee commented on another title, while comparing English erotic authors unfavourably with their French counterparts, 'the copulations which occur at every page are of the most tedious sameness; the details are frequently crapulous and disgusting, seldom voluptuous ... gross, material, dull and monotonous'.[50]

So keen was 'Walter' to conceal autobiographical details that little is known of the author's public life, although his memoir offers some clues. Like Henry Spencer Ashbee, 'Walter' was born in London to a prosperous middle-class father and went into business. He inherited a small fortune on the death of his father, and, when the money ran out, married a rich woman whom he despised, and he evidently had some success in business. Ashbee founded and became senior partner in a firm of London merchants called Charles Lavy & Co., and married his partner's daughter, Miss Lavy, a wealthy Jewish woman, while 'Walter' also married a Jewess, his boss's daughter. It was not a happy union, although it did provide enough money to spend on prostitutes. 'Walter's' wife died when he was thirty-five, much to his delight: 'Hurrah, I was free at last!'[51] 'Walter' then met Helen Marwood, a woman with whom he 'did, said, saw and heard, well nigh everything a man and a woman could do with their genitals',[52] and who inspired him to keep writing the sex diary which he had begun in his twenties.

The parallels between the life and interests of Henry Spencer Ashbee and 'Walter' have been commented upon and more than one authority has suggested that 'Walter' may have been Ashbee. Although both writers demonstrate a certain obsessive-compulsive attitude towards matters of a sexual nature, the theory does beg one question: if Ashbee was 'Walter' then why, as a self-professed connoisseur of pornography, would he have taken refuge in a pseudonym? Was he, like Pepys, writing primarily for his own pleasure, so that he could dwell on his conquests in his old age? Did *My Secret Life* perform the function Oscar Wilde required of a diary, in that it was 'something sensational to read on the train'? 'Walter' found himself one sympathetic reader in the form of Helen Marwood, who enjoyed telling him about her 'former tricks' in return for hearing about his own 'amatory career'. 'She had read a large part of the manuscript, or I had read it to her whilst in bed and she laid quietly feeling my prick. Sometimes she'd read and I listen, kissing and smelling her lovely alabaster breasts, feeling her cunt, till the spirit moved us both to incorporate our bodies.'[53] It is a curiously domestic, even cosy, conclusion for a man whose preferred sexual encounters took place for money, with strangers, down dark alleyways.

While 'Walter' took a certain degree of homosexual play in his stride, never questioning his essentially heterosexual nature, the lives of genuine homosexual men continued to be overshadowed by prosecution and even death, as becomes evident in the following chapter.

11

THE LOVE THAT DARE NOT SPEAK ITS NAME

'Does it really matter what these affectionate people
do – so long as they don't do it in the streets and
frighten the horses?'

Mrs Patrick Campbell

In 1833, William Bankes, MP for Dorset, was discovered 'standing
behind the screen of a place for making water against Westminster
Abbey walls, in company with a soldier named Flower, and of
having been surprised with his breeches and braces unbuttoned at
ten at night, his companion's dress being in similar disorder'.[1]
Bankes was lucky to escape a jail sentence. Aristocrats, professors
and clergymen testified to the effect that 'he was never yet known to
be guilty of any expression bordering on licentiousness or profaneness and the jury acquitted him despite incriminating evidence on
the grounds that his character was not that associated with
sodomites'.[2] This appears to be a clear example of how far the establishment would go to protect an open secret, and Bankes's reputation

seemed safe. Unfortunately for him, however, in 1841 he was caught in a compromising position with a guardsman in Green Park, and fled the country before he could go on trial for a second time. Under the Buggery Statute of 1533, initiated by Henry VIII, homosexual activity was technically punishable with death, although conviction was difficult, as the witness had to have seen penetration.[3] Leaving scandal in his wake, Bankes died abroad in 1855. Like many homosexuals of this era, he was condemned to end his days in exile.

There have been many words for homosexuality and gay sex, but the actual term 'homosexual' originates with a Hungarian physician named Benkert in 1869.[4] Of course the expression covers an entire range of sexual behaviour, but, for the duration of this chapter, 'homosexual' best serves to describe the personalities and activities

A nineteenth-century male brothel, from a French study of prostitution, where boys from the street are made available to clients. Here one man is passionately kissing a boy's foot (1884).

depicted. In some respects, the homosexual underworld operated like a parallel universe. Just as the top-drawer whores went unacknowledged and unmolested by the police, so a blind eye was often turned to homosexuality in high places if the protagonists were sufficiently well connected, and cover-ups to protect the reputation of the culprits were not unknown. If William Bankes MP had been a little more discreet, perhaps he would not have been forced to flee abroad and leave his beloved stately home, Kingston Lacey in Dorset, and his considerable collection of Egyptian antiquities.

Other politicians sailed close to the wind without falling foul of the legal system. For instance, George Canning, briefly Prime Minister back in 1827, was said to make advances to any pretty young man around the House of Commons, while future Prime Minister Benjamin Disraeli was, if not actually homosexual, then outrageously camp, noting in his novel *Coningsby* that 'at school friendship is a passion. It entrances the being; it tears the soul.'[5] Disraeli's reference to 'school' is significant here. Institutionalized homosexuality had long been a feature of the English public-school system. Commenting on the fate of Oscar Wilde, the editor William Stead noted: 'Should everyone found guilty of Oscar Wilde's crime be imprisoned, there would be a very surprising emigration from Eton, Harrow, Rugby and Winchester to the jails of Pentonville and Holloway. Until then, boys are free to pick up tendencies and habits in public schools for which they may be sentenced to hard labour later on.'[6] Despite the best efforts of individual headmasters to stamp it out, homosexuality was a recurrent element of public-school life.

The classical traditions which formed the basis of the educational curriculum extolled the virtues of love between young men – or a young man and an older one – as the ideal, in keeping with the original text of Plato's *Phaedrus*. The Old Testament also supplied an example, in the relationship between David and Jonathan, which was considered 'wonderful, passing the love of women'.[7] On a more earthy level, the system lent itself to abuse, with its 'fagging' (not a reference to homosexuality but the tradition by which younger boys became the slaves of older pupils), flogging, 'beating, buggery and boredom' as Ronald Pearsall so eloquently expresses it.[8] At Harrow, for instance, pretty boys were given girls' names, such as 'Nancy', and became the 'bitches' of older boys. Very few boys had the strength of character, or the desire, to withstand the combination of social pressure and temptation, although William Gladstone, stalwart as ever, insisted that he did not succumb during his time at Eton. According to his biographer, he 'did not stand aside from the harmless gaiety of boyish life, but he rigidly refused any part in boyish indecorums'. The harmless gaiety, for the record, consisted of playing chess and cards in the evenings, and taking a boat out on the river without authorization.[9]

While relationships between pupils were commonplace, affairs between pupils and teachers were not unknown. Dr Charles Vaughan, appointed headmaster of Harrow in 1844 in his late twenties, noticed early on that the boys were passing compromising notes to one another, and attempted to put an end to these activities by forbidding the use of feminine names and threatening his charges with flogging. But Vaughan himself was tempted: in 1858, he became involved with a boy named Alfred Proctor. Proctor confided in another boy, John Addington Symonds, telling him he was having an affair with the headmaster. Although homosexual himself, Symonds was so shocked that he eventually revealed this information to his tutor at Oxford, and Vaughan had to resign.[10]

Oscar Browning (1837–1923) experienced violent crushes at Eton. 'Why I should love Prothero as I do I cannot tell, but I do love him and I believe that that love ennobles me and purifies me,' he confided to his diary;[11] and, a year later, he was in love with 'Dunmore', entranced by everything about him, from his eyes and his manner to the fact that he was a lord.[12] Browning went on to become a master at Eton, where he became helplessly attracted to the young George Nathaniel Curzon, to such an extent that his 'irrepressible attentions' caused hilarity among the boys. As Pearsall tells us, '"spooning" [caressing and kissing] between master and boy was a subject for cruel jest, but it was also accepted as part of the order of things'.[13]

Obvious homosexual tendencies did little to harm Browning's reputation. He went on to become a fellow and tutor at King's College, Cambridge, and a member of the Apostles, the exclusive Cambridge debating society. Browning had found his niche. At Cambridge, he was fortunate enough to inhabit a realm in which institutionalized homosexuality flourished. Dons at Oxford and Cambridge were free to indulge their eccentricities. These ancient seats of learning were exclusively male (Girton, the first residential college for women, did not open until 1869) and the majority of dons were bachelors, as they were deprived of their fellowships if they married. The only women to penetrate the hallowed portals were bedders (chambermaids) and cooks. For intelligent, worldly, upper-class men, college life was a homosexual haven, a continuation of public school and an entrée to the establishment: the only requirement being that one must be reasonably discreet.

The homosexual scene in London was rather different. Instead of the Platonic ideal of master and boy, which flourished at Oxford and Cambridge, London had a ready supply of 'renters', or rent boys, and an avid clientele of men ready to take advantage of them. As the author of *The Yokel's Preceptor* described the situation in 1855, 'these monsters actually walk the streets the same as the whores, looking for a chance'. Fleet Street, Holborn and the Strand were favourite cruising grounds, and, according to the *Preceptor*, signs in the pubs around Charing Cross warned drinkers to 'Beware of Sods'. The *Preceptor* was, of course, written as a guidebook for out-of-town homosexuals, and contained useful tips such as the observation that if you were actually going in search of a 'sod', the favoured signal consisted of 'placing their fingers in a peculiar manner underneath the tails of their coats' and waggling them about, which was apparently 'their method of giving their office'.

In addition to being referred to as 'sods' (short for 'Sodomite'), homosexuals were also known in vulgar slang as 'margeries' and 'poofs', while any homosexual act was referred to as 'backgammon', which must have proved confusing for those pub-goers who anticipated nothing more exciting than a board game. There were homosexual brothels, such as the one next to Albany Street barracks run by a Mrs Truman, and there were clubs, such as The Hundred Guineas, where, in the tradition of molly houses, the members were given girls' names. For the most part, this twilight world flourished discreetly, but being a homosexual in London had its dangers, as the example of William Bankes MP has already illustrated. The stakes were higher: the illegality of the act made every homosexual a target for blackmail, either by his renter or a third party. Exposure meant public humiliation, family shame, exile or jail. As though predicting his own downfall, Oscar Wilde likened hanging out with his renters to 'feasting with panthers'. And of course it was Wilde who was engulfed in the greatest scandal of all.

But before I turn to the trials of Oscar Wilde, let us consider three other cases which cast a bright and unwelcome spotlight on London's homosexual underworld.

In April 1870, three men appeared in the dock of Bow Street Magistrates' Court, charged with attending the Strand Theatre with intent to commit a felony. There was nothing unusual about such an event, although the addresses given by the accused were from the smart end of town: one of them lived in Berkeley Square, Mayfair; another resided at Buckingham Palace Road. What did make this scene unusual was the way two of these men were dressed.

Ernest Boulton, twenty-two, wore a cherry-coloured silk evening dress trimmed with white lace; his arms were bare, and he had on bracelets. He wore a wig and plaited chignon. The costume of Frederick William Park, twenty-three, consisted of a dark green satin dress, low-necked and trimmed with black lace, of which material he also had a shawl round his shoulders. His hair was flaxen and in curls. He had on a pair of white kid gloves. The third gentleman, Alexander Mundell, also twenty-three, was more conventionally attired.

Superintendent Thomson, of E Division, was called by the prosecution and stated that at half past ten o'clock on Thursday evening, he went to the Strand Theatre and saw the prisoners in a private box, Boulton and Park being in female costume. He noticed their conduct and saw one of them repeatedly smile and nod to gentlemen in the stalls. As they left the theatre the prisoners were arrested and taken to Bow Street police station. Thomson's colleague Sergeant Kerley added that on their way to the station, Boulton and Park begged him to let them go and offered a bribe if he would listen to them, any sum he required. Boulton and Park were defended by a Mr Abrams who argued that the charge of felony was without foundation, and that the prisoners were guilty of nothing more than 'having a bit of a lark'. For the prosecution, Mr Flowers retorted that they had indulged in this so-called 'lark' for a very long time, and that he suspected the prisoners had a more serious purpose, such as enticing gentlemen to their apartments to extort money from them. Mr Abrams denied this suggestion.[14]

The court case which followed demonstrated that this 'lark' had indeed been of a long duration, and the story itself was so bizarre that it attracted considerable attention. In May 1871, a year after their first appearance at Bow Street Magistrates' Court, Boulton and Park made their debut in the High Court charged with 'conspiring and inciting persons to commit an unnatural offence'. It was a big case, with the attorney-general and the solicitor-general appearing for the prosecution. The attorney-general started by saying that it was an unpleasant duty to have to conduct such a prosecution against such well-educated young gentlemen, but that he had no alternative.[15] So who were these two well-educated young gentlemen, and how on earth did they end up in court?

Ernest Boulton came from a respectable background and was employed by his uncle, a stockbroker. He was an attractive young man with a good singing voice, described as a soprano. Frederick William Park, meanwhile, was articled to a solicitor. In their spare time, the young men enjoyed amateur dramatics, and their favourite activity was dressing up as women. This again seems to have been regarded as a relatively blameless pastime. The trouble was that these 'larks' began to dominate their everyday lives, and they started hanging around in music halls such as the Alhambra, in Leicester Square, and in the Surrey Theatre, south of the river. John Reeves, manager of the Alhambra, told the court that they had been summarily ejected for causing a disturbance by being dressed up as women and trying to pick up men.[16]

It emerged that a Mr Cox had flirted with Boulton in a City pub, mistaking him for a woman, and had even invited him back to his office to drink champagne. Thinking that he had pulled, Mr Cox admitted that 'I kissed him, she, or it, believing at the time it was a woman.'[17] This did not prevent Mr Cox from setting up another meeting, but at some point he realized that Boulton, who called himself 'Stella', was not all he seemed. Bumping into Boulton and his companion Lord Arthur Clinton in a pub in Covent Garden, he exclaimed: 'You damned set of infernal scoundrels, you ought to be kicked out of this place!'[18]

Boulton, meanwhile, had been living with Lord Arthur at his house in Berkeley Square, and they had exchanged many explicit letters, which were read out by the prosecution for the delectation of the court. One typical example, written following a separation, read: 'I am consoling myself in your absence by getting screwed.' Frederick Park played the role of peacemaker during such lovers' tiffs, and tried to mediate between the couple. Sounding like an old mother hen, he protested in one letter that he wanted to come over to see the couple but he needed an umbrella 'as the weather has turned so showery that I can't get out without a dread of my back hair coming out of curl'. Other more explicit letters must have titillated the court with their explicit references to homosexual activities: 'I have as usual left a few little things behind, such as the glycerine, &c, but I cannot find those filthy photos, I do hope they are not lying about your room!'[19]

As well as hanging around theatres and music halls, Boulton and Lord Arthur enjoyed parading up and down the Burlington Arcade alongside the high-class whores. According to George Smith, the beadle (security guard), Boulton had been cruising Burlington Arcade for about two years, face covered very thickly with rouge and every type of cosmetic. Boulton always created such a commotion when he entered the arcade that it was impossible to miss him. He would wink and pucker up at the men, and even referred to the beadle himself as 'you sweet little dear!'

The pair never made any secret of their shenanigans. During the trial, a large chest was brought into court. When it was opened, a gasp of amazement went up from the spectators as it contained sixteen silk dresses, twenty wigs and a variety of boots.

Alexander Mundell, who appeared as a witness at the trial of Boulton and Park, first met the couple at the Surrey Theatre during a performance of a play called *Clam*. On that occasion, they were wearing male attire but appeared so effeminate that Mundell believed they were women dressed as men. Completely taken in, Mundell even tried to give them instruction on how to be convincing 'drag kings', suggesting that they would seem more masculine if they were to swing their arms. Mundell arranged to meet them again, whereupon they turned up dressed as women.

Boulton told Mundell that they were really men, but Mundell treated this as a fine joke, and invited 'Stella' Boulton and 'Mrs Jane Graham' (as Park liked to call himself) out to dinner at the Globe, near the Haymarket. But time was running out for the pair. On 28 April 1870, they were followed by another detective, William Chamberlain, to the Strand Theatre, where they had arrived dressed as ladies. Park even visited the ladies' room during the interval to have some lace pinned up on his dress. As they got into a cab outside the theatre, Chamberlain pounced. They were arrested and taken to Bow Street.

Following their arrest, Boulton and Park were examined by the magistrate and the police surgeon, James Paul. Dr Paul ordered

Boulton, who was wearing knickers and silk stockings, to strip, then examined his anus for signs of buggery, noting 'extreme dilation of the posterior' and relaxed muscles, which he took to be evidence of anal intercourse. Dr Paul then examined Park and found what he told the court were 'the same symptoms in these men as I should expect to find in men that had committed unnatural crimes', although he admitted that he had no experience in the field of unnatural vice.[20] Dr Paul's cavalier attitude towards the prisoners irritated the judge, who called for an independent medical examination. Conducted by J. R. Gibson, surgeon to Newgate gaol, this found no evidence of buggery and concluded that the anal dilation could have been the result of natural causes. Boulton and Park went one further, and had another examination by Le Gros Clark, of the Royal College of Surgeons, who gave them a clean bill of health.

In summing up this curious case the judge, Lord Chief Justice Cockburn, was left with a dilemma. With no witnesses to give evidence of anal penetration, the offence of buggery could not be proved. The police surgeon had behaved in a crass and improper manner by subjecting Boulton and Park to a medical examination. George Smith, the beadle of Burlington Arcade, had admitted to taking bribes from shopkeepers to let whores into the arcade and had clearly turned a blind eye to the antics of Boulton and Park. There was no evidence that the pair had attempted to rob or blackmail their male admirers. They had been flagrantly open about their cross-dressing activities, but Park's landlady testified to the effect that there had been no evidence of immorality.

So what was left? A couple of drag queens who enjoyed roaming the West End 'for a bit of a lark'.[21] Although in his summing-up the judge felt compelled to condemn the young men's 'frolic' as 'an outrage not only of public morality but also of decency, which would offend a member of either sex and ought not to be tolerated', the jury returned a verdict of not guilty. Boulton and Park sank back into relative obscurity, although their case lived on in popular culture as illustrated by this limerick:

> There was an old person of Sark
> Who buggered a pig in the dark;
> The swine in surprise
> Murmured: 'God blast your eyes,
> Do you take me for Boulton or Park?'

Two years later, in 1873, London was rocked by another homosexual scandal, but this had none of the bizarre cross-dressing comedy of Boulton and Park. Instead, it was the tragic tale of Simeon Solomon, a gifted painter, who paid a high price for coming out of the closet – if indeed it could be said that he was ever in the closet in the first place.

Simeon Solomon, born in 1841, was the younger brother of the respectable Royal Academician Abraham Solomon. His father, an importer of hats, had been the first Jewish freeman of the City of London, and his friends included the Oxford don Walter Pater and the Pre-Raphaelite painter Burne-Jones. According to the poet Algernon Swinburne, Solomon's paintings displayed 'the latent relations of pain and pleasure, the subtle conspiracies of good with evil, of attraction and abhorrence'.[22] By his own admission, Solomon was homosexual and an enthusiastic sado-masochist, confiding that 'I will at once candidly unbosom to my readers, my affections are divided between the boy and the birch.'[23]

Solomon's life consisted of a tragic decline from respectability, fame and financial security, to disgrace, infamy and poverty. He was the darling of the Pre-Raphaelites until 1873, when, on 11 February, he was arrested in a public urinal at Stratford Place Mews, off Oxford Street, for having sex with a sixty-year-old stableman, George Roberts. Both men were charged with indecent exposure and attempting to commit sodomy. They were both fined £100 and sentenced to eighteen months in prison, but Solomon's wealthy cousin Mary intervened and his sentence was reduced to police supervision. Roberts, however, was not so fortunate and went to jail. Solomon headed for Paris, but was arrested there a year later on similar charges, although this time his companion was a nineteen-year-old. Sentenced to three months in prison, Solomon returned to find that he had been ostracized from polite society and his career was in ruins. Former patrons, galleries and friends shunned him, and the deaths of several family members followed in quick succession. Solomon became increasingly depressed and began to drink heavily. He even lost the support of Swinburne, having become, in the poet's words, 'a thing unmentionable alike by men and women, as equally abhorrent to either, nay, to the very beasts',[24] on the grounds that, heading for financial ruin, he had sold the letters Swinburne had written to him. This was an embarrassment for Swinburne as they contained 'much foolish burlesque and now regrettable nonsense never meant for any stranger's eye'.[25]

Solomon continued to paint, however, until the mid-1890s, although his later works express feelings of hopelessness, alienation and despair, as indicated by the titles: *Love at the Waters of Oblivion* (1891), *Tormented Soul* (1894), *Death Awaiting Sleep* (1896) and *Twilight and Sleep* (1897). Suffering from bronchitis and alcoholism, Solomon was admitted to St Giles's Workhouse in Covent Garden as 'a broken-down artist', and died penniless in 1905, after collapsing in High Holborn. Solomon had flouted Victorian morality and had been punished for it, in the most Victorian of ways: he had faced financial ruin and loss of social status and, as a result, he died an outcast.

Victorian homosexuals faced further persecution with the passing of the Criminal Law Amendment Act in 1885. Designed to protect under-age girls, this Act had the further effect of outlawing consensual homosexual acts between men. The purity campaigners who had forced this legislation through regarded homosexuality as one variety of male lust run amok.

Section 11 of the Act reads:

Any male person who, in public or private, commits, or is a party to the commission of, or procures or attempts to procure the commission by any male person of any act of gross indecency with another male person, shall be guilty of a misdemeanour, and, being convicted thereof, shall be liable, at the discretion of the Court, to be imprisoned for any term not exceeding two years with or without hard labour.

There is no reference to homosexual acts between women, allegedly because when it was pointed out to Queen Victoria that women were not mentioned in this legislation, she replied, 'No woman would do that.'[26]

Given the prevalence of homosexuality in public schools and at universities, a public perception developed that homosexuality was almost exclusively an aristocratic vice practised at the expense of honest working-class young boys who were corrupted by their rich patrons. The next scandal illustrates how this idea gained credibility.

In September 1889, a modest north London weekly broke the news that a peer of the realm was a regular customer at a male brothel which had been shut down by Scotland Yard in July. A follow-up story in November even hinted that the scandal could reach all the way to His Royal Highness Prince Eddy (Albert Victor, son of the Prince of Wales), and that the matter was being covered up by palace officials to protect the Prince's reputation.

This sensational story had begun two months earlier, on 6 July 1889, when Inspector Frederick Abberline, who had previously been assigned to the Jack the Ripper case in Whitechapel, arrived at a house at 19 Cleveland Street, near Fitzroy Square, with a warrant for the arrest of thirty-five-year-old Charles Hammond. The warrant stated that Hammond and his eighteen-year-old accomplice Henry Newlove 'did unlawfully, wickedly, and corruptly conspire, combine, confederate and agree' to procure rent boys 'to commit the abominable crime of buggery'. But he was too late: the house was locked and empty, and Hammond had fled to France. Inspector Abberline had more success with Newlove, however. He found him at his mother's house at 1.30 p.m. and escorted him to the police station.

The Cleveland Street brothel had been discovered by pure chance after the police had been summoned to investigate the theft of cash at the Central Telegraph Office. During this routine investigation, it was found that a telegraph delivery boy was carrying 18 shillings on his person. Telegraph boys were forbidden to carry any cash of their own, in case it became mixed up with telegraph money; and this was a considerable sum, too, the equivalent of several weeks' wages. When questioned, the boy, Thomas Swinscow, answered that he had earned the money working for a man named Hammond. When pressed to describe the kind of work he had carried out for Hammond, the boy hesitated for a moment and then blurted out the truth: 'I got the money from going to bed with gentlemen at his house.' According to Swinscow, another telegraph boy, Henry Newlove, had introduced him to Hammond. At Hammond's house, he had sex with one man, and in exchange received 4 shillings. He only admitted to servicing two clients, but he named two other boys who he claimed worked for Hammond more often.

Under police questioning Newlove, Swinscow and the other boys named names. Newlove himself implicated Lord Arthur Somerset, head of the Prince of Wales's stables, and two other prominent men, Henry Fitzroy, the Earl of Euston, and a British army colonel. As the investigation continued, the telegraph boys confirmed that Lord Somerset was a regular and hinted that Prince Eddy was involved too. Newlove was rewarded for his co-operation. When he and another accomplice were sentenced for gross indecency and procuring, Newlove received four months' hard labour, while his more reticent colleague served nine. As for Lord Somerset, he had time to flee to a comfortable exile in Bad Homburg, a spa town in Germany.

At first, the story attracted no interest from the press. But then Ernest Parke, editor of the *North London Press*, picked up the story. The *North London Press* was a small radical weekly which usually covered council meetings and campaigned for better pay for the working man. But Parke was a first-class investigative journalist with a nose for a good story. He became intrigued when one of his reporters handed him a story about Newlove's conviction in September, and he wondered why Newlove and his associate had escaped so lightly, when, just months previously, a clergyman from Hackney had been sentenced to prison for life for similar offences. This was clearly a case of one law for the rich and one for the poor. And how, Parke asked, did Hammond know that the police were coming in time to make good his escape? This had all the hallmarks of a conspiracy, and no mistake. Using his contacts in the Metropolitan Police, Parke discovered that the telegraph boys had named prominent aristocrats among their clients. On 28 September, Parke ran a story to the effect that 'the heir to a duke and the younger son of a duke' were involved in the scandal; on 16 November, he ran a follow-up naming the Earl of Euston and Lord Arthur Somerset, younger son of the Duke of Beaufort, and alleging that they had been allowed to leave the country to conceal the involvement of a personage even more 'distinguished and more highly placed'.

This scoop would have been enough to impress Parke's readers; it certainly irritated more conservative newspapers, such as the *Birmingham Daily Post*, which commented 'the less that has to be said in these columns of the terrible scandal in London the better we shall be pleased'.[27] One Tory MP even referred disparagingly to the case as 'hideous and foetid gangrene'.

Although Lord Arthur Somerset had fled to the continent, Parke was mistaken when he wrote that the Earl of Euston had left the country. The Earl was still in England and had no intention of leaving. Instead, he launched a libel action against Parke on 26 October. Parke was not in the least perturbed and was convinced this was a case he could win. He knew that the Earl had visited Cleveland Street and that he had been acquainted with Lord Somerset.

The Earl had indeed visited Cleveland Street, but his account of

the proceedings was somewhat different from that of the male prostitutes, or 'renters'. According to the Earl, he had been walking in
Piccadilly late one May evening, when he had been offered a card
inviting him to a display of *poses plastiques* (striptease) in Cleveland
Street. He had retained the card and, several nights later, called on
the house to watch the said display. When he knocked on the door,
he was asked for a sovereign, which he paid. And then the man who
had answered the door made 'an indecent proposal'. At this point,
according to the Earl, he had called the man a scoundrel, threatened
to knock him down if he did not allow him to leave and had
stormed out of the house in a mood of self-righteous indignation.[28]
Several newspapers believed the Earl's version. The *New York
Herald* pointed out that several such gentlemen had probably visited
the house in all innocence, curious to see what happened there and
believing it to be a casino.

Parke was convinced that the jury would believe his version
of events and that when he won this case, he would be striking a
blow for the freedom of the press. Other newspapers had fought shy
of the case, he observed. Notable scandal sheets such as William
Stead's *Pall Mall Gazette* and *Lloyd's Newspaper* had remained silent;
Reynold's Newspaper had only quoted, reticently, the first stories of
the *North London Press*. Parke could also take consolation in the
fact that a 'Fair Trial Fund' was being raised on his behalf by H. W.
Massingham (later one of the most famous journalists of his day)
with signatories such as the Liverpool MP T. P. O'Connor, another
journalist and a campaigner for Irish nationalism. Nothing could go
wrong, could it?

The case opened in January 1890. Lord Euston was cross-
examined, with the lawyers insinuating that there was something
degenerate about his decision to go to watch a striptease act at his
advanced age (Euston was then aged forty-one). Lord Euston
replied with exasperation that such displays could be quite artistic,
actually, and created the impression of being a suave heterosexual
man about town. And then Parke's witness was called. This was

John Saul, a rather camp twenty-six-year-old with 'a stagey manner and a peculiar effeminate voice'. Saul told the court that in May 1887 he had taken Lord Euston to 19 Cleveland Street, and he knew Lord Euston as 'The Duke'.

But far from being the star witness, Saul was torn apart by the prosecution. Where, they demanded, had Saul come by the ring on his finger? Surely it must be worth a pretty penny. Was it a gift from a rich protector? No, replied Saul in some confusion, the ring was paste, and as to having a protector, he lived with a Mr Violet, a respectable man, in Brixton. And what about the silver-headed cane? Was that a gift from a grateful admirer? No, replied Saul, he had bought it for one and six in the Brixton Road. And finally, the prosecution wanted to know, what exactly was Mr Saul's occupation? When Saul replied that he had been an actor at the Drury Lane Theatre, the prosecutor rubbed his hands in glee. As a witness, Saul appeared perverted, histrionic and unreliable. Parke, realizing that the case was not going his way, interrupted the proceedings and said that other witnesses could testify to events at 19 Cleveland Street. But when Lord Justice Hawkins invited him to bring them to court, Parke stalled: he could not produce these witnesses, he said, as this would mean betraying his sources.

Lord Justice Hawkins, in his summing-up, declared that Lord Euston was accused of 'heinous crimes revolting to one's common notions of all that was decent in human nature',[29] but invited the jury to come to their own conclusions and decide whether Parke's allegations were correct. The jury's verdict proved Parke correct: there was a conspiracy, and there was one law for the rich and one for the poor; Parke was found guilty of libel and Lord Euston was exonerated. Parke received a year's imprisonment, regarded as harsh by the *North London Press*, which, without its editor, swiftly went under. Far from being acclaimed as a campaigner for free speech, Parke was condemned by other newspaper editors. He was 'a miscreant' who should be whipped at the cart's tail from one end of London to the other, according to the *People*; and the *Labour*

Elector, which had supported Parke's campaign for better pay and conditions for dockers and postmen, complained that his sentence was not severe enough and 'if Lord Euston had gone into the *Star* office and there and then physically twisted the little wretch's neck, nobody would have blamed him'.[30]

Parke's conviction exonerated Euston, but another trial began on 12 December that proved Parke's conspiracy theory. The prosecutor charged Arthur Newton, Newlove's defence lawyer, with obstructing justice by warning Hammond to flee the country. When the case went to trial, Newton was easily convicted. After the verdict was reached, the presiding judge addressed the court and concluded that Newton had helped Hammond escape to prevent him from testifying against his aristocratic clientele. Then, he sentenced Newton to six weeks in prison.

Henry Labouchère, the radical Member of Parliament who drafted the law against Gross Indecency in 1885, watched the Newton trial closely. He suspected that the cover-up went beyond a lawyer's efforts to protect his clients and believed that the Prime Minister had arranged for Lord Arthur Somerset to be warned of his impending arrest to give him time to escape. Labouchère voiced his suspicions in Parliament on 28 February 1890 and moved that a committee be formed to investigate the government. The ensuing debate was so fractious and Labouchère was so provocative that he was suspended for a week, but his efforts to expose the government failed. By a vote of 204 to 66, Parliament rejected his motion. At the highest levels, the cover-up had succeeded.

The Cleveland Street affair gradually faded away as the English press and public turned their attention to more routine news stories, but the uproar had lasting effects on the public perception of homosexuals. The prostitutes were 'innocent' telegraph boys who had been 'corrupted' by Hammond in service of the unrestrained lusts of a wealthy aristocratic clientele. 'Working men,' proclaimed one radical, John Knifton, 'are free from the taint' (of homosexuality), although he did grudgingly admit that 'for gold laid down our boys might be tempted to their fall'.[31] However, the most significant impact of the Cleveland Street scandal was to intensify the hatred for homosexuality which culminated in the sensational trials of Oscar Wilde in 1895.

When Wilde arrived at Oxford in 1874, it was clear that a brilliant career awaited him. He had already made his mark, winning a scholarship to Magdalen College after studying classics at Trinity College, Dublin. An excellent scholar, he soon fell under the spell of Walter Pater, an eccentric don who had endured endless bullying in his youth on account of his wizened, hunch-backed appearance. Pater delighted in surrounding himself with attractive young men 'of a remote and unaccustomed beauty, somnambulistic, frail, androgynous, the light almost shining through them', among whom 'exotic flowers of sentiment' expanded.[32] Pater was at the forefront of the Aesthetic Movement, which could be summed up in the phrase 'Art for Art's sake'. Aestheticism constituted a complete rejection of the Victorian notion that art should be pressed into the service of morality to provide edification for the middle classes and the poor. Instead, the role of the aesthete was to burn with a clear, gemlike flame, and turn his own appearance, personality and even life into a work of art. This artistic sensitivity went hand in hand with a Platonic appreciation of male beauty, particularly young male beauty. Exotic friendships flowered under these hothouse conditions, and being perceived as homosexual was no great drawback; indeed, Platonic tendencies were almost mandatory for young men entering aesthetic and artistic circles. The worst they had to fear was a mild form of gay-bashing consisting of being 'debagged' (having one's trousers ripped off) by 'hearties' (jocks) and dumped in the college fountain. The young Oscar Wilde was kidnapped by such a group and deposited on a hill outside Oxford, but seemed to have been little the worse for it, confiding to his tormentors that he had enjoyed the experience and that the view was very charming.

Wilde threw himself into the aesthetic scene with characteristic gusto, decorating his college rooms with sunflowers and peacock feathers, growing his hair long and dressing flamboyantly in velvet coats with silver buttons, white stockings and buckled shoes. Just how far he went with his Platonic tendencies is debatable. Although he may have been aware of his own sexuality, Wilde was cautious enough to be shocked when he saw a fellow undergraduate, Charles John Todd, ensconced in a private box with a choirboy.[33] And yet, just over a decade later, it was Wilde who threw caution to the winds and became Britain's most scandalous homosexual.

In many respects, Oscar Wilde was the first modern celebrity. On graduating from Magdalen, his mission statement was: 'I'll be a poet, a writer, a dramatist. Somehow or other I'll be famous, and if not famous, I'll be notorious.' In the words of Wilde's rival, the painter James McNeill Whistler, it was a matter of 'You will, Oscar. You will.' But Wilde was to fall from grace like Icarus, flying too close to the sun. One of the first players of the fame game, Wilde was ignorant of the golden rule: Pride goeth before a fall.

Arriving in London with the intention of becoming a 'professional aesthete', Wilde soon found himself with a stalled career, two young sons from his marriage to Constance Lloyd, and increased financial responsibilities. Far from being an overnight success, he bowed to the inevitable, became the editor of a women's magazine and seemed like many a middle-aged journalist, beaten into submission by domesticity and artistic failure. But Wilde was beginning to find satisfaction elsewhere. His flamboyant, charismatic personality ensured a devoted entourage, and in 1886, Wilde was introduced to a seventeen-year-old fan, a Cambridge drop-out named Robbie Ross who idolized Wilde and intended to seduce him. Somewhat embarrassed by Ross's persistence, Wilde permitted him to do so. As for the sex itself, this would probably have fallen into the category referred to in the Criminal Law Amendment Act 1885 as 'gross indecency', for which read mutual masturbation and fellatio.

Once Ross became his lover, Wilde began to accept his own sexuality and have multiple male partners. He avoided sex with Constance by telling her that he had contracted syphilis. The affair with Ross provided more than sexual release; it inspired the novel *The Picture of Dorian Gray*, published in 1890. This was a stylish tale of a hedonistic young man who retained his youthful beauty while his portrait, hidden in the attic, grew daily more hideous with every act of vice committed; it was also an aesthete's handbook, every line endorsing Wilde's world view, such as 'all art is quite useless'[34] and 'there is no such thing as a moral or an immoral book. Books are well written, or badly written.'[35]

Dorian Gray became a best-seller, and Wilde attracted ever more besotted admirers. One of these young men was Lord Alfred Douglas or 'Bosie', an Oxford undergraduate who had been so enthralled by *Dorian Gray* that he claimed to have read it fourteen times. He first visited Wilde's home in Tite Street in 1891, and Wilde was entranced by the combination of Bosie's flaxen hair, alabaster skin and total infatuation. What Wilde did not realize at this point was that Bosie was a spoilt brat, a manipulative hysteric who enjoyed living in a permanent state of emotional meltdown. Far from being the love of his life, Bosie was to become Wilde's nemesis.

Bosie proved to be Wilde's *bête noire* in more ways than one. It was not merely his histrionic personality which brought trouble; it was also his subterranean private life. In the spring of 1892, Bosie was at his wits' end, because an indiscreet love letter he had written to another young man had fallen into a blackmailer's hands. Unbeknown to Wilde, Bosie was a regular customer of young male prostitutes. Many had police records, which should have been enough to deter him, but instead it only added to their appeal. As an experienced man of the world, Wilde knew exactly what to do. He instructed his solicitor to pay the blackmailer £100 and Bosie was rescued. It seems that at this point, they became lovers, but the pair were not exclusive, and soon Wilde found himself initiated into the twilight world of renters; Wilde was 'feasting with panthers' and enjoying the experience every bit as much as Bosie.

Bosie and Wilde were soft targets for the renters. Bosie was naive, and mistook the renters' easy camaraderie for true friendship; he was also careless. When he gave one of the boys, Alfred Wood, one of his old suits, he had overlooked the fact that the pockets were stuffed with passionate love letters from Wilde. As soon as he discovered the letters, Wood planned to blackmail the pair, but Wilde was able to resolve the matter with a one-off payment of £30. This time, he did not involve his solicitor. There can be no doubt that Wilde enjoyed the additional frisson that criminality brought to his liaisons. Like his creation Dorian Gray, Wilde believed that he was leading a double life, indeed that he had almost elevated it to an art form. A wife and two sons formed an effective smokescreen. But Wilde's personality was so flamboyant that rumours about his relationship with Bosie circulated around London, and worse was to come. One of the love letters to Bosie which Alfred Wood had discovered somehow found its way to Bosie's father, the Marquess of Queensberry.

Wilde had observed that 'a man cannot be too careful in the choice of his enemies';[36] he had certainly followed his own advice by offending John Sholto Douglas, 9th Marquess of Queensberry. An eccentric little man, so belligerent that his colleagues in the House of Lords would have nothing to do with him, Queensberry's only claim to fame was to agree the Queensberry Rules for boxing championships, and to secure the adoption of weight differences, so that boxers might be evenly matched.[37] Queensberry's first wife had deserted him on grounds of cruelty and, just to complete the picture, he was a raving homophobe. Queensberry was the boyfriend's father from hell. Queensberry's relationship with his own son was scarcely any better. He regarded Bosie as a sissy, and he also suspected that his oldest son, Drumlanrig, was having an affair with the Foreign Secretary, Lord Rosebery. When Queensberry saw the love letter from Wilde to Bosie, he flew into a rage and demanded that Bosie break off the relationship there and then. Bosie, who also had a filthy temper, responded in kind, and an exchange of letters concluded with Queensberry threatening to thrash him and Bosie offering to take him on, with a pistol.

Queensberry believed that Wilde had led Bosie astray, whereas, of course, it was Bosie who had initiated Wilde into the delights of 'feasting with panthers'. The relationship between father and son deteriorated, not helped by the fact that Bosie proved to be an indifferent student and dropped out of Oxford without sitting his Finals. In an effort to break up the relationship with Wilde, Bosie's parents sent him abroad; but these trips did nothing to curb his appetites, as he spent his vacations in France and Egypt cruising for rough trade.

At one point, in 1894, however, it looked almost as if the Marquess had started to relent and accept the relationship between Wilde and Bosie. Chancing upon the pair lunching at the Cafe Royal, he was invited to join their table and was completely overwhelmed by Wilde's charisma. As he got up to leave, the Marquess commented to his son: 'I don't wonder you are so fond of him. He is a wonderful man.'[38] But this mellow mood did not last. The same day, he returned home and wrote to Bosie that his relationship with Wilde was 'loathsome and disgusting' and that it must cease or he would be disinherited.[39] Queensberry had heard rumours that Wilde's wife was planning to divorce him, and, if this was true, Queensberry felt that he would be entirely justified in shooting him on sight.[40]

Bosie, who could not tolerate even the mildest form of criticism, fired back a brief response in the form of a telegram 'of which the commonest street-boy would have been ashamed'[41] as Wilde put it. Addressed to his father, it read, simply: 'WHAT A FUNNY LITTLE MAN YOU ARE.' Provoked beyond endurance, Queensberry replied, threatening to give Bosie a good thrashing and warning that if he caught him again with Wilde, 'I will make a public scandal in a way you little dream of.'[42] Queensberry was as good as his word: it was a scandal of nightmare proportions.

Queensberry visited Wilde's house in Tite Street unannounced on 30 June. Wilde later described the scene to Bosie: 'in my library at Tite Street, waving his small hands in the air in epileptic fury, your father, with his bully, or his friend, between us, had stood uttering every foul word his foul mind could think of, and screaming the loathsome threats he afterwards with such cunning carried out'.[43] Wilde faced him down on this occasion, and threw him out, commenting that 'I do not know what Queensberry rules are, but the Oscar Wilde rule is to shoot on sight.'[44] Queensberry was not to be stopped. He went from restaurant to restaurant, looking for Wilde, forcing him into a confrontation where Wilde would either retaliate 'in such a manner that I would be ruined' or 'not retaliate in such a manner that he would also be ruined'. It is a real testimony to Wilde's powers of concentration that, in the middle of such constant pressure, he was able to sit down and write his masterpiece, *The Importance of Being Earnest*. Far from being the flamboyant dilettante, Wilde had a strong dose of the Protestant work ethic. 'Work never seems to me a reality,' he wrote to a friend, 'but a way of getting rid of reality.'[45] As Wilde put the finishing touches to his production, Queensberry *père* grew more unhinged by the minute, planning to disrupt the first night of *The Importance of Being Earnest* by pelting the stage with rotten vegetables and inciting a protest which would lead to a press investigation into Wilde's private life. Mercifully, his plans were detected in time and thwarted.

Events in October 1894 conspired to drive the Marquess over the edge. He was already in the throes of a divorce from his second wife, who accused him of impotence, when news came that his eldest son, Drumlanrig, heir to the title, had been found dead. The official verdict was a 'shooting accident', but the Marquess saw straight through this euphemism for suicide. Drumlanrig had killed himself after a blackmailer threatened to reveal his affair with Rosebery. *In extremis*, Queensberry's attacks on Wilde escalated, culminating in a letter on 28 February 1895 addressed 'To Oscar

Wilde, ponce and sodomite', or 'posing as a sodomite', as Queensberry later interpreted it. Finally, it appeared that Wilde had been forced to retaliate. But Wilde was a shrewd man. He was aware that the law of libel rests on one basic principle: if the allegation is found to be true, then it is not libel. If Wilde lost the case, and the allegation of his homosexuality was proved to be correct, he faced the loss of his reputation and two years in jail at hard labour, as spelt out in the Criminal Law Amendment Act. Although Wilde's theatrical success had brought some wealth, he did not command the vast financial resources of the Marquess, who could afford to instruct the most experienced counsel. Wilde refused to take the matter to court, and it might have ended there, had it not been for Bosie. When Wilde complained that he did not have the funds to fight a libel suit, Bosie declared that he and his mother, the Marquess's first wife, Lady Queensberry, would be delighted to pay the costs.[46] Bosie also embarked on a campaign of scenes, sulks, tantrums and downright nagging which eventually drove Wilde into suing Queensberry for libel.

Wilde engaged his solicitor, Humphreys, to represent him, and instructed him that he was innocent of the charges. Humphreys, for his part, was somewhat naive. He cannot have been ignorant of Wilde's sexuality, but he undertook the case as a great career move: what lawyer could resist a courtroom battle between two celebrities over a sensational sexual innuendo? Wilde was also confident that the prosecuting barrister, Edward Carson, would prove sympathetic, as he had been a fellow student of Wilde's at Trinity College, Dublin. Surely the fact that they shared this august Alma Mater counted for something?[47] Trusting that the case would go in his favour, Wilde whisked Bosie off to Monte Carlo, where they could forget their troubles in the casino, although a news story in the *Observer* claimed that they were thrown out of their hotel at the request of other guests.[48] On his return, Wilde sought the advice of two good friends, the writer Frank Harris, and George Bernard Shaw. Over lunch at the Cafe Royal, Harris urged Wilde to drop the case. 'You are sure to lose,' Harris told him. 'You haven't a dog's chance. Don't commit suicide!' Harris's advice was for Wilde to depart for Paris immediately, taking Constance Wilde with him, and Shaw agreed. Wilde rose to his feet, ready to leave. He was convinced by their arguments and wanted to go home and pack, but, at the last moment, Bosie overruled his friends' suggestions and persuaded Wilde to stay and fight.[49]

Events began to develop the ghastly momentum of a nightmare. On 1 April, like a sick April Fool's joke, Wilde was shown Queensberry's plea of justification for the charges he had made against him. The document was absolutely damning. Queensberry's legal team had hired detectives to look into Wilde's private life, one of whom, named Littlejohn, had spoken by chance to a West End prostitute during the course of his routine investigations. When asked how business was, she had replied, dourly, that it was bad for the girls at the moment as there was so much competition from rent boys, under the influence of Oscar Wilde.[50] 'All you have to do is break into the top flat at 13 Little College Street, and you will find all the evidence you require,' she told him.

Littlejohn went to the flat, which turned out to be the home of Alfred Taylor, a former pupil of Marlborough College who had introduced Wilde to dozens of renters. Taylor was arrested, and the names and addresses of the renters found at his flat meant that they were easily tracked down, locked in a house, and 'terrified into giving evidence against Wilde'.[51] The resulting evidence consisted of fifteen different counts accusing Wilde of soliciting more than twelve boys, of whom ten were named, to commit sodomy. It is, however, noticeable that the alleged offences were not in date order, and that apparently testimony varied as to the number of offences and the number of boys involved, which suggests that much of the evidence was indeed faked or tampered with. There were so many holes in the prosecution case you could have driven a carriage through it, leading to the inevitable conclusion that Wilde was set up.

1. Edward Shelley, between February and May 1892.
2. Sidney Mavor, in October 1892. (Mavor testified that Wilde had done nothing wrong.)
3. Freddie Atkins, on 20 November 1892, in Paris. (His evidence was thrown out.)
4. Maurice Schwabe, on 22 November 1892. (Did not testify.)
5. Certain (unnamed) young men, between 25 January and 5 February 1892, in Paris.
6. Alfred Wood, in January 1893.
7. A certain young man, about 7 March 1893, in the Savoy Hotel.
8. Another young man, on or about 20 March 1893, in the Savoy Hotel.
9. Charles Parker, in March and April 1893.
10. Ernest Scarfe, between October 1893 and April 1894. (Did not testify.)
11. Herbert Tankard, in March 1893 at the Savoy Hotel. (Did not testify.)
12. Walter Grainger, in June 1893 in Oxford and in June, July and August at Goring [Wilde's country house].
13. Alfonso Harold Conway, in August–September 1894 at Worthing and about 27 September in Brighton.

Any qualms Edward Carson might have had about prosecuting Wilde were dispelled by this wealth of evidence. Carson knew he would win this case, and it would be the making of him. As for Wilde, who had expected to go into court to defend his reputation as an aesthete and as the author of a handful of love letters, nothing could have prepared him for such a damning indictment. But, given the choice between leaving the country, which he regarded as a cowardly retreat, or going to court, Wilde resolved to face down his enemies. When he entered the courtroom on 3 April 1895, he knew that he had no chance of winning the case. But he embraced martyrdom with courage and wit, comparing himself with St

Sebastian. Carson set out to demolish Wilde's reputation by condemning *Dorian Gray* as an immoral book, although Wilde had already countered that argument in print.

After reading an extract from the novel, Carson asked Wilde: 'Did you write that?' Wilde replied that he had the honour to be the author. Carson put down the book with a sneer and turned over some papers. Then he read out a verse from one of Wilde's articles. 'And I suppose you wrote that also, Mr Wilde?' Wilde waited until you could have heard a pin drop in the court. And then, very quietly, he replied, 'No, Mr Carson, Shakespeare wrote that.'[52] Carson turned scarlet, and then read another extract. 'And I suppose Shakespeare wrote that also, Mr Wilde?' 'Not as you read it, Mr Carson.' There was such an uproar that the judge threatened to clear the court.

Carson regained his composure and returned to the topic of *Dorian Gray* being a 'perverted' book. Surely the nature of the book, and its sensational subject matter, might lead the ordinary reader to suppose that its author might have 'a certain tendency'? Wilde responded that the novel would appear perverted only to 'brutes and illiterates'; he had 'no knowledge of the views of ordinary individuals', a response which must have alienated many of his more conventional supporters. Carson persevered with his interrogation, but he was up against the most formidable wit in England. When he enquired, 'Have you ever adored a young man madly?' Wilde instantly hit back with: 'I have never given adoration to anybody except myself.' It was clear that Carson would never get the better of Wilde in this verbal fencing match. However, when it came to presenting the evidence, Carson gained the upper hand. As he began to enumerate the number of young men who had given evidence against Wilde, it was clear that Wilde would lose the case. The list of names was read out, with instance after instance of illicit sex with 'homeless and shiftless boys'.[53]

As Wilde's biographer Richard Ellman states, the panthers had been defanged by Queensberry's men; toothless pussycats, they had been ready to say anything to stay out of jail. If they could not tell the difference between what they had done with Bosie and what they had done with Wilde, so much the better.[54] Further damning evidence took the form of Queensberry's letters to Bosie, in which he had pleaded with his son to end the relationship with Wilde, and accounts of Wilde's relationships with Charley Parker, a valet, and his brother, a groom. When Carson suggested that a valet and a stable boy were strange companions for an artist, Wilde retorted that he had not known what they did for a living, but if he had known, he would not have cared. 'I didn't care twopence what they were. I liked them. I have a passion to civilize the community.' Whatever the evidence he was confronted with, Wilde had a talent for discounting points against him which in different circumstances would have been the making of him as a Queen's Counsel. Unfortunately, Carson had one card left to play, in the form of Walter Grainger, a servant at the house in Oxford where Bosie had rooms.

CARSON: Did you ever kiss him?
WILDE: Oh, dear no. He was a peculiarly plain boy. He was, unfortunately, extremely ugly. I pitied him for it.
CARSON: Was that the reason why you did not kiss him?
WILDE: Oh, Mr Carson, you are pertinently insolent.
CARSON: Why, sir, did you mention that this boy was extremely ugly?

Wilde had stumbled. He had as good as admitted that, had Grainger been an attractive youth, he would have made advances to him. In attempting to recover himself, he blustered and spluttered, before coming out with: 'For this reason. If I were asked why I did not kiss a door-mat, I should say because I do not like to kiss door-mats. I do not know why I mentioned that he was ugly, except that I was stung by the insolent question you put to me and the way you have insulted me through this hearing.'[55]

After this cross-examination, Carson concluded with a reminder to the court that the Marquess of Queensberry had been motivated to condemn Wilde as a 'sodomite' in 'one hope alone, that of saving his son',[56] whereas Wilde was guilty of consorting with 'some of the most immoral characters in London'. While he had no proof that Wilde had had an improper relationship with Bosie (Queensberry was adamant that his son's reputation must be protected), Carson proposed to bring in the boys who would testify to 'shocking acts' with Wilde. Alfonso Conway, in particular, would give evidence that Wilde had dressed him up in gentlemen's clothes, so that he would appear a fit companion. Clearly, this last challenge to the class system was more than Wilde's team could bear: Carson was taken aside by Wilde's barrister, Sir Edward Clarke, and asked if he would accept a plea of 'not guilty' as in 'not guilty of posing as a sodomite', if Wilde dropped the charges. But Carson refused, and insisted that Queensberry was justified in calling Wilde a sodomite in the public interest.

Wilde himself was not in court. With the case going against him, he had been given the opportunity to make a dash for France. But he had been adamant that he would stay. Back in the courtroom, the judge instructed the jury to rule in Queensberry's favour, which they did, instantly. The Marquess of Queensberry left the court to loud cheers, while the judge simply folded up his papers and left, but not before sending a message to Carson: 'I never heard a more powerful speech nor a more searching crossXam [*sic*]; I congratulate you on having escaped the rest of the filth.'[57] The case had been the making of Carson, and the destruction of Wilde.

With such damning evidence, Wilde could have been arrested straight away, but the police did not have a warrant ready. He retreated to the Cadogan Hotel, with Robbie Ross and his friends to console him. They urged him to leave for France while he could, but Wilde sat in a state of paralysis, almost unable to comprehend his fate as the last train for Dover left without him.

Wilde went on trial for gross indecency on 26 April 1895, careworn and anxious after a month in jail, and with his hair cut short.

The proceedings covered the same ground as the Queensberry trial, with the same witnesses presented to testify that they had committed 'indecencies' with Wilde. The only strategy Wilde's barrister, Sir Edward Clarke, could pursue was to discredit the witnesses, a plan which was doomed to failure.

One notable feature of this trial was that for the first time Wilde seemed to find his own voice and take the proceedings seriously. When, with reference to a poem by Bosie, Wilde was asked, 'What is the "Love that dare not speak its name"?' he finally dropped the posturing and posing and replied, from the heart:

> The 'Love that dare not speak its name' in this century is such a great affection of an elder for a younger man as there was between David and Jonathan, such as Plato made the very basis of his philosophy, and such as you find in the sonnets of Michelangelo and Shakespeare. It is the deep, spiritual affection that is as pure as it is perfect . . . It is in this century misunderstood, so much misunderstood that it may be described as the 'Love that dare not speak its name' and on account of it I am placed where I am now. It is beautiful, it is fine, it is the noblest form of affection. There is nothing unnatural about it. It is intellectual, and it repeatedly exists between an elder and a younger man, when the elder man has intellect, and the younger man has all the joy, hope and glamour of life before him. That it should be so the world does not understand. The world mocks at it and sometimes puts one in the pillory for it.[58]

Wilde had never sounded so superb. Here stood this man, frail and ill after imprisonment, who had been loaded with insults and crushed and buffeted, standing there sounding perfectly self-possessed, dominating the Old Bailey with his fine presence and musical voice. He carried the entire court away and had never experienced such a triumph as when the gallery burst into applause. It was Wilde's defining moment, and his swan song. According to Max

Beerbohm, Oscar stood up to hear the verdict looking magnificent and sphinx-like, only to be informed that the jury had failed to reach a verdict. The jury was still not convinced as to the evidence. A third trial was scheduled, and this time the prosecution checked the backgrounds of its witnesses and won guilty verdicts on eight of nine counts of gross indecency. On 24 May, the judge addressed the courtroom and complained that it was the worst case he had ever tried and that he felt compelled to pass 'the severest sentence that the law allows'.[59] With that, he sentenced Wilde to the maximum: two years' hard labour. Wilde turned white and looked as though he might faint. As the warders seized him by the arms and led him away, he seemed to want to speak, but the judge ignored him. That night, the Marquess of Queensberry held a celebration dinner with two of Wilde's former friends, Charles Brookfield and Charles Hawtrey, the men who had conspired to betray him.[60]

Wilde went into exile as soon as he had completed his prison sentence. There could be no return to his old life. He lost custody of his sons, and an attempt to patch things up with Constance ended in tragedy when she died after an operation on her spine. Shunned by his former friends, who were terrified of being associated with him, Wilde died in Paris in 1901, in the arms of Robbie Ross, whose ashes were later placed in Wilde's flamboyant tomb at the cemetery of Père Lachaise. Even Wilde's memorial was not without its element of black comedy: designed by Jacob Epstein, the tomb was inspired by Wilde's poem 'The Sphinx', but looks less like a sphinx than an art deco angel, with genitals on proud display. The tomb, and particularly the angel's genitals, became the object of veneration by Wilde's legions of fans, some of whom chipped away and removed the impressively proportioned equipment. Speculation continues to surround their whereabouts.

Over a century later, it is possible to make a case for Wilde as our greatest sexual martyr, but it also seems as if he was punished for that great British sin of being 'too clever by half'. Wilde's subversive attitude towards institutions such as marriage and the law provoked the wrath of the establishment, as did his breathtaking arrogance and apparent lack of contrition. Few, if any, writers would take the stand against an eminent lawyer today. Wilde certainly remains the world's most famous homosexual. With his exclamatory manner and witty putdowns, he established a stereotype for gay men which echoes down the years and found its expression in characters as diverse as Anthony Blanche in Evelyn Waugh's novel *Brideshead Revisited* and the comic creations of Kenneth Williams and John Inman. Although it is tempting to deride these figures as unwelcome caricatures which expose the homosexual to ridicule, it is worth remembering that Wilde inadvertently paved the way for awareness, if not acceptance, of homosexuality in a way that it had never been recognized before. For this reason, Wilde deserves his status as a sexual martyr, a St Sebastian shot through with the last arrows of Victorian hypocrisy.

12

THE HOUR OF OUR DEATH

'They might all be killed tomorrow. Surely you don't mind them
having a good time with the girls?'

From the days of the Romans to the twentieth century, London had
always offered rest and relaxation to visiting military. From the *lupanaria* of the Bankside to Damaris Page, 'the great bawd of sailors',
and the docklands whores recorded by Mayhew, there had always
been plenty of action for men who wanted to forget the terrors of
battle. But London reached its zenith as a city of pleasure during and
between the two world wars. The impact of these wars transformed
a generation's attitude to sex and swept away many of the tattered
remnants of Victorian morality at all social levels, from the aristocracy (who had always done what they liked anyway) to the working
classes. The wars also changed the status of women dramatically,
permitting them to develop sexual and social autonomy.

The young men arriving in London from France and Belgium
were desperate for distraction after the horrors of trench warfare;
the young women waiting to greet them back in Blighty were going

through upheavals of their own, many exhilarated by their own new-found freedom but also devastated by grief. Young widows, married less than a year, found themselves as eager for sexual solace as the men on leave, while the threat of sudden death, in the form of Zeppelin raids, loomed above the city like an evil shadow. (A total of 600 people were killed by Zeppelin raids in London during the First World War.) The prospect of imminent annihilation was a tremendous aphrodisiac, and of course London's sex workers rose to the challenge, as one contributor to the *Weekly Dispatch* observed:

> A young officer from Scotland was accosted sixteen times in the course of walking from his hotel near Regent Street to Piccadilly Tube, a walk of a few hundred yards. Sometimes by those who appeared to be mere children. To a relative who met him later he said: 'No healthy lad could withstand this kind of temptation.' There is no city so absolutely vicious as London has been since the outbreak of the war . . . We do not wait for dark in the West End to open this dance of death. From the early hours of the afternoon the soldiers' steps are dogged by women. In the tea-shops, in the hotels, in kinemas [*sic*], in music-halls they wait for them. He must jostle them upon the pavement and have them at his elbow whenever he stands to greet a friend. And 70 per cent of them are diseased, as one great authority computes . . . [1]

Purity campaigners, struggling to retain their hold on the nation's morals, seized the opportunity to swoop on any unlawful sexual activity, ostensibly in the interests of preventing the spread of venereal disease, but essentially in a desperate attempt to gain social control. With the men away at war, it was left to a battalion of hatchet-faced killjoys to patrol the streets of London seeking out acts of gross indecency. In the name of the NCCVD (the National Council for the Control of Venereal Disease) eagle-eyed women broke up courting couples, berated prostitutes and on one occasion reported a couple of homosexuals to the authorities for having sex in a cemetery. But the sex spies were impotent when it came to controlling the sheer scale of prostitution and the unrepentant activities of the amateurs of all classes, and the women who, experiencing more freedom than at any other time in history, were also discovering the freedom to have sex like men. Bored, frustrated debutantes at last got the opportunity to do something constructive in the form of nursing or performing clerical duties for the army, while working-class women found themselves pressed into service in the factories, railways or on the land, performing the tasks forsaken by the men who had signed up 'to have a go at the Bosch'. For all the hard work and the danger, the freedom these women enjoyed was unparalleled: restricting gowns were exchanged for uniforms, and silk slippers replaced with stout boots; hats with long trailing veils were laid away, in favour of caps. The scores of widows were discouraged from wearing full Victorian-style mourning on the grounds that heavy veils and black crepe dresses were impractical, and also because the returning soldiers did not want to see dozens of girls in widows' weeds as they walked through the city. Practical dress and a welcoming attitude towards men on leave were considered good for British morale. Girls learnt to smoke cigarettes and even carry condoms, as eager as the men to experience every pleasure before they died. Armistice Day, when it eventually arrived, developed into a bacchanalian festival worthy of the days of Roman London: as crowds celebrated the end of the war to end all wars by dancing in the street and drinking the pubs dry, men and women embraced freely. The writer Norman Douglas wistfully recalled seeing scenes of wild lovemaking on the streets of the West End.[2]

While the First World War offered liberation for straight women, it proved a godsend for lesbians. Hitherto caricatured as 'mannish' women with Tyrolese hats and waistcoats, and reviled as 'the shrieking sisterhood',[3] lesbians had inherited a new, exciting world where being physically courageous and practical were positively encouraged and having cropped hair and work boots passed without comment. The writer Vita Sackville-West, who had always been something of a tomboy, experienced an epiphany one afternoon in 1918, when a parcel of land girl's clothes arrived at her country home. Dressed in breeches and gaiters, 'I went into wild spirits; I ran, I shouted, I jumped, I climbed, I vaulted over gates, I felt like a schoolboy let out on a holiday.'[4] This episode was just the beginning of an outrageous affair with Violet Keppel (daughter of Alice, mistress of Edward VII) during which Vita regularly dragged up in men's clothes and paraded along the streets of Mayfair, smoking a cigarette and being addressed by newsvendors as 'Sir'. The fact that she was almost six foot tall was a great advantage in this escapade, and she recalled later that she looked rather like a scruffy undergraduate. 'The extraordinary thing was, how natural it all was for me,' she remembered. 'I never felt so free as when I stepped off the kerb, down Piccadilly, alone, and knowing that if I met my own mother face to face she would take no notice of me.' Vita and Violet regularly spent the night together in a hotel as 'man and wife', and Vita relished her double life, always returning home to Knole (her stately home) in time to greet her husband, Harold Nicolson, when he returned from London.

Vita continued to wear mannish clothes for the rest of her life; years later, the writer Peter Quennell described her wearing a pearl necklace, lacy blouse, tweedy gardening trousers and knee-high boots and concluded that she looked like Lady Chatterley to the waist, while beneath was all the gamekeeper's.

Vita and Harold's relationship survived her entanglement with Violet, and many other affairs on both sides, through a mixture of genuine love and mutual regard, wonderfully chronicled by their son Nigel Nicolson in his memoir *Portrait of a Marriage*. Vita and Harold were typical members of a set informally known as 'the Bloomsbury Group', an assortment of writers, artists and intellectuals which included Virginia Woolf and her publisher husband Leonard, Woolf's sister Vanessa Bell, the economist Maynard Keynes, and the writers Lytton Strachey, E. M. Forster and David

Garnett. In some ways, these individuals were similar to the 'privileged wantons' of the Elizabethan court, permitted a great deal of irregular behaviour on the grounds of wealth and social position. They also owed much of their sexual freedom to the recently translated works of Sigmund Freud, the father of psychoanalysis, whose theories on sexuality were wilfully misinterpreted by an entire generation as an incitement to sexual licence. As we have seen throughout this book, the wealthier and more influential members of society have always permitted themselves greater freedom, and in some respects the Bloomsburys were a recent manifestation of this phenomenon. If it seems to the outsider that the Bloomsbury men appeared to be extraordinarily tolerant of their wives' romantic liaisons, it is worth noting that the Bloomsbury men were predominantly homosexual. There was consternation among the set when the hitherto gay Maynard Keynes married Lydia Lopokova, a Russian ballet dancer; Leonard Woolf appears to have been the only truly heterosexual man in the group. D. H. Lawrence, the provincial working-class novelist taken up by the

A delightful vignette of a lesbian couple from 1913.

Bloomsburys, was genuinely scandalized by the antics of this arty crowd, an irony given that his most notorious book, *Lady Chatterley's Lover*, would become the subject of an obscenity trial.

These homosexual intellectuals did not have complete freedom, of course, due to the existing legislation which had remained unchanged since the Criminal Law Amendment Act 1885, and the fate of Oscar Wilde continued to act as a deterrent to all but the most blasé. Public humiliation was still the fate of those who got found out; William Lygon, 7th Earl Beauchamp, was driven into permanent exile in Europe when his vindictive cousin, the Duke of Westminster, threatened to ruin his political career by exposing his homosexuality. Lygon was subsequently the inspiration for Lord Marchmain, the patriarch in *Brideshead Revisited*, although Waugh reflected the climate of the times by making Marchmain an urbane heterosexual adulterer rather than a homosexual. E. M. Forster, author of celebrated novels such as *A Room with a View*, abandoned publishing fiction in despair because the existing laws meant he could not write about the subject matter which really interested him: sexual relationships between men. His autobiographical novel *Maurice* was eventually published in 1971, after his death.

Despite the continuing drawbacks of 'feasting with panthers', London offered solace for homosexual men to an unparalleled degree. They were drawn to London like moths to a flame, aware that the city presented them with a plethora of public and private arenas in which to explore their sexuality and obtain a level of acceptance inconceivable in the provinces. In London, many elements converged to create a world in which homosexuality was acknowledged, if not legally condoned; the theatre, light entertainment, the media and the rag trade all offered opportunities for a lonely boy who had grown up thinking he was the only one in Barnsley, or Gainsborough, or Port Talbot. The establishment itself, with its guardsmen's barracks, lawyers' chambers and the palaces of Westminster and Buckingham, provided rich pickings. In 1916, a young student, Robert Hutton, arrived in London and had his first sexual encounter with a man who picked him up in Victoria Station. After they had sex underneath the trees in Belgrave Square, Hutton wrote: 'it was as if a curtain had been drawn back. I could see clearly what had been partially obscured before. This was what I had been looking for. I knew now, that other people felt the same way as I did. I was no longer alone.'[5]

And there was no need to be alone. London was a gay paradise during the war years, with Piccadilly Circus its glittering hub. Just as, decades earlier, prostitutes of every caste had been drawn to the Haymarket, 'the Dilly', with its distinctive statue of Eros and flashing bright lights, became the centre of the universe for homosexual men. Baedeker described the district as 'the centre of London' for the 'pleasure seeker' and this was certainly the case. There was Oscar Wilde's former haunt, the Cafe Royal on Regent Street; the Empire and the Alhambra, music halls still going strong despite the passage of the years; there was the Trocadero and the Regent's Palace Hotel, and pubs like the Bunch of Grapes, the Wellington and the Griffin, while the bar at the Strand Hotel attracted a wide range of men, from servicemen on leave to clerks and 'respectable' married men. Lyons Corner House on Coventry Street (known to the cognoscenti as 'the Lilypond') was to all intents and purposes a gay café, where shop assistants and labourers rubbed shoulders with intellectuals and 'pansy boys', and the waitresses, aware of the nature of their clientele, discreetly steered women away from the homosexual patrons. 'Pansies' or 'queens' represented one public face of homosexuality, the unrepentantly flamboyant homosexuals such as Quentin Crisp who risked a beating by parading along Piccadilly in lipstick and rouge. One Alex Purdie recalled that he was 'a swine for make-up; my perfume was called *Soir de Paris* . . . if I could scrounge together half a crown to have a bottle of this, my day was made'.[6] With powdered faces and eyebrows 'plucked to hell' these boys ventured out to battle. As one of them observed, 'it's not make-up, it's ammunition!' and sometimes ammunition was what one needed. Quentin Crisp recalled: 'If I was compelled to stand still in the street . . . to wait for a bus or on the platform of an Underground station, people would turn without a word and slap my face, if I was wearing sandals passers-by took care to stamp on my toes, housewives hissed and workmen spat on the ground.'[7]

Despite the experience of homophobia, London's homosexual scene was not so much an underworld as a flourishing alternative universe, and it even had its own language, 'Polari', derived from Romany and thieves' slang. 'Heterosexual people didn't know what we were talking about,' one man recalled. 'We didn't want people to know.' Instead of saying 'there's a copper coming into the bar', one man would tip off another with 'there's a sharping omi'; if a pretty boy was spotted, he was referred to as 'bona', meaning attractive.[8]

And, just as in Roman times, the bath houses flourished, in the form of Turkish baths, and municipal bath houses, the latter built in the Victorian era for London's poor to wash their clothes and their bodies, but soon an irresistible attraction for homosexual men. Robert Hutton celebrated the Armistice in the Turkish baths, 'which came as near to killing me as the war ever had . . . I slept for a week in a Turkish bath, which meant, virtually, that I did not sleep at all.'[9] When the writer Christopher Isherwood was pursuing the young composer Benjamin Britten he took him to the Savoy Turkish baths in Jermyn Street, notorious for the amount of cruising and sexual activity which went on. Whether or not anything happened, the experience seemed to make Britten more comfortable with his emerging sexuality.

Extending outwards from Piccadilly, like the spokes on a wheel, were London's other venues for homosexual encounters, the clubs of Soho, the bohemia of Fitzrovia, the pubs of Earl's Court and everywhere, throughout London, the network of meeting points in the public conveniences and the parks.

*

Whilst lesbians had experienced a reasonable degree of tolerance, due partially to Queen Victoria's refusal to believe in their existence, and received liberation of a kind during the First World War, sexual tolerance towards homosexual women was severely tested by the publication of *The Well of Loneliness* in 1928. This novel was a *cri de coeur* from Radclyffe Hall (1880–1943), concerning the lonely and masculine Stephen Gordon, a lesbian who eventually finds happiness and acceptance with a female partner after years of misery. Hall had decided to 'put my pen at the service of some of the most misunderstood people in the world', citing the theories of the sexologist Havelock Ellis that 'inverts' were 'a part of Nature, made that way by God, and then punished by a cruel and uncomprehending world. Their suffering cried out for redress and an end to persecution.'[10]

Sir Chartres Biron, the chief magistrate at Bow Street, would have preferred 'inverts' and their kind to remain silent and ruled that the novel was an 'obscene libel' and all copies should be destroyed. Hall's publisher, Jonathan Cape, immediately launched an appeal, while E. M. Forster mobilized eminent supporters including Leonard and Virginia Woolf to defend the book on aesthetic grounds. Unfortunately, Leonard claimed that the book 'failed completely as a work of art', while Virginia found it unreadable. Cape's attempt to defend the book was doomed, since the judge had already formulated his views on what constituted obscenity and was not prepared to listen to London's literati queuing up to defend it.

In a desperate bid to ban the book on health grounds, the Director of Public Prosecutions, Sir Archibald Bodkin, wrote to several doctors asking for a clinical analysis of what he called 'homo-sexualists'. Sir Archibald was worried that women would be inspired to practise lesbianism after reading the book: 'a large amount of curiosity had been excited among women, and I am afraid in many cases curiosity may lead to imitation and indulgence in practices which are believed to be somewhat extensive having regard to the very large excess in numbers of women over men,' he wrote to Dr J. A. Hadfield of Harley Street.[11] Sir William Henry

Willcox, consulting medical adviser to the Home Office and physician at St Mary's Hospital in London, gave Sir Archibald the evidence he needed, declaring that lesbianism 'is well known to have a debasing effect on those practising it, which is mental, moral and physical in character. It leads to gross mental illness, nervous instability, and in some cases to suicide in addicts to this vice. It is a vice which, if widespread, becomes a danger to the well-being of a nation.' Publication of the book, he said, would risk its being read 'by a large number of innocent persons, who might out of pure curiosity be led to discuss openly and possibly practise the form of vice described'.[12]

It is doubtful whether *The Well of Loneliness* sparked a Sapphic recruitment drive. The protagonists' sexual activities get no more explicit than the statement 'she kissed her full on the lips like a lover', and an observation that 'that night, they were not divided', implying that two women shared a bed. Despite the comments from the judiciary that the book featured 'two women making beasts of themselves', any reader looking for hot lesbian action would be deeply disappointed. But it was to be almost twenty years before *The Well of Loneliness* was eventually published in Britain, in 1949. By then Hall was dead and buried in Highgate cemetery, secure in a tomb in the Lebanon Circle with her lover Mabel Batten.

Sex, gay and straight, thrived in London during the interwar years, despite all the best efforts of the authorities. The upper classes, particularly the men who had survived the trenches, became notorious partygoers, dubbed 'the bright young things' by the newspapers and enjoying an elite social scene of debutantes' balls, cocktail parties, nightclubs and country house weekends. Some individuals found these bright young things completely insufferable. The iconic screen star Louise Brooks visited London in 1925 as a seventeen-year-old, before her career took off. Employed as a dancer at the Café de Paris in Coventry Street, Piccadilly, where she became the first person to dance the Charleston in London, Brooks had plenty of opportunity to meet the 'fast set' and was not impressed; indeed, Brooks dismissed them as 'a dreadful, moribund lot', adding that Evelyn Waugh must have been a genius to make them seem so fascinating in *Vile Bodies*.[13]

But this was a minority view. After the tedium and danger of the war, hitherto respectable young women were busy reinventing themselves as 'flappers', shingling their hair, smoking cigarettes and painting their faces, in unconscious imitation of the genuine whores. They drank cocktails (an American development, derived from the fact that the illegal alcohol circulating during Prohibition tasted so disgusting that it had to be 'cut' with other substances such as fruit juice or soda) and danced until dawn. This early example of binge-drinking among young women led, inevitably, to a certain amount of sexual experimentation. While married women began to have access to affordable birth control, in the form of diaphragms and condoms, thanks to the pioneering Marie Stopes (1880–1958), who opened her first clinic in London in 1921, female promiscuity still brought with it the unavoidable risk of unwanted pregnancy. The novelist Rosamond Lehmann presented a realistic account of an abortion in *The Weather in the Streets* (1936) in which the protagonist, Olivia Curtis, undergoes an illegal termination. Lehmann's account of events is not shocking in the visceral sense; it is tastefully written up without melodramatic descriptions of knitting needles or haemorrhages. The abortionist who sets things in motion is presented as an avuncular figure who makes enough from the miscarriage trade to send his son to Harrow, while the doctor who attends Olivia after the subsequent miscarriage is gruffly efficient, warning her not to 'monkey about with herself' if she wants to have children in future. The shock for modern readers consists of the subterfuge Olivia has to resort to in order to get an abortion: she poses as a married woman, then sells her lover's emerald ring (for less than its actual value) to cover the £100 cost of the operation (£2,500 in today's money). When the second doctor is called out, Olivia's male friend passes himself off as her husband to avoid awkward questions from the physician or the prospect of criminal

Marie Stopes, birth control pioneer and author of Married Love,
one of the first sex manuals (1919).

proceedings. The book was considered outrageous at the time of publication; as an account of a disastrous affair with a married man, it was years ahead of its time.[14]

Despite the panic to raise funds for her abortion, Olivia Curtis and her friends were relatively affluent compared with other Londoners. Britain in the 1930s was blighted by the Depression, an economic downturn which saw millions of people out of work and starving; it would take another war before the safety net of the welfare state was in place. One response to this financial crisis was that more women than ever before resorted to prostitution, and the sex trade flourished in London, where conditions for prostitutes were better than at any time within living memory. Inspector Sharpe of the Flying Squad recalled that the majority of girls worked for about four hours a night (or day) receiving fifteen to twenty clients for between 10 shillings to £1 (£25 at today's prices) per customer. A working girl's weekly income of around £80 to £100 compared well with the average shopgirl's wage of just £2 a week. Inspector Sharpe, counting around sixty-seven streetwalkers standing along Piccadilly, observed that this was seen as an acceptable way to get on in life. 'If they had gone straight they must have contented themselves with a seventy-shillings-a-week husband and a semi-detached house in the suburbs. They would have had to pinch for their cheap finery and within a few years a brood of squalling children would have surrounded them. On the streets they make five times what a husband could have brought them, and three quarters of their talk is of the money.' One woman in her thirties whom the inspector often met in Piccadilly looked like a little servant girl, with her pug-face and severe taffeta frock. 'Before she went on the game she was married to a fifty-shillings-a-week railwayman and had five children. Now, she had a five-pound-a-week flat and a maid.'[15]

There were inevitably less fortunate women. The writer George Orwell noted down-and-out prostitutes in Trafalgar Square selling themselves for sixpence a time, although towards morning they would settle for a cigarette and a cup of tea. For these women, Trafalgar Square had become the twentieth-century equivalent of Gropecunt Lane. Nevertheless, the appeal of prostitution to working-class women had never been stronger. In Simon Blumenfeld's novel *Jew Boy* (1935) a young woman who has given up work as a domestic servant to become a whore in the West End tells the protagonist: 'It's not so terrible. Really, I'm lots better off than I was before. When I was in service, the master would always be after me, or if it wasn't the master, there was sure to be a son . . . And they expected all that thrown in buckshee, with scrubbing the house, and clearing out the slops. And I couldn't say anything, or I'd lose my job. Now if I have to do that, I get paid for it, and at least I get SOME time for myself.'[16]

The streetwalkers were notable for their camaraderie. One WPC remarked that 'they are a friendly lot, ready to help one another, exchanging clothes with each other, and even loaning small sums to a rival down on her luck and out of business for the time being'.[17]

Meanwhile, in the upper echelons a new development was under way: the emergence of the call-girl. These women operated out of houses and flats in the fashionable parts of London, servicing clients who sought discretion and comfort. One such operation was run by a dress designer in Grosvenor Square. Men would telephone and ask for a girl, and the designer would fix them up with one; she had 52 young women on her books, and a client list of over 154. The girls tended to be young, and avoided looking like prostitutes; the objective was to be classy and sophisticated, so that they would not attract attention in a Knightsbridge restaurant or a Mayfair hotel, on the arm of their powerful older clients. Special tastes were catered for: a raid on a house near the BBC headquarters at Langham Place revealed pornography, three flagellation canes, one of which had tin tacks secured to the end, a birch and two whips. Prosecutions were rare as the police had to rely on evidence from the neighbours or underworld rivals before they could raid a house.[18]

As in Victorian London, prostitutes often shared apartments, or took their clients to seedy hotels which specialized in renting by the hour. Renting a flat together had its own problems, as even two women could be accused of running a disorderly house and living on immoral earnings. Caution and discretion became the key, but if the girls did get arrested, relationships with magistrates were generally cordial. In 1939 one girl, a waitress, who shared a flat in Baker Street with a girlfriend to halve the substantial costs (£3 a week) was told by the judge that 'if she chose to pursue that form of life she must take care not to break the law, that is, share with another prostitute'.[19] Alexander Wollcott, an American writer and broadcaster, noted during a visit to Bow Street Magistrates' Court that the major difference between Britain and the US was 'the old-world courtesy with which your magistrates treat your whores'.[20] Perhaps this had something to do with the fact that so many of the judiciary patronized whores themselves. One notable exception to these affable relations was the Savidge Case.

Sir Leo Chiozza Money and a prostitute, Irene Savidge, were arrested on charges of indecent behaviour in Hyde Park in May 1928.

Sir Leo was an eminent economist with friends in high places, and thanks to his influence the pair were eventually acquitted in the magistrates' court, but not before Irene Savidge had undergone a lengthy police interrogation at New Scotland Yard at the hands of Archibald Bodkin, Director of Public Prosecutions. A female police officer had been dismissed and the interview had lasted several hours, with Bodkin twisting Irene's words and even forcing her to reveal the red petticoat she had on at the time. Although Bodkin and the police were exonerated, the case led to questions in the House of Commons about the roles of the police and the Department of Public Prosecutions. Shortly afterwards, a prostitute named Helene Adele filed a complaint about two uniformed officers from Y Division who, finding her asleep in the back of a cab, attempted to have sex with her. When Helene refused, she was arrested and charged with insulting words and behaviour. Helene maintained her innocence, however, and the courts decided in her favour; she was acquitted at Clerkenwell Magistrates' Court and the policemen were charged with perjury.[21]

The parks were also a major pick-up point, but the whores on parade were not the downtrodden 'park women' of Mayhew's day. These prostitutes, dressed in their little black suits, walked their poodles along the Bayswater Road and through Marble Arch, in search of prey. (Poodles had long been the dog of choice for prostitutes, a French tradition dating back to the late nineteenth century when top courtesans would ride through the Bois de Boulogne in their carriages, pet dogs proudly on display.) The blackout turned London into one massive Hyde Park, and made it impossible to police. In 1938 there had been over 3000 arrests for prostitution in the Metropolitan Police District; in 1939 there were only 1,865 and in 1940 1,505.[22]

The outbreak of the Second World War ushered in the years of plenty as far as prostitutes were concerned and the trade was transformed. Demand outstripped supply and prices rose accordingly. Another development was the change in attitude by the authorities:

at the beginning of the war, the police were so overstretched dealing with air raids, looting and civilian casualties that they had less time to arrest prostitutes. The impact of the war upon London's prostitutes was apparent from the outset. British men may have complained that their US rivals were 'oversexed and over here' but they were welcomed with open arms by the prostitutes. Huge numbers of soldiers, sailors and airmen converged on the city, along with foreign military; first the Canadian and then the US armies arrived in town looking for sex. The Americans represented the greatest foreign presence in London; even before the attack on Pearl Harbor in December 1941, which brought the United States into the war, there were over 2000 service personnel based at the American Embassy in Grosvenor Square, and within six months that number had doubled.[23] Billeted in the West End, at the Hotel Splendide Piccadilly, the Badminton Club and the Grosvenor House Hotel, these handsome young men fanned out into the city in search of entertainment; according to Quentin Crisp, this 'army of occupation flowed through the streets of London like cream on strawberries, like melted butter over green peas, labelled "With Love from Uncle Sam" and packaged into uniforms so tight that in them their owners could fight for nothing except their honour'.[24] This benign army of occupation was also highly paid, with far more disposable cash than the British. A US sergeant, for instance, received four times the wages of his British equivalent, which led to resentment among British officers and men. One British officer was horrified to be charged 14 shillings for a carafe of wine, muttering that no doubt an American private could afford those prices.[25] London's prostitutes were quick to seize the opportunity to raise their prices: a £1 trick had risen to £3 or £4 by 1943 and by 1945 US soldiers were parting with £5 (£125) for a quickie. Rising prices had no impact on turnover: as the Allied armies gathered in London and Southern England to prepare for the invasion of France, they visited prostitutes in scores. One plainclothes police officer observed thirty-three US or Canadian soldiers visit one brothel in a night, forty-two on another, thirty-five on a third and twenty-nine on the fourth.[26] When one house in Brighton was raided, the madam appealed to the police: 'The boys belong to a bomber crew. They might all be killed tomorrow. Surely you don't mind them having a good time with the girls?'[27]

While many of the professionals made a killing, other women drifted into prostitution as a means of survival. Young girls, orphaned and homeless after being bombed out, found they had no alternative but to go on the game. Wives of men in the Forces also dabbled in the trade, such as the wife of an army sergeant discovered by the police with a houseful of prostitutes and soldiers.[28] When a sergeant in the Royal Engineers came home unexpectedly to his house in Camden Town in December 1944, he found two African-American soldiers in bed with two women. His five children were in the Morrison shelter, and his wife was in another room with the door locked. When he eventually persuaded her to open up he found her in bed with a black soldier. The sergeant was granted a separation order, the children were taken into care by the London County Council and their mother was sentenced to two months' hard labour.[29]

There was also no shortage of enthusiastic amateurs. The novelist Evelyn Waugh noted in his characteristic grumpy fashion that 'for [the US servicemen's] comfort there swarmed out of the slums and across the bridges multitudes of drab, ill-favoured adolescent girls and their aunts and mothers, never before seen in the squares of Mayfair and Belgravia. There they passionately and publicly embraced, in the blackout and at high noon, and were rewarded with chewing-gum, razor-blades and other rare trade goods.'[30] Female commentators were quick to condemn their sisters for licentious behaviour. One Vivienne Hall described the young girls who flocked around the US servicemen as 'the crudest specimens of womanhood, doing anything they want them to do and fleecing them in payment, cheapening themselves and screaming about the West End!'[31], while another critic, Hilda Neal, regarded these good-time girls as 'awful little flappers', seizing on the Americans 'like limpets; many look about fifteen or younger; the girls were of the factory type and loud at that'.[32]

London's nightlife expanded to cater for the free-spending American military. Despite the Blitz, the Café de Paris remained open, with 25,000 bottles of champagne in its extensive cellars and the guarantee that, twenty feet below ground level, it was safe even from enemy action. This glittering nightclub was a magnet for officers, diplomats, aristocrats and beauties; the professionals were also of course in attendance. At a slightly less elevated level, there was the Windmill Theatre in Soho. Opened in 1931 on the site of a windmill dating back to the reign of Charles II, the Windmill specialized in *tableaux vivants*, or tasteful nude scenes in which the models remained motionless. Any movement or gesture which smacked of burlesque would have aroused the wrath of the Lord Chamberlain, an official appointed to crack down on sleaze in the theatre. During the dark days of the Second World War the triumphant motto of the proprietor, Vivian Van Damm, was 'We never closed' (although at one point during the Blitz he and his troupe were reduced to sheltering in the cellar), and it provided quintessentially English entertainment in its morale-boosting displays of naked young women.

In Soho, tactics designed to appease the American servicemen included a series of sleazy clubs offering cold beer and hot jazz, run by proprietors who either verged on criminality or were outright gangsters. No matter how much effort the authorities expended in closing these clubs down, others soon sprang up, mushroom-like, an inevitable draw to homesick servicemen. One of the most popular was Percival Murray's Cabaret Club in Soho, which featured 'exotic dancers' or burlesque acts. After the war, Murray's was to play a crucial role in the Profumo affair.

Many of these clubs also operated as brothels. One, in Coram's Fields, Bloomsbury, was a hotel with a club in the basement. The girls solicited in the bar and then took their clients upstairs. But the proprietors were good at covering their tracks. When the police attempted to raid it, they discovered only an elderly man on his own and a barmaid (also on her own). At a period when corruption was rife, it was obvious that the management had been tipped off before the raid.

While theatres and cinemas were frequently closed in wartime London due to the bombing raids, other venues insisted on business as usual. On the night of 9 March 1941, 150 debutantes, dressed in white, were curtseying to the cake in the ballroom of the Grosvenor House Hotel as part of the peculiar British ritual known as 'coming out' during which the daughters of the nobility were presented to the Queen. On this occasion, the event went ahead without a royal presence. Despite the fact that red warning lights shone through the windows to indicate an air raid, and the floor shook from bombs landing nearby, the instinctive impulse was to keep calm and carry on. Elsewhere in London, in pubs and clubs and church halls, people got on with their lives, drank beer and talked about the weather. Over at the Café de Paris in Piccadilly, manager Martin Poulsen promised that 'the good times are just around the corner'. The tables were occupied by 'handsome flying Johnnies, naval Jacks in full dress', guardsmen, territorials and civilians, the servicemen making the most of their leave while the civilians made the most of the lull in bombings. As West Indian band leader Ken 'Snakehips' Johnson put his orchestra through their paces with a stirring rendition of 'Oh, Johnny!', the air-raid sirens rang out and bombs started to fall nearby. 'Snakehips' upped the ante and the orchestra played 'Oh, Johnny!' a little louder. But then came the hit. Heaps of wreckage crushed dead and injured, reducing the nightclub to a shambles of silver slippers, broken magnums, torn sheet music, dented saxophones and smashed discs. As young men carried out the bodies of their dead girlfriends, a special constable named Ballard Berkeley (who later found fame as the Major in *Fawlty Towers*) was one of the first on the scene. In a chilling vignette, Berkeley spotted the decapitated body of 'Snakehips' Johnson, while elegantly dressed people were still sitting at tables, apparently in conversation, but actually stone dead. Meanwhile, firemen and civilians coming to the rescue were horrified to see looters rifling through pockets and handbags, tearing the rings off the fingers of the dead and dying. A grim end to London's determination to party on through its darkest hour.[33]

Despite such blows to the city's morale, the prostitutes kept working. Indeed, there was such a demand for their services that, towards the end of the war, the girls were running short of space and fights broke out between streetwalkers over strips of pavement, while new girls were forced to 'buy' a beat from retiring whores. In 1944, the authorities felt impelled to take draconian measures against prostitution, with the magistrates of London eager to clean up their city, claiming that there was a public outcry that the menace of prostitution was not being dealt with severely enough and that brothels brought London into disrepute. The *Evening Standard* launched a clean-up campaign, leading to the closure of one hundred nightclubs, although it was harder to control the streetwalkers; the prostitutes themselves were not impressed. Doing their bit for the war effort, welcoming the servicemen with open arms, they told the newspaper in no uncertain terms that they were most disgruntled. 'First time I've ever had any trouble' was one woman's response to the clean-up campaign. 'Behavin' like that for no reason at all!' protested another.[34] There was also the age-old tendency to blame the girls, not the clients: prostitutes were told by the judiciary, 'girls like you are a very great menace to many otherwise excellent young men who are serving their country'.[35]

One anecdotal historian of wartime prostitution was Marthe Watts, a French prostitute who arrived in London shortly after the beginning of the war and married the elderly Mr Watts to gain a passport. An experienced prostitute, Marthe was no stranger to the law herself: over the years she made more than 400 appearances before the magistrates. To hurry clients along, she ensured that her room was as bleak and functional as possible. When one American glimpsed her hard wooden bed, he exclaimed: 'Huh, a workbench!' Marthe's finest hour came on VE Day, when she took home forty-nine clients, working through the night until six o'clock the following morning. Marthe's lover was Gino Messina, a brutal, greedy gangster who controlled London's sex industry for a generation. She claimed that Gino introduced the 'ten-minute rule' for punters, on the grounds of economy and jealousy; he could never last longer than ten minutes himself. Despite Gino's unpleasant personality, Marthe was devoted to him, throwing a party when he got out of jail.

Perhaps Marthe's loyalty to Gino derived from the fact that the Messina family had come to dominate London's sex trade by the 1940s. Gino had arrived in London in 1934, having heard that the city offered opportunities to the enterprising criminal. He had received an excellent training in the sex trade from his father, who had trafficked women in Alexandria, Egypt. Despite their Sicilian surname, the Messinas maintained that they were of Egyptian and Maltese descent. Gino had shrewd business instincts and soon realized that London's sex trade was chaotic, and that fines for prostitutes were comparatively low; the penalty for soliciting cost little more than a parking ticket. [36]

Within a year, he had built an empire in the West End and his brothers – Salvatore, Carmelo, Alfredo and Attilio – had come over to join him. On paper, the family business appeared to be legitimate; the brothers described themselves as antique dealers and diamond brokers and if pressed replied that they were in the 'import' trade. What they actually imported was women, sourced from the continent and further afield. As these women had their own passports and had arrived in Britain of their own volition, the Messinas could not be convicted of trafficking. And no expense was spared in tempting girls to throw in their lot with the brothers. One prostitute, taken out to dinner and sweet-talked by Gino, described him as a perfect gentleman.[37]

By 1950, the Messinas were running 500 girls in the West End.

'We Messinas are more powerful than the British government,' Attilio Messina told the press. 'We do as we like in England.' In 1947, the Messinas' grip on the trade was challenged by Carmelo Vassallo, a Maltese pimp, and during a violent encounter Gino slashed Vassallo's face with a razor, which earned him two years in jail. He celebrated his release by spending £10,000 on a two-tone Rolls Royce. Hefty backhanders to the police also assured immunity from prosecution, until the legendary crime reporter Duncan Webb of the *People* began to investigate allegations of leaks from Scotland Yard to Alfredo Messina. On 3 September 1950, the *People* carried a front-page lead on prostitution, containing all the information necessary for a police investigation into corruption, including names, dates, photographs and interviews with over one hundred prostitutes. Edna Kallman was one such woman. At thirty-nine, she had been working for the Messinas for ten years and was ill and exhausted. She told police that Attilio had hired a maid to watch her and enforce the ten-minute rule. When Edna complained about her working conditions, Attilio retorted that she was lucky to have the work. 'I could get a seventeen-year-old who would work harder than you,' he told her, 'and I could fuck her as well!'[38]

Superintendent Guy Mahon of Scotland Yard set up a task force and engaged in such an aggressive campaign against the Messina brothers that, by the end of the 1950s, Alfredo Messina had been imprisoned on bribery and prostitution charges. Attilio Messina was sentenced to four years' imprisonment after being caught illegally attempting to re-enter the country in April 1959. The remaining Messina brothers fled abroad. Gino and Carmelo resurfaced in Belgium; subsequently arrested, Gino was sentenced to six years while Carmelo was deported to Italy, where he died in 1959. The authorities had investigated the tangled roots of the Messina family tree and discovered that the brothers were not, as they claimed, Maltese, but Sicilian. In true gangster fashion, Gino continued working. A journalist visiting him in his Belgian jail found him signing cheques for rent and taxes on his London properties, which, according to the *Sunday People,* were still being used for immoral purposes. Meanwhile, the remaining brother, Salvatore, had disappeared, and was the only Messina never to be brought to justice.[39]

The Messina brothers' brutal methods were typical of the London underworld in the mid-twentieth century. The next generation of gangsters, the Krays, inherited the Messinas' empire and ensured its survival through a terrifying reign of intimidation and violence. But, as we will see in the next chapter, London's sexual underworld was about to change yet again.

13

SWINGING LONDON

From *Lady Chatterley* to Belle de Jour

When the Director of Public Prosecutions turned to the jury during the Chatterley trial and demanded, 'Is it a book you would wish your wife or servants to read?' he demonstrated extraordinary arrogance in his ignorance of popular opinion and modern life. The disastrous attempt to ban Lawrence's novel represented the last desperate attempts of the establishment to police artistic expression and popular culture. It was a losing battle, and those waging it were soon to lose credibility themselves; in the wake of the Chatterley trial, the government and high society faced a series of scandals and revelations which made *Lady Chatterley's Lover* appear positively tame by comparison.

In this journey into London's sexual history, I will look at the Chatterley trial and its consequences, the high-society scandals of the 1960s and 70s, the links with organized crime, and subsequent developments in the sex industry, including the prostitutes taking control of it and the recent phenomenon of 'Belle de Jour', a call-girl who posted an account of her exploits on the internet, and her many imitators.

But first, let us revisit the Chatterley trial and try to understand, from the perspective of the twenty-first century, what all the fuss was about. *Lady Chatterley's Lover* (1928) was Lawrence's most famous novel but far from his best. The narrative follows the relationship between Constance, a sex-starved young aristocrat whose husband was crippled in the First World War, and Oliver Mellors, the gamekeeper on her estate. Lurking beneath the tsunami of swearing and coital grunts was Lawrence's genuine moral message: the book is a plea for physical and spiritual intimacy between couples, rather than brutal animalistic sex or a retreat into lofty celibacy. Not for nothing was Lawrence's alternative title 'Tenderness'.

Lawrence's graphic descriptions of sex meant he was no stranger to controversy. In 1915, police raided the offices of his publishers, Methuen, and seized and burned 1,011 copies of *The Rainbow*; in 1929, a book of poems, *Pansies*, was deemed so offensive that Lawrence had to withdraw twelve verses; an exhibition of his paintings was closed on the grounds of 'indecency'; but this was nothing compared with the outrage following the appearance of *Lady Chatterley's Lover*, which, when it did not find a British publisher, was printed in Florence in 1928, and seized at customs when attempts were made to bring it into England. Imported copies inevitably got through, however, and were available upon application from booksellers prepared to risk a prison sentence (one bookseller went to jail for two months in 1955) and from the many 'sex shops' which had sprung up in Soho.

Soho had replaced Holywell Street as the home of pornography, and while some of the magazines sold in the early days, such as Harrison Marks's *Spic and Span*, would be regarded as mild by modern standards, most shops had a back room specializing in hardcore material, gay and straight, and Olympia Press editions of classic erotica such as *Fanny Hill*, *The Story of O* and *The English*

Governess. It was in these unlikely surroundings that the aspiring novelist or Cambridge don might track down an unexpurgated edition of *Lady Chatterley's Lover*.

When, in May 1960, Penguin Books proudly announced that they planned to publish a paperback of the novel, complete and unexpurgated, for 3s 6d (17.5p), the Director of Public Prosecutions, Mervyn Griffith-Jones, swung into action. He declared that the unexpurgated version was obscene and that 'a prosecution for publishing an obscene libel would be justified. Indeed if no action is taken in respect of this publication it will make proceedings against any other novel very difficult.'[1]

The attorney general, Sir Reginald Manningham-Buller, had only to read the first four chapters before he agreed: 'If the remainder of the book is of the same character I have no doubt you were right to start proceedings – and I hope you get a conviction.'[2] The solicitor general, Sir Jack Simon, reached the same conclusion.

Just as Jonathan Cape had done in the 1928 *Well of Loneliness* obscenity trial, Penguin recruited a number of expert witnesses, in the form of eminent writers and academics. Under the Obscene Publications Act of 1959, it was possible for publishers to escape conviction if they could prove that a work had literary merit. While thirty-five witnesses, including luminaries such as E. M. Forster, Richard Hoggart, Cecil Day Lewis and Raymond Williams, were prepared to testify to Lawrence's artistic genius, the prosecution desperately scrabbled around, intending to match the defence 'bishop for bishop and don for don'. The DPP's office approached Sir David Cecil, an Oxford don who had dismissed Lawrence back in 1932 as a 'guttersnipe', and Graham Hough, a fellow of Christ's College, Cambridge, who had deplored the number of four-letter words in the novel, but they refused to testify. Noel Annan, Provost of King's College, Cambridge, and Helen Gardner, Reader in Renaissance English Literature at St Hilda's College, Oxford, were also approached, but also refused to appear for the prosecution, Gardner replying by return of post that she was 'unwilling to give any assistance to those who are desirous of suppressing the work of a writer of genius and complete integrity'. Gardner subsequently appeared as a witness for the defence.[3]

The DPP's staff were reduced to a page-by-page analysis of the book looking for 'filth' (an indispensable guide to any reader short of time but keen to find 'the naughty bits'). A typical extract ran: 'pp. 177–185. Connie goes to the hut the same day after tea. Intercourse unsatisfactory to Connie to start with but all right the second time (full details and four-letter words).' Under the heading 'Gratuitous filth', the DPP's office had tried to keep a running count of the offending words. It notes on page 204 a 'fucking', a 'shit', a 'best bit of cunt left on earth' and three sets of 'balls'. At the trial, Griffith-Jones told the jury that the word 'fuck' or 'fucking' appeared no fewer than thirty times.[4]

The trial of *Regina v. Penguin Books* opened at the Old Bailey on 27 October 1960. While the literary establishment turned out in force for the defence, the prosecution called only one witness: Detective Inspector Charles Monahan, the police officer to whom Penguin had 'published' the book by sending him a copy. A major indication of just how ill-advised this prosecution had been was the moment when Mervyn Griffith-Jones rose to his feet and asked the jury: 'Would you approve of your young sons, young daughters – because girls can read as well as boys – reading this book? Is it a book that you would have lying around the house? Is it a book you would wish your wife or servants to read?'[5]

The jury took just three hours to return a verdict of not guilty. Lawrence's stepdaughter, Barbara Barr, summed up the popular response when she declared that 'I feel as if a window has been opened and fresh air has blown right through England.' Within a year, *Lady Chatterley's Lover* had sold two million copies.

The verdict horrified the establishment. While *The Times* was appalled at the failure to produce witnesses for the prosecution, the Archbishop of Canterbury complained and fourteen Conservative MPs tabled an amendment to the Queen's Speech (due the following month) demanding the repeal of the new Obscene Publications Act. This collective handwringing proved futile; the trial had been an expensive waste of time and taxpayers' money and the authorities had misjudged the public mood.[6]

This was just the beginning. Within three years, the establishment would be rocked by political and sexual scandals which would bring down the government and leave the highest in the land without so much as a fig-leaf to preserve their modesty. The first, in 1963, featured all the vital ingredients for a major sex scandal: high society, sexual perversion, prostitution, violence and espionage. One of its principal players, Stephen Ward, deserves a place in our narrative as one of the few male bawds.

A society osteopath who numbered Winston Churchill, Ava Gardner and Douglas Fairbanks Jr among his clients, Ward was a social climber who ensured a constant stream of invitations by supplying a steady flow of attractive girls to the establishment. Ward sought out pretty working-class girls, claiming to be 'sensitive to their needs and the stresses of modern living'. As he roamed the cafés and bars of the West End looking for new recruits, Ward's technique would have been familiar to the wise old bawds of Covent Garden. And the rewards were considerable: a cottage on Lord Astor's country estate and admission to the highest ranks of society. Ward appeared urbane and charming on a superficial level, although the actress Diana Dors saw straight through him, and referred to him as that 'slick society doctor among the jet set'.[7]

In 1959, Ward met Christine Keeler at Murray's Cabaret Club in Soho. Christine, an 'exotic dancer', was a beautiful 17-year-old with the face of a Madonna. Within weeks, she had moved into Ward's flat in Wimpole Mews and befriended another of Ward's party girls, Mandy Rice-Davies, whose lovers included the slum landlord Peter Rachman and Lord Astor.

In July 1961, Ward took Christine to a pool party at Cliveden, Lord Astor's country estate, where he introduced her to Sir John

Profumo, the Secretary of State for War, and his wife, the actress Valerie Hobson. Christine and Profumo enjoyed a brief liaison, although Profumo ended it after a few weeks. And that might have been the end of the matter but for an incident with a gun in December 1962. Christine had moved out of Ward's flat but had returned to visit Mandy, who was still living there. On 14 December, one of Christine's boyfriends, Johnny Edgecombe, a petty criminal, arrived at the flat in a jealous rage and tried to gain entry, firing at the door several times with a gun. As a result of Edgecombe's subsequent trial, Christine and Mandy's relationship with Stephen Ward and many rich and powerful men was exposed; there were juicy rumours in the Sunday papers about two-way mirrors, whips and canes, and kinky sex among the jet set, including allegations about a party in Bayswater attended by Keeler, Rice-Davies and Ward, at which a cabinet minister had served a dinner of roast peacock while wearing nothing except a mask and a bow tie . . . The man also had a card round his neck: 'If my services don't please you, whip me.' Another rumour concerned a cabinet minister being fellated by a prostitute in Hyde Park, while further speculation included an orgy which involved eight High Court judges. 'One, perhaps,' groaned Harold Macmillan to a colleague, 'two, just conceivably. But eight – I just can't believe it.'[8]

Quite apart from the affront to public morality of the Secretary for War engaging in sex with a call-girl, another aspect of the affair propelled it into a different league altogether. This was the revelation that, while sleeping with Profumo, Christine had also been involved with Yevgeny 'Eugene' Ivanov, a senior naval attaché at the Soviet Embassy. It was the height of the Cold War and the security implications for Harold Macmillan's Conservative government were catastrophic.

The public lapped it up, and Profumo was forced to make a statement to the House of Commons. In March 1963, he told the House that there was 'no impropriety whatever' in his relationship with Christine and that he would issue writs for libel and slander if the allegations were repeated outside the House. Christine, meanwhile, had become a celebrity; a photograph of her sitting astride a chair, with nothing but the plywood back to preserve her modesty, became an instant classic when it was leaked to the *Sunday Mirror*. Endlessly republished, copied and parodied, the photograph has come to epitomize the Profumo affair.

It must have come as something of a relief to Profumo when another scandal hit the headlines in May 1963. This also took the form of a photograph, but far more graphic and sensational than 'La Keeler' posed on a chair. This photograph surfaced as the result of acrimonious divorce proceedings between the Duke and Duchess of Argyll, wealthy West End socialites. The Duke was divorcing the Duchess, a former Deb of the Year, on the grounds of her serial adultery, as revealed in her diaries and collections of photographs. One series of pictures in particular proved outrageous. Snapped in the bathroom of her home in Upper Grosvenor Street, Mayfair, these revealed 'Marg of Arg' wearing nothing but a string of pearls, performing fellatio on an unknown man, his head not shown on the photograph. Other pictures depicted the same 'unknown man' masturbating for the camera, with handwritten labels testifying to the different states of arousal, from 'before' to 'thinking of you', 'during – oh!' and 'finished'. There was wild press speculation as to the identity of 'the headless man', including rumours that he was a government minister or a film star. Candidates for Marg of Arg's lover included the Defence Secretary Sir Edwin Duncan Sandys (son-in-law of Winston Churchill) and the American actor Douglas Fairbanks Jr.

The headless man was one of many. It emerged that during the course of her marriage Margaret had sex with over eighty men, including two cabinet ministers and two members of the royal family. When asked to explain her behaviour, Margaret maintained that she had never been the same since plunging forty feet down a lift shaft during the war, this experience triggering off an extraordinary neurological condition which left her without the sense of taste or smell but with a voracious sexual appetite. The judge's verdict was damning. He described Margaret as

> a highly sexed woman who has ceased to be satisfied with normal sexual activities and has started to indulge in disgusting sexual activities to gratify a debased sexual appetite. A completely promiscuous woman whose sexual appetite could only be satisfied by a number of men, whose promiscuity had extended to perversion and whose attitude to the sanctity of marriage was what moderns would call enlightened, but which in plain language was wholly immoral.

As a result of the divorce, Margaret lost everything: her reputation, and her beautiful house in Mayfair.[9]

The scandal of Marg of Arg was overshadowed two weeks later on 5 June, when John Profumo was forced to stand up in the Commons once again. This time he confessed that he had misled the House and lied in his testimony. Profumo resigned from the cabinet and from his post as an MP. During a stormy cabinet meeting on 20 June, Duncan Sandys also offered to resign, admitting that he was in the frame as Marg of Arg's 'headless man'. An exhausted Macmillan, fearing further scandal, refused to accept his resignation. (The identity of Margaret's headless lover was never fully revealed, although handwriting experts concluded in 2001 that he was Douglas Fairbanks Jr.)

In the wake of John Profumo's confession to the House of Commons, Stephen Ward was arrested and charged with living off immoral earnings. When Ward went on trial at the Old Bailey on 22 July, Christine Keeler and Mandy Rice-Davies were called to testify against him. It was while giving evidence that Mandy Rice-Davies made her famous quip: when the prosecuting counsel pointed out that Lord Astor denied having an affair or having even met her, Mandy replied, with great spirit, 'Well, he would, wouldn't he?'

Mervyn Griffith-Jones (the unsuccessful prosecutor in the Chatterley case) turned his forensic skills against Ward in his closing speech, a character assassination so devastating that Ward went home and took an overdose of sleeping pills. Three days later, on Saturday 3 August, he died. The trial was formally closed the following Monday, with no sentence pronounced, although Ward had been found guilty of living off immoral earnings, a verdict which the writer Ludovic Kennedy later concluded was a miscarriage of justice. After all, Christine received more money from Ward than he did from her; if anyone had been living off immoral earnings, it was her. Christine did not escape prosecution. She was found guilty of perjury, and sentenced to nine months in prison. Ward's lonely death was followed by an equally forlorn funeral: nobody came.

In September 1963, Lord Denning released an official government report into the Profumo affair. It was a best-seller, with hundreds of men queuing outside HM Stationery Office at midnight to get hold of a copy. A month later the Prime Minister, Harold Macmillan, resigned on the grounds of ill health.

The Profumo affair was the most spectacular example of the curious relationship between the establishment and the twilight world of the sex industry. (It was to have echoes a decade later, when Lord Lambton, a Tory MP, was forced to resign after evidence emerged that he had been seeing prostitutes and smoking cannabis with them. The revelations were enough to drive Lord Lambton into exile in Italy.) A more sensational revelation was to come in July 1964 when rumours of another compromising photograph began to circulate. The *Sunday Mirror* claimed that the photograph of 'the peer and the gangster' was 'the picture we dare not print' for fear of the libel laws. This was scarcely surprising: the paper's outrageous claim was that 'the peer', a household name, was conducting a homosexual affair with London's most notorious villain.

A day or two later the German magazine *Stern* published a photograph of the mysterious couple, comfortably ensconced on a sofa, accompanied by a handsome if rather feral young man, whose name was Leslie Holt. Holt was a cat burglar. The gangster staring into the camera with those troubling eyes was Ronnie Kray. And the 'household name' was Lord Boothby, an eminent Tory peer.[10]

When the photograph appeared, Boothby was faced with a dilemma. He admitted to having met Ronnie Kray during two or three business meetings, but flatly denied that they were having an affair. If he did nothing, it might seem as if he was admitting to the accusation; if he took the *Sunday Mirror* to court, he would endure a lengthy and expensive legal battle during which the tabloid hacks would rake up every aspect of his private life. And Boothby had a great deal to hide. He had fathered at least three children by the wives of other men, and conducted a long affair with Harold Macmillan's wife. The resulting daughter was brought up as the long-suffering Macmillan's own. Boothby was cheerfully unrepentant of his wicked ways. When Boothby's cousin, Ludovic Kennedy, called him 'a shit of the highest order' to his face, Boothby merely rubbed his hands, chuckled and said, 'Well, a bit. Not entirely.' But while high-society adultery was not uncommon, accusations of homosexual flings with career criminals were potentially lethal. The cabinet trembled and there was a council of war at Chequers as ever more ludicrous rumours flew around the House. Two backbenchers claimed they had seen Boothby and the Labour MP Tom Driberg cruising at a dog-track; worse still, it was claimed the pair were involved in a money-laundering scam with the gangs which operated at the track. Driberg, blatantly homosexual (he went after anything in trousers and refused to take no for an answer), was also close to the Krays. He was a regular at Ronnie's parties, where, according to his biographer, Francis Wheen, rough but compliant East End lads were served 'like so many canapés'.[11]

With an election looming, the rumours about Boothby's private life must have seemed like a gift to the Labour Party, but Harold Wilson's shadow cabinet were in no position to take advantage of the situation. With a Labour victory on the cards, the last thing they wanted was to bring press attention to Driberg's antics. Labour leader Harold Wilson set his personal solicitor, Arnold Goodman, on the case. Goodman, known as 'Mr Fixit', instructed Boothby to write an open letter to *The Times* denying the allegations in the *Sunday Mirror,* denying that he was homosexual and saying that he had met Ronnie Kray on only two or three occasions, by appointment, and in the company of other people. Boothby also wrote to the Home Secretary explaining that he had not known Kray was a criminal, and that he had responded to Kray's request to be photographed with him because he was a celebrity; the Krays' legitimate business consisted of running a string of nightclubs in the West End, and Ronnie adored having his picture taken with the rich and famous, from Judy Garland to Rocky Marciano.

After *The Times* published the letter, Goodman obtained an out-of-court settlement of £40,000 from IPC, owners of the *Sunday Mirror,* and a grovelling apology from the chairman. The cover-up spared Boothby's blushes, and it also protected the Krays; years later, veteran tabloid journalist Derek Jameson recalled that Fleet Street knew that the Krays were trouble and gave them a wide berth, referring to them only in passing as 'those well-known sporting brothers'.

While the Commissioner of the Metropolitan Police denied that there had been a police investigation of the Boothby–Kray affair, it later emerged that the Krays had been under investigation by Detective Chief Inspector 'Nipper' Read since the beginning of the year. The Kray twins were arrested on 10 January 1965, charged with demanding money with menaces from a club owner in the West End and sent to court. But the Krays had friends in high places; not only were any potential witnesses too intimidated to testify against them in court, but Boothby himself stood up in the House of Lords and demanded to know how long the police intended keeping the Krays in custody. The only explanation for this behaviour, which resulted in uproar, is that the Krays were blackmailing Boothby. After a farcical trial and retrial (which found in favour of the defendants), the Krays were released. The twins maintained their grip over the establishment for another three years until they were eventually arrested and convicted in 1968 for the murder of a minor gang member, Jack 'the Hat' McVitie.

While the Krays and other criminal gangs represented the most sensational aspects of London's criminal underworld, the prostitutes who worked for them continued to take massive risks with their personal safety and face arrest and imprisonment on a daily basis. The most vulnerable of these women were those who worked in Soho, which had continued to be the heart of the red-light district. In the 1940s and 50s, the girls worked the streets in time-honoured fashion. With the introduction of the Sexual Offences Act 1956 and the Street Offences Act 1959, they were compelled to change their tactics.

The Sexual Offences Act criminalized any house or flat 'resorted to or used by more than one woman for the purposes of prostitution' and made it illegal to live off immoral earnings (as in the case of Stephen Ward). Unfortunately, this law was no respecter of relationships, so anybody whom the woman supported – be it mother, children or boyfriend – was liable to the charge.[12] Meanwhile, the Street Offences Act was designed to force prostitutes off the street in much the same way as the Criminal Law Amendment Act of 1885. Under the Street Offences Act, a woman could be convicted of soliciting on the 'uncorroborated word of a single policeman'. 'Soliciting' was interpreted as covering 'not only spoken words but also various movements of the face, body and limbs such as a smile, a wink, making a gesture and beckoning or wriggling the body in a way that indicates an invitation to prostitution'. After two cautions, a woman could be labelled 'a common prostitute', a description which stayed on her record for life and could be read out in court, even during a rape or child-custody case.[13]

Challenged by these draconian new regulations, London's whores and their pimps hit on a solution. Instead of patrolling the streets, they took single rooms referred to as 'walk-ups' and advertised their services on the doorway, just as the Roman prostitutes had done two millennia earlier. There were new descriptions for old acts: 'French polishing' (fellatio) was a favourite, while punters were also offered 'French lessons' or tempted with a little postcard that announced 'Large Chest for Sale'. Prostitutes employed a maid, often a retired prostitute, whose task was to usher the punter upstairs and see him out again after the transaction had been completed.

One woman who learnt her trade in Soho was Cynthia Payne, or 'Madam Cyn'. But when the authorities began to crack down on prostitution in central London, she cannily moved her operation to the suburbs, far from prying eyes. However, even Cynthia did not escape detection. In 1978, police raided her house in Ambleside Avenue, Streatham. Inside, they found a cross between a vicarage tea party and an orgy in full swing, with queues of middle-aged and elderly men, including clergymen, MPs and lawyers, waiting to

*'Madam Cyn' (Cynthia Payne), the bawd of
Streatham, leaving court in 1987.*

exchange their 'luncheon vouchers' for food, drink, strip shows and a trip upstairs with the girl of their choice. Charged with running the biggest disorderly house in London, 'Madam Cyn' was sentenced to eighteen months in prison (reduced on appeal to six months and a fine). Cynthia, whose motto really should have been 'Help the Aged', swiftly became a national treasure, partly as a result of her brilliant soundbites: 'I always seem to fall for police-men,' she commented. 'After every raid I got a new boyfriend.' Cynthia was up in court again in 1987, on nine charges of control-ling prostitutes. The thirteen-day trial kept the nation entertained with tales of sex capers, slaves, transvestites and undercover police-men while many establishment figures sympathized with her plight, such as the Conservative MP Geoffrey Dickens who found it 'astounding that all this public money should be poured into bringing these charges'. When, after just five hours of deliberation, the jury acquitted Cynthia of all charges the courtroom burst into applause. In a trial costing £117,000, the judge ordered costs to be paid from central funds, and Cynthia's £5000 legal aid costs to be reimbursed. As Cynthia emerged from court, she told a crowd of over a hundred well-wishers, 'This is a victory for common sense. But I have to admit all this has put me off having parties for a bit.'[14]

While entrepreneurs such as Cynthia had fled, Soho continued to have a raffish reputation throughout the 1950s and 60s. There were the clip-joints, where unsuspecting tourists were lured into paying £300 a bottle for champagne which tasted suspiciously, in the words of the Kinks, 'just like cherry cola'. There were the prostitutes themselves, the peep shows and the fifty-eight sex shops. There were the 'private' cinemas, which operated like clubs, allowing patrons to watch films which had not got past the British Board of Film Censors; and there were the strip clubs. While the Windmill was forced to renege on its claim that 'we never closed' by closing for good in 1964 and becoming the Compton Street Cinema, Raymond's Revue Bar opened on 21 April 1958 with a garish sign proclaiming it to be the 'World Centre of Erotic Entertainment'.

Raymond's first job in show business had been as a mind-reader on Clacton Pier, and this early exposure to male psychology must have provided some useful insights, as he became a millionaire by exploiting the public's fascination with sex. The 'King of Soho's' empire included pornography, property development and the magazines *Razzle*, *Men Only* and *Mayfair*.

The Revue Bar closed in 2004, a victim of the new permissiveness; soft-porn 'lads' mags', the internet, cable television and DVDs rendered such venues superfluous; lap-dancing clubs offered more salacious entertainment; and Soho itself had been cleaned up by Westminster City Council on the orders of Dame Shirley Porter in the 1980s. Proprietors were forced to adopt discreet shop fronts and all blatant displays of nudity or sexual activity were banned. Just as New York's raunchy Times Square was sanitized under Mayor Giuliani, London's Soho lost its raffish quality beneath a tide of creeping gentrification, coffee shops and wine bars. Media types replaced alcoholic painters and dissolute journalists in the old pubs, and the *milieu* became just another part of the London heritage experience.

London's prostitutes responded by starting to fight back. Supported by the English Collective of Prostitutes (a lobbying organization founded in 1975), one group of whores from Shepherd Market put up a spirited resistance to Westminster City Council's clean-up campaign in May 2009. Shepherd Market is a small quarter of Mayfair between Curzon Street and Piccadilly. Mayfair has always been one of the smartest addresses in London, realm of the super-rich and, traditionally, of the prostitute. From the eighteenth century onwards, Shepherd Market had been associated with high-class prostitutes. For years, the working girls and the aristocrats lived side by side; in the mid-1970s, up to one hundred girls walked the streets of the district every night, waiting for their regulars. Commissionaires in the grand hotels of Park Lane would tell families of tourists not to go to Shepherd Market because of the gauntlet of girls they would have to run. On one

Focus Cinema, Brewer Street, W1, in 1976, before Westminster City Council imposed advertising restrictions on the sex trade.

occasion, a gang of girls set upon and beat up an American tourist. They were convinced she was a new prostitute trying to move in on their territory. In fact, the unfortunate woman was just a little provocatively dressed.

As organized crime strengthened its grip on London, many of the Shepherd Market girls became targets for pimps and petty criminals. With corruption rife in the Metropolitan Police, particularly the vice squad, local residents felt helpless in the wake of a crime wave. 'A girl was financing three people from the game as well as herself: her landlord, her ponce and the local police,' remembers one local resident, when interviewed by the *Independent*.

Things became so bad that in 1978 we established the Save Shepherd Market Campaign and took a murder map along to the House of Commons. This showed the position of every murder, act of arson and defenestration of prostitutes that had taken place in the previous 12 months. It was a horrific document. Three days after that, I had my restaurant raided and turned over by the police. It was a public statement, not so much to me as to those who lined their pockets.[15]

Eventually, enforcement action from Westminster City Council and an anti-corruption drive by the Metropolitan Police resolved the issue. These days, you are more likely to walk past expensive bars and restaurants than brothels, and the shabby old pub the Maisonette has been replaced by a mosque serving the quarter's wealthy Arab residents. However, not all the prostitutes have fled. In 2009, when police raided flats in Shepherd Market and reported the prostitutes to the council's planning department, council officials wrote to them accusing them of 'a change of use from residential accommodation' – in other words, running a business from a private address, which constitutes a breach of planning law. According to Niki Adams of the English Collective of Prostitutes (ECP), 'the women have been working here safely for more than a decade, which means they haven't "changed use" of the properties. The women are a welcome part of the community here and should be allowed to run their businesses without hassle from the police or council.'[16]

Niki Adams's statement represented a fight-back by prostitutes against the council. In February 2009, when the Metropolitan Police closed a brothel in Dean Street, Soho, the decision was overturned by the magistrates following lobbying from the ECP. This body also campaigned against the closure of the estimated sixty to a hundred flats used by prostitutes across the borough, supported by residents who maintained that the working girls were an integral feature of the diverse local community.

Back in Shepherd Market, the ECP's argument was that evicting prostitutes from their flats would mean that they were forced to work the streets, where they faced increased danger. 'Megan', a London prostitute for twenty-five years, has worked out of a

Shepherd Market flat for fifteen years and was reluctant to go anywhere else.

'It's a little village here and we couldn't work in a better place,' she told the *London Informer* newspaper. 'Over the years we have had a great relationship with the police. Whenever they need help tracing a girl who has gone missing they come up and ask our help, because we are open and know everybody. The eight girls here in the flats have all been working for a long time. I don't know why suddenly we have become the enemy. The community supports us and perhaps the council did not realise that when they started sending threatening letters out.'[17]

Megan appreciated that there were problems with the sex industry, and young girls being coerced into working as prostitutes, but pointed out that by being driven onto the street, she and her colleagues would be put at risk. 'It's a hard time for us, the recession is hitting our clients and the new laws are making them scared to come to us – even if they've been with us for years.'[18]

The new laws Megan referred to represented yet another attempt to clean up prostitution, but for the working girls they may prove as punitive as previous legislation. The Policing and Crime Bill, passing through Parliament at the time of writing, aims to curb sex trafficking and protect women from being coerced into the sex trade. However, according to opponents, it would potentially criminalize men paying for consensual sex with a prostitute and women who employed maids or other workers to help them, damaging their business and forcing them to take greater risks. While in theory the bill appears to defend prostitutes, in practice it may become oppressive. According to Megan: 'If the police carry on raiding us, we will lose customers and then be forced onto the streets. We will then be in the same danger as the women the police say they want to protect. It doesn't make sense. But we will stand firm and fight any attempts to close us down.' And so they did. In May 2009, the working girls successfully overturned Westminster City Council's attempts to oust them from their flats in Shepherd

*A 'West End Girl' illustrates an investigation
into the sex trade, 1966.*

Market. Megan's parting shot to her interviewer on the *London
Informer* proved prophetic: 'This is the oldest business in the world
and we're not going anywhere.'[19] Indeed, it was business as usual,
'the oldest business in the world', in one of the oldest cities in the
world.

14

PLUS ÇA CHANGE

Sex in the twenty-first century

As I wandered around the West End retracing the footsteps of the Victorian 'Cyprians' in Burlington Arcade, Megan's rallying cry rang in my ears. She was not going anywhere. Or at least she was not intending to go far from her present flat in Mayfair. And neither were thousands like her. There would always be prostitution in London, just as there would be many other expressions of sexuality, and it seems reasonable that the girls get the protection and support they need from the authorities, rather than having to rely on pimps; they obviously provide a much needed service and deserve better conditions than those poor wretches we met at the beginning of the book, shivering on the Bankside in their chains.

One thing that our sexual odyssey of London over the past two millennia has proved to me is that *plus ça change, plus c'est la même chose* – the more things change, the more they remain the same. As we emerge, blinking, into the sunlit uplands of the twenty-first century it is tempting to believe that we have progressed. Away with sexual guilt, priggish repression and Victorian Puritanism! With the advent of Sigmund Freud, Marie Stopes and the torrent of sex manuals which their disciples unleashed upon the world, from *Married Love* to the unintentionally hilarious *Joy of Sex*, and the sexual licence unleashed by two world wars, it might be reasonable to think that our secret sins and peculiar vices have disappeared in favour of briskly clinical couplings. Mercifully, nothing could be further from the case. London continues to yield its own rich crop of secret affairs, obscenity trials and sex scandals, every bit as byzantine as those of the preceding years. There will always be a boy in Piccadilly, leg hooked up on the wall behind him, indicating availability; there will always be a comely matron, prowling the Arcade, with a welcoming smile for the right man; or a slender brunette eyeing up a silver-haired old charmer. The bawds, the rogues, the villains and the beauties weave their eternal dance through London as they always did. These days, the Mother Needhams greet the trains at St Pancras; calculating pimps size up the trusting Scottish boys who arrive at Euston and are drawn, mothlike, to the bright lights of Piccadilly Circus; and resilient young women decide that lap-dancing or two years in a brothel represent a better way to fund their PhDs than yet another bank loan.

Such is the case of 'Belle de Jour', whose lucrative but short career in the oldest profession was made possible by that most recent phenomenon, the internet. With the advent of cyberspace, pornography took on a radical, electronic form, and proved impossible to control, eroding conventional methods of censorship. Prostitutes and writers of erotica were quick to seize on its potential and none more so than 'Belle de Jour', who first came to public attention in 2003 when she began to post her 'Diary of a London Call Girl'. With a pseudonym derived from Luis Buñuel's 1967 film starring Catherine Deneuve as a bourgeois housewife who works in a brothel to relieve her *ennui,* 'Belle' soon built up an enormous fanbase.

Subsequently issued in book form and inspiring a television

series, *Diary of a London Call Girl* represented a development in the history of sex, a collision between the world's oldest profession and the latest technology. But the result was familiar enough, an attractive young woman confiding her exploits just as Fanny Hill had breathlessly narrated her adventures two centuries earlier. 'Belle' inspired a slew of imitators, a new genre of popular erotica untroubled by the harsh censorship which had plagued writers such as D. H. Lawrence; it is a sign of the times that one can purchase books with titles such as *Confessions of a New York Call Girl* at the supermarket alongside the weekly grocery shop. Many attempts were made to unmask 'Belle', and she had been variously suspected of being the author Toby Young, Rowan Pelling, former editor of the *Erotic Review* and chick-lit writer Isabel Wolff. Finally, in November 2009, threatened with exposure by the *Daily Mail*, the real 'Belle de Jour' stepped forward in the glamorous form of research scientist Brooke Magnanti. Just as Cleland had written *Fanny Hill* to get out of debt, so Magnanti had worked as a high-class prostitute to subsidize her PhD in forensic pathology. Given the choice of £200 an hour on the game or a fraction of that wage working in a bookshop, Magnanti had chosen the more lucrative option; she also maintained that she had paid her taxes, so was not guilty of tax evasion. Magnanti's employers took an enlightened attitude: while such a revelation might once have been a sacking offence, the University of Bristol stood by her, arguing that her past was not an issue.

Magnanti's experience of the sex trade seems to have been a positive one; she has benefited and has moved on, just like Sarah Tanner, the Victorian prostitute interviewed by Arthur Munby in the 1850s who went into streetwalking as a professional venture, quit while she was ahead and opened a coffee shop out of the proceeds. Magnanti's experiences seem to bear out the words of a young woman interviewed by Mayhew, who told him pertly that she wasn't at all worried about what would become of her, and could marry tomorrow if she liked. Perhaps Dr Acton, the Victorian reformer, had been correct when he wrote that 'once a harlot always a harlot' was a myth.

But many commentators believe that there are also victims among the hard-working working girls, the twenty-first-century equivalents of the Roman sex slaves. Just a month before the unmasking of 'Belle de Jour' dominated the headlines, a moral panic broke out over sex trafficking. When government minister Denis MacShane appeared on *Newsnight* arguing that the new Policing and Crime Bill was necessary to prevent trafficking, fellow guest Niki Adams, of the English Collective of Prostitutes, challenged MacShane to produce one shred of evidence that women from Eastern Europe, Africa and the Far East were being brought into the United Kingdom to work as prostitutes. Adams's scepticism at MacShane's claims prompted an investigation by the *Guardian* newspaper which concluded that not one single trafficker had been arrested during a six-month investigation into the sex trade and that trafficking had been overstated as one of the reasons women entered prostitution. Campaigners such as Niki Adams responded that the investigations into sex trafficking served no purpose and merely added to the demonization of young women, many of whom were mothers, and who had gone into prostitution because they had no other means of earning a living.[1] For these women, prostitution was business as usual, 'the oldest business in the world', in the words of Megan from Shepherd Market.

And then there are the rest of us, the amateurs, seeking affirmation in the form of fast love, cruising, cottaging, passionate sex with a complete stranger, longing for the love of women, the love of men, searching for similarity and comfort and the satisfaction of physical and emotional needs. Sexual desire is the most basic of human impulses, the desire for the 'little death' ('*la petite mort*', or orgasm) which will distract us from the inevitable event, the hour of death that lies in store for every one of us. In the words of Andrew Marvell in his 'Ode to His Coy Mistress', it is our way of defying the tomb:

Had we but world enough, and time,
This coyness, lady, were no crime . . .
But at my back I always hear
Time's wingèd chariot hurrying near;
And yonder all before us lie
Deserts of vast eternity.
Thy beauty shall no more be found,
Nor, in thy marble vault, shall sound
My echoing song; then worms shall try
That long preserv'd virginity,
And your quaint honour turn to dust,
And into ashes all my lust.
The grave's a fine and private place,
But none I think do there embrace.

Now therefore, while the youthful hue
Sits on thy skin like morning dew,
And while thy willing soul transpires
At every pore with instant fires,
Now let us sport us while we may;
And now, like am'rous birds of prey,
Rather at once our time devour,
Than languish in his slow-chapp'd power.
Let us roll all our strength, and all
Our sweetness, up into one ball;
And tear our pleasures with rough strife
Thorough the iron gates of life.

Bibliography

Acton, William, *Prostitution, Considered in Its Moral, Social, and Sanitary Aspects* (2nd edn), 1870

Aubrey, John, *Aubrey's Brief Lives*, edited from the original manuscripts and with an introduction by Oliver Lawson Dick, Penguin, London, 1949

Bailey, Paul (ed.), *The Oxford Book of London*, Oxford University Press, New York, 1995

Barnfield, Richard, *The Complete Poems*, ed. George Klawitter, Susquehanna University Press, Selinsgrove, 1990

Borris, Kenneth, *Same-sex Desire in the English Renaissance: Sixteenth to Mid-Seventeenth Century Texts*, Routledge, London, 2003

Burford, E. J., *Bawds and Lodgings*, Peter Owen, London, 1976

— *The Orrible Synne*, Calder and Boyars, London, 1973

— and Wotton, Joy, *Private Vices – Public Virtues: Bawdry in London from Elizabethan Times to the Regency*, Hale, London, 1995

Chaucer, Geoffrey, *The Poetical Works*, ed. F. N. Robinson, Houghton Mifflin, Boston, 1933

Cleland, John, *Fanny Hill, or, Memoirs of a Woman of Pleasure*, ed. Peter Wagner, Penguin, London, 1985

Crawford, Katherine, *European Sexualities 1400–1800*, Cambridge University Press, Cambridge, 2007

Cruikshank, Dan, *The Secret History of Georgian London*, Random House, London, 2009

Davenport-Hines, Richard, *Sex, Death and Punishment, Attitudes to Sex and Sexuality in Britain since the Renaissance*, Fontana, London, 1990

Elfenbein, Andrew, *Byron and the Victorians*, Cambridge University Press, Cambridge, 1995

Ellman, Richard, *Oscar Wilde*, Vintage, London, 1988

Fabricius, Johannes, *Syphilis in Shakespeare's England*, J. Kingsley, London, 1994

Foucault, Michel, *The History of Sexuality*, translated from the French by Robert Hurley, Penguin, London, 1992

Fryer, Peter, *Staying Power – The History of Black People in Britain*, Pluto Classics, London, 1984

Gaunt, William, *The Pre-Raphaelite Dream*, Jonathan Cape, London, 1943

Gibson, Ian, *The English Vice: Beating, Sex and Shame in Victorian England and After*, Duckworth, London, 1978

Glendinning, Victoria, *Vita: the Life of Vita Sackville-West*, Orion, London, 2005

Greenberg, David F., *The Construction of Homosexuality*, University of Chicago Press, Chicago, 1988

Greene, Graham, *Lord Rochester's Monkey: Being the Life of John Wilmot, Second Earl of Rochester*, Viking, London, 1974

Greenwood, James, *Low-Life Deeps*, 1881

Guilpin, Everard, *Skialetheia*, 1598

Harrison, Fraser, *The Dark Angel: Aspects of Victorian Sexuality*, The Sheldon Press, London, 1977

Haynes, Alan, *Sex in Elizabethan England*, Sutton, Stroud, 2006

Henriques, Fernando, *Prostitution and Society*, Vol. 1, MacGibbon and Kee, London, 1963

Hilton, Tim, *John Ruskin: The Later Years*, Yale University Press, New Haven, 2000

Houlbrook, Matt, *Queer London, Perils and Pleasures in the Sexual Metropolis 1918–1957*, University of Chicago Press, Chicago, 2005

Kaplan, Morris, *Sodom on the Thames: Sex, Love and Scandal in Wilde Times*, Cornell University Press, Ithaca, 2005

Lehmann, Rosamond, *The Weather in the Streets,* Collins, London, 1936

Linnane, Fergus, *London the Wicked City*, Robson Books, London, 2003

Marcus, Steven, *The Other Victorians: A Study of Sexuality and Pornography in Mid-nineteenth-century England*, Weidenfeld and Nicolson, London, 1970

Merians, Linda E. (ed.), *The Secret Malady: Venereal Disease in Eighteenth-century Britain and France*, University of Kentucky, Lexington, KY, 1996

Nashe, Thomas, *The Unfortunate Traveller: and Other Works*, Penguin Classics, London, 2006

Nicolson, Nigel, *Portrait of a Marriage*, Athenaeum, London, 1991

O'Donoghue, E. G., *Bridewell Hospital*, John Lane, The Bodley Head, London, 1929

Pearsall, Ronald, *The Worm in the Bud: The World of Victorian Sexuality*, Sutton, Stroud, 2003

Picard, Lisa, *Elizabeth's London: Everyday Life in Elizabethan London*, Weidenfeld and Nicolson, London, 2003

Porter, Roy, *The Facts of Life: The Creation of Sexual Knowledge in Britain, 1650–1950*, University of Yale Press, London and New Haven, 1995

— (ed.), *Rewriting the Self: Histories from the Renaissance to the Present Day*, Routledge, London, 1997

— and Roberts, Marie Mulvey, *Pleasure in the Eighteenth Century*, Macmillan, London, 1996

Quennell, Peter, *London's Underworld: Being Selections from Henry Mayhew*, Spring Books, London, 1950

Roberts, Nickie, *Whores in History, Prostitution in Western Society*, Harper Collins, London, 1993

Rochester, John Wilmot, Earl of, *The Complete Poems*, ed. David M. Vieth, Routledge and Keegan Paul, London, 1953

Rousseau, G. S., and Porter, Roy, *Sexual Underworlds of the Enlightenment*, Manchester University Press, Manchester, 1987

Rubenhold, Hallie (ed.), *Harris's List of Covent Garden Ladies*, Tempus, Stroud, 2005

Salgado, Gamini, *The Elizabethan Underworld*, Sutton, Stroud, 2006

Scott, Maria Margaret, *Re-presenting 'Jane' Shore: Harlot and Heroine*, Ashgate, Aldershot, 2005

Showalter, Elaine, *Sexual Anarchy: Gender and Culture at the 'Fin de Siècle'*, Bloomsbury, London, 1991

Smithies, Edward, *Crime in Wartime: a Social History of Crime in World War II*, Allen and Unwin, London, 1982

Srebnick, Amy Gilman, and Lévy, René (eds.), *Crime and Culture. An Historical Perspective*, Ashgate, Aldershot, 2005

Stanford, Derek, *Aubrey Beardsley's Erotic Universe*, New English Library, London, 1967

Stone, Lawrence, *The Family, Sex and Marriage in England, 1500–1800*, Penguin, Harmondsworth, 1979

Taylor, Timothy, *The Prehistory of Sex: Four Million Years of Human Sexual Culture*, Fourth Estate, London, 1996

Tomalin, Claire, *Samuel Pepys: The Unequalled Self*, Viking, London, 2002

Traub, Valerie, *The Renaissance of Lesbianism in Early Modern England*, Cambridge University Press, Cambridge, 2002

Waller, Maureen, *1700: Scenes from London Life*, Sceptre, London, 2001

Warnicke, Retha M., *The Rise and Fall of Anne Boleyn*, Cambridge University Press, Cambridge, 1991

Wheen, Francis, *The Sixties*, Ebury Press, London, 1982

Ziegler, Philip, *London at War, 1939–1945*, Sinclair Stevenson, London, 1995

WEBSITES

http://ancienthistory.about.com/library/bl/bl_prostitutionnotes2.htm

http://www.bigeye.com/sexeducation/romanempire.html

http://www.elizabethan-era.org.uk/famous-elizabethan-women.htm

http://freepages.genealogy.rootsweb.ancestry.com/~gowenrf/husseyms _003.html

http://rictornorton.co.uk/eighteen/index.htm

http://www.independent.co.uk/news/uk/this-britain/a-brief-history-of-brothels-523962.html

http://www.lib.rochester.edu/camelot/medsex/medsexfrm.htm

http://www.my-secret-life.com/

http://www.met.police.uk/history/ripper.htm

http://www.nickelinthemachine.com/

http://www.victorianlondon.org/

http://sederi.org/docs/yearbooks/07/7_14_shaw.pdfhttp://freepages.gen
ealogy.rootsweb.ancestry.com/~gowenrf/husseyms_003.html

Notes

CHAPTER ONE

1. See Burford, *Bawds and Lodgings*, p. 14
2. Ibid., p. 11
3. See Burford, *The Orrible Synne*, p. 12
4. Ibid.
5. See Burford, *Bawds and Lodgings*, p. 12
6. See Burford, *The Orrible Synne*, p. 13
7. Ibid., p. 17
8. Ibid., p. 13
9. See Burford, *Bawds and Lodgings*, p. 14
10. Ibid., p. 15
11. Ibid.
12. Ibid., p. 17
13. Ibid., p. 16
14. See Burford, *The Orrible Synne*, p. 20
15. See Burford, *Bawds and Lodgings*, p. 17
16. Ibid.
17. See Burford, *The Orrible Synne*, p. 11
18. Ibid., p. 15
19. See Roberts, *Whores in History*, p. 36
20. See Burford, *The Orrible Synne*, p. 23
21. See Roberts, op. cit., p. 38
22. See Burford, *Bawds and Lodgings*, p. 18
23. Ibid., pp. 18–19
24. Ibid.
25. Ibid.
26. Ibid.
27. See Taylor, *The Prehistory of Sex*, pp. 206–7
28. See Burford, *Bawds and Lodgings*, p. 20

29. Ibid.
30. See Roberts, op. cit., p. 42
31. See Burford, *Bawds and Lodgings*, p. 22
32. See Burford, *The Orrible Synne*, p. 23
33. Ibid., p. 19
34. See Roberts, op. cit., p. 41
35. Ibid., p. 44
36. See http://www.museumoflondon.org.uk/English/Collections/Online Resources/Londinium/Lite/classifieds/bikini.htm
37. See Roberts, op. cit., p. 43
38. See Burford, *The Orrible Synne*, p. 24
39. Ibid., p. 25
40. Ibid.
41. See Burford, *Bawds and Lodgings*, p. 26
42. Ibid.

CHAPTER TWO

1. See Burford, *Bawds and Lodgings*, p. 32
2. See Roberts, *Whores in History*, p. 88
3. See Burford, *Bawds and Lodgings*, p. 37
4. See Roberts, op. cit., p. 61
5. See Burford, *The Orrible Synne*, p̄. 68
6. See Roberts, op. cit., p. 83
7. Ibid.
8. Ibid., p. 86
9. See Burford, *The Orrible Synne*, pp. 49–50
10. See Roberts, op. cit., p. 67
11. See Chaucer, *The Canterbury Tales*, lines 165–205
12. Ibid., lines 205–50
13. Ibid., lines 622–90
14. Ibid., lines 118–66
15. See Burford, *The Orrible Synne,* p. 52
16. See Roberts, op. cit., p. 63
17. Ibid., p. 88
18. Ibid., p. 89
19. See Burford, *The Orrible Synne*, p. 53
20. See Burford, *Bawds and Lodgings*, p. 49
21. See Burford, *The Orrible Synne*, p. 56
22. Ibid., p. 83
23. Ibid., p. 69
24. Ibid., p. 71
25. See Burford, *Bawds and Lodgings*, p. 31

26. Ibid.
27. See Burford, *The Orrible Synne*, pp. 155–6
28. See Burford, *Bawds and Lodgings*, p. 69
29. See Burford, *The Orrible Synne*, p. 67
30. Ibid., p. 66
31. Ibid., p. 74
32. Ibid., p. 85
33. Ibid., p. 84
34. Ibid., p. 76
35. Ibid., p. 129
36. Ibid., p. 130
37. Ibid., p. 76
38. Ibid.
49. Ibid., p. 77
40. Ibid.
41. Ibid., p. 80
42. Ibid., p. 76
43. Ibid., pp. 86–7
44. Ibid., p. 112
45. Ibid.
46. Ibid., p. 89
47. Ibid., p. 79
48. See http://www.bbc.co.uk/history/british/middle_ages/black_07.shtml
49. See Burford, *The Orrible Synne*, p. 92
50. Ibid., p. 96
51. Ibid., p. 109
52. See Scott, *Re-presenting 'Jane' Shore: Harlot and Heroine*
53. See http://www.middle-ages.org.uk/jane-shore.htm

CHAPTER THREE

1. See Burford, *The Orrible Synne*, p. 142
2. See Fabricius, *Syphilis in Shakespeare's England*, p. 1
3. See Burford, op. cit., p. 207
4. See Fabricius, op. cit., p. 5
5. Ibid., pp. 14–15
6. Ibid., p. 20
7. Ibid., p. 22
8. See Waller, *1700: Scenes from London Life*, quoted Linnane, *London the Wicked City*, p. 27
9. Ibid.
10. See Fabricius, op. cit., p. 33
11. See Burford, op. cit., p. 205

12. Ibid., p. 204
13. See Aubrey, *Brief Lives*, p. 11
14. Ibid., p. 86
15. See Warnicke, *The Rise and Fall of Anne Boleyn*, p. 193
16. Ibid., p. 194
17. See Haynes, *Sex in Elizabethan England*, p. 176
18. See Warnicke, op. cit., pp. 191–221
19. See Hussey manuscript at http://freepages.genealogy.rootsweb.ancestry. com/~gowenrf/husseyms_003.html
20. See Warnicke, op. cit., p. 194
21. See Burford, op. cit., p. 167
22. See Aubrey, op. cit., p. 11
23. See Haynes, op. cit., p. 129
24. See Borris, *Same-Sex Desire in the English Renaissance*, p. 98
25. Ibid., p. 339
26. Ibid.
27. Ibid.
28. See Aubrey, op. cit., pp. 253–4
29. Ibid., pp. 255–6
30. Ibid., p. 138
31. Ibid.
32. Ibid., pp. 100–101

CHAPTER FOUR

1. See Fabricius, *Syphilis in Shakespeare's England*, p. 104
2. Ibid.
3. Ibid.
4. Ibid., p. 165
5. Ibid.
6. Ibid.
7. See Burford, *The Orrible Synne*, p. 190
8. See Burford, *Bawds and Lodgings*, p. 140
9. See Burford, *The Orrible Synne*, p. 174
10. See Fabricius, op. cit., p. 105
11. Ibid.
12. Ibid., p. 128
13. See Burford, *The Orrible Synne*, p. 195
14. Ibid.
15. See Salgado, *The Elizabethan Underworld*, p. 42
16. See Picard, *Elizabeth's London: Everyday Life in Elizabethan England*, p. 169
17. See Haynes, *Sex in Elizabethan England*, p. 175

18. See Burford, *The Orrible Synne*, p. 195
19. See Salgado, op. cit., p. 45
20. See Burford, *The Orrible Synne*, p. 180
21. See Salgado, op. cit., p. 49
22. Ibid.
23. See Burford, *The Orrible Synne*, p. 198
24. See Salgado, op. cit., p. 38
25. Ibid., p. 49
26. See Burford, *The Orrible Synne*, p. 135
27. See Salgado, op. cit., p. 41
28. See O'Donoghue, *Bridewell Hospital*, p. 145
29. Ibid., p. 155
30. See Shakespeare, *King Lear*, IV. xi. 175–9
31. See Burford, *The Orrible Synne*, p. 209
32. Ibid.
33. See Linnane, *London the Wicked City*, p. 21

CHAPTER FIVE

1. See Burford, *Private Vices – Public Virtues*, p. 217
2. Ibid.
3. Ibid., p. 218
4. Ibid., p. 220
5. Ibid.
6. See *Social History*, January 1994, vol. 19, no. 1, p. 104
7. See Burford, op. cit., pp. 221–2
8. See Burford, op. cit., pp. 222–3
9. See Roberts, *Whores in History*, p. 156
10. Ibid., p. 136
11. See Burford, *Bawds and Lodgings*, p. 181
12. Ibid.
13. See Burford, *The Orrible Synne*, pp. 232–3
14. Ibid.
15. See Burford, *Private Vices – Public Virtues*, p. 43
16. See Roberts, op. cit., p. 142
17. See Burford, *Private Vices – Public Virtues*, p. 54
18. See Roberts, op. cit., p. 142
19. Ibid., p. 146
20. Ibid., p. 144
21. See Burford, *Private Vices – Public Virtues*, p. 98
22. See Roberts, op. cit., p. 145
23. See Greene, *Lord Rochester's Monkey*, p. 38
24. See Roberts, op. cit., p. 148

25. See http://muse.jhu.edu/journals/eighteenth-century_studies/summary/v035/35.2conway/html
26. See Roberts, op. cit., pp. 148–9
27. See Greene, op. cit., p. 58
28. Ibid., p. 10
29. See http://rictornorton.co.uk/social12.htm
30. See Rochester, *The Complete Poems*, pp. 76–7
31. See Greene, op. cit., pp. 72–3
32. See Rochester, op. cit.
33. See Greene, op. cit., p. 58
34. Ibid., p. 183
35. See Burford, *Private Vices – Public Virtues*, p. 56
36. See Tomalin, *Samuel Pepys*, p. 201
37. Ibid., p. 202
38. See Pepys, *Diary*, 16 January 1664 and 16 February 1667
39. Ibid.
40. See Tomalin, op. cit., p. 201
41. See Burford, *Private Vices – Public Virtues*, pp. 63–4
42. See Pepys, *Diary*, 16 January 1664 and 16 February 1667
43. See Burford, *Private Vices – Public Virtues*, pp. 63–4
44. Ibid.
45. Ibid., p. 65
46. See Linnane, *London the Wicked City*, p. 73
47. See Burford, *Private Vices – Public Virtues*, p. 67
48. Ibid., p. 70
49. See Linnane, op. cit., p. 73
50. See Burford, *Private Vices – Public Virtues*, p. 79
51. Ibid., p. 70
52. Ibid., p. 75
53. Ibid., p. 77

CHAPTER SIX

1. See Burford, *Private Vices – Public Virtues*, p. 121
2. Ibid., p. 122
3. See Roberts, *Whores in History*, p. 170
4. Ibid.
5. Roberts, op. cit., p. 171
6. Ibid.
7. See Burford, op. cit., p. 123
8. See Roberts, op. cit., pp. 172–3
9. Ibid., p. 173.
10. See Burford, op. cit.

11. See Burford, op. cit., p. 97
12. See Linnane, *London the Wicked City*, pp.102–111
13. See Burford, op. cit., p. 124
14. See Roberts, op. cit., p. 177
15. Ibid.
16. See Cruikshank, *The Secret History of Georgian London*, pp. 117–18
17. See Burford, op. cit., p. 104
18. Ibid.
19. See Roberts, op. cit., p. 124
20. Ibid.
21. See Linnane, op. cit., pp. 100–101
22. See Porter and Roberts, *Pleasure in the Eighteenth Century*, pp. 26–7
23. See Linnane, op. cit., p. 92
24. Ibid.
25. See Porter and Roberts, op. cit.
26. See Linnane, op. cit., p. 104
27. Ibid.
28. See Roberts, op. cit., p. 171
29. Ibid.
30. Ibid., p. 172
31. See Boswell, *The London Journal*, 25 November 1762
32. See http://www.fandmpublications.co.uk/pages/westminster.htm
33. See Roberts, op. cit., p. 168
34. See Linnane, op. cit., p. 116
35. See Roberts, op. cit., p. 158
36. See Burford, op. cit., pp. 154–5
37. See Roberts, op. cit., pp. 121–2
38. See Linnane, op. cit., p. 122
39. Ibid.
40. See Cleland, *Fanny Hill*, p. 173
41. See Fryer, *Staying Power*, p. 76
42. See http://www.jrank.org/cultures/pages/562/Prostitution.html
43. See Burford, op. cit., p. 109
44. Ibid., p. 113
45. Ibid., p. 53
46. Ibid., pp. 141–2
47. Ibid.
48. See Rousseau and Porter, *Sexual Underworlds of the Enlightenment*, pp. 78–9
49. See Merians, *The Secret Malady*, pp. 190–5
50. See Rousseau and Porter, op. cit., p. 80
51. See Linnane, op. cit., p. 149
52. Ibid.
53. Ibid., p. 151

CHAPTER SEVEN

1. See Linnane, *London the Wicked City*, p. 189
2. Ibid., p. 192
3. See Porter and Roberts, *Pleasure in the Eighteenth Century*, pp. 68–9
4. See Linnane, op. cit., p. 192
5. Ibid., p. 190
6. Ibid., pp. 192–3
7. Ibid., p. 190
8. Ibid., p. 191
9. See Rousseau and Porter, *Sexual Underworlds of the Enlightenment*, pp. 108–23
10. See Cruikshank, *The Secret History of Georgian London*, pp. 373–5
11. Ibid.
12. See Rousseau and Porter, op. cit., pp. 244–6
13. See Rubenhold, *Harris's List of Covent Garden Ladies*, pp. 46–7
14. See Burford, *Private Vices – Public Virtues*, p. 184
15. See Rousseau and Porter, op. cit., p. 235
16. Ibid., p. 248
17. See Norton, *Two Kissing Girls of Spitalfields*, http://www.rictornorton.co.uk
18. See Traub, *The Renaissance of Lesbianism in Early Modern England*, p. 316
19. See Rousseau and Porter, op. cit., p. 59
20. See Norton, *A Game at Flats*, http://www.rictornorton.co.uk
21. See Rousseau and Porter, op. cit.
22. See Traub, op. cit., p. 315
23. See Rousseau and Porter, op. cit., p. 52
24. Ibid., p. 53
25. Ibid., p. 54
26. Ibid.
27. Ibid.
28. Ibid., p. 55
29. Ibid., p. 57
30. Ibid.
31. See Roberts, *Whores in History*, p. 162
32. See Linnane, op. cit., p. 247
33. Ibid., p. 250
34. Ibid., pp. 250–1
35. See Pearsall, *The Worm in the Bud*, p. 335
36. See Ashbee, *The Flogging Whores of Old London*, http://public.diversity.org.uk/deviant/ssflg1.htm
37. See Burford, op. cit., p. 184
38. Ibid.

39. See Roberts, op. cit., p. 162
40. See Rousseau and Porter, op. cit., p. 51
41. Ibid., p. 107
42. See Linnane, op. cit., p. 145
43. Ibid., p. 147

CHAPTER EIGHT

1. See Quennell, *London's Underworld*, p. 13
2. Ibid., p. 14
3. Ibid.
4. See www.tate.org.uk
5. See Quennell, op. cit., p. 15
6. See A. T. Quiller-Couch, *The Oxford Book of English Verse*, Clarendon, Oxford, 1939, pp. 162–178
7. See T. Hardy, *The Poems of Thomas Hardy*, ed. James Gibson, Macmillan, London, 1976, pp. 193–4
8. See Pearsall, *The Worm in the Bud*, p. 246
9. See Acton, *Prostitution, Considered in Its Moral, Social and Sanitary Aspects*, www.victorianlondon.org
10. Ibid.
11. Ibid.
12. See Roberts, *Whores in History*, p. 238
13. See Marcus, *The Other Victorians*, p. 31
14. Ibid., pp. 91–2
15. See Parent-Duchâtelet, A. J. B., *De la prostitution dans la ville de Paris*, Société encyclographique des science médicales, Brussels, 1838 I, pp. 339–40
16. See Pearsall, op. cit., p. 245
17. See Quennell, op. cit., p. 19
18. Ibid., pp. 35–6
19. Ibid., p. 19
20. See Sebba, 'Kissing and Telling with Gusto', *The Spectator*, 30 August 2003
21. See Linnane, *London the Wicked City*, pp. 136–7
22. See Quennell, op. cit., p. 44
23. See Acton, op. cit.
24. See Pearsall, op. cit., p. 247
25. See Roberts, op. cit., p. 217
26. See Pearsall, op. cit., p. 249
27. See Quennell, op. cit., p. 34
28. Ibid., p. 118
29. Ibid., p. 21
30. See Marcus, op. cit., p. 98

31. See Quennell, op. cit., p. 40
32. Ibid., pp. 37–8
33. See Harrison, *The Dark Angel*, p. 221
34. See Quennell, op. cit., p. 44
35. Ibid., p. 74
36. See Roberts, op. cit., pp. 193–4
37. Ibid., p. 194
38. See Quennell, op. cit., p. 22
39. See Roberts, op. cit., p. 193
40. Ibid.
41. See Quennell, op. cit., p. 21
42. See Linnane, op. cit., p. 210
43. Ibid., p. 212
44. See Marcus, op. cit., p. 99
45. See Quennell, op. cit., p. 42
46. Ibid.
47. See Roberts, op. cit., p. 237
48. See Quennell, op. cit., p.46
49. Ibid., p. 43
50. See Marcus, op. cit., p. 105
51. Ibid.
52. Ibid., p. 106
53. Ibid., p. 107
54. See Quennell, op. cit., p. 47
55. Ibid. pp. 82–3
56. Ibid., p. 84
57. Ibid., pp. 121–7
58. Ibid., pp. 36–7
59. See *The Times*, London, 25 February 1858
60. See Roberts, op. cit., p. 243

CHAPTER NINE

1. See Roberts, *Whores in History*, p. 232
2. See Harrison, *The Dark Angel*, p. 162
3. Ibid., p. 163
4. Ibid., p. 206
5. Ibid., p. 195
6. See *The Times*, London, 25 February 1858
7. See Roberts, op. cit., p. 238
8. See Pearsall, *The Worm in the Bud*, p. 288
9. See Greenwood, *Low-Life Deeps*, p. 56
10. Ibid.

11. Ibid., pp. 56–63
12. See Ewing Ritchie, *The Night Side of London*, London, 1861, pp. 46–51
13. See Quennell, *London's Underworld*, p. 45
14. Ibid., p. 55
15. Ibid., p. 56
16. Ibid., pp. 69–70
17. See Pearsall, op. cit., p. 282
18. Ibid.
19. Ibid., p. 283
20. Ibid.
21. Ibid., p. 282
22. Ibid., p. 284
23. See Quennell, op. cit., p. 67
24. Ibid., pp. 88–93
25. See Roberts, op. cit., p. 246
26. Ibid.
27. Ibid., p. 247
28. Ibid., p. 246
29. Ibid., p. 251
30. Ibid., pp. 252–3
31. Ibid., p. 253
32. Ibid., pp. 253–4
33. See Pearsall, op. cit., p. 290
34. See Harrison, op. cit., pp. 223–4
35. Ibid., p. 226
36. See Pearsall, op. cit., p. 291
37. See Linnane, *London the Wicked City*, p. 298
38. See Roberts, op. cit., p. 256
39. See Pearsall, op. cit., p. 300
40. Ibid., p. 298
41. Ibid., p. 300
42. See Roberts, op. cit., p. 256
43. See Pearsall, op. cit., p. 301
44. Ibid.
45. Ibid., pp. 301–2
46. See Roberts, op. cit., pp. 256–7
47. Ibid., p. 257
48. See Pearsall, op. cit., p. 302
49. Ibid., p. 304
50. Ibid., p. 303
51. Ibid.
52. Ibid.
53. Ibid., p. 304
54. Ibid.

55. See Roberts, op. cit., p. 258
56. See Pearsall, op. cit., pp. 307–8
57. Ibid.
58. Ibid., pp. 308–9
59. See Metropolitan Police records at http://www.met.police.uk/history/ripper.htm
60. Ibid.
61. See Pearsall, op. cit., p. 310
62. Ibid.
63. Ibid.
64. See Metropolitan Police records at http://www.met.police.uk/history/ripper.htm
65. Ibid.
66. See Pearsall, op. cit., p. 313

CHAPTER TEN

1. See Pearsall, *The Worm in the Bud*, p. 371
2. See Porter, *Rewriting the Self*, p. 183
3. See Pearsall, op. cit., pp. 377–8
4. Ibid., p. 369
5. See Marcus, *The Other Victorians*, pp. 69–70
6. Ibid., p. 69
7. Ibid., p. 74
8. Ibid. p. 75
9. See Pearsall, op. cit., p. 364
10. Ibid.
11. Ibid., p. 335
12. Ibid., p. 332
13. Ibid., p. 342
14. See Marcus, op. cit., pp. 256–7
15. Ibid., p. 257
16. See Pearsall, op. cit., p. 336
17. Ibid.
18. Ibid.
19. Ibid., p. 335
20. Ibid., p. 342
21. See http://www.my-secret-life.com
22. See Pearsall, op. cit., pp. 365–6
23. Ibid., p. 384.
24. Ibid., p. 385
25. Ibid.
26. Ibid., p. 382

27. Ibid., p. 370
28. Ibid., p. 384
29. Ibid., p. 381
30. Ibid., p. 382
31. See Stanford, *Aubrey Beardsley's Erotic Universe*, p. 29
32. Ibid., pp. 15–16
33. Ibid., p. 17
34. Ibid.
35. Ibid., p. 16
36. See Pearsall, op. cit., p.392
37. Ibid., p. 289
38. See Marcus, op. cit., p. 37
39. Ibid., p. 36
40. Ibid.
41. Ibid., p. 42
42. Ibid., p. 43
43. Ibid., p. 48
44. Ibid., p. 82
45. Ibid., p. 188
46. Ibid., pp. 93–4
47. See http://www.my-secret-life.com
48. See Harrison, *The Dark Angel*, pp. 258–9
49. Ibid., pp. 261–2
50. See Pearsall, op. cit., p. 370
51. See Harrison, op. cit., p. 260
52. See Marcus, op. cit., p. 83
53. Ibid., pp. 186–7

CHAPTER ELEVEN

1. See Pearsall, *The Worm in the Bud*, p. 450
2. See Elfenbein, *Byron and the Victorians*, p. 210
3. See Pearsall, op. cit., p. 450
4. Ibid., p. 448
5. Ibid., p. 455
6. Ibid., p. 456
7. Ibid., p. 452
8. Ibid., p. 453
9. Ibid., p. 454
10. Ibid.
11. Ibid., p. 455
12. Ibid.
13. Ibid., p. 456

14. See *The Times*, London, 30 April 1870
15. See Pearsall, op. cit., p. 461
16. Ibid.
17. Ibid., p. 462
18. Ibid.
19. Ibid.
20. Ibid., p. 464
21. Ibid., p. 465
22. Ibid., p. 451
23. Ibid.
24. Ibid., p. 452
25. Ibid.
26. See Ellman, *Oscar Wilde*, p. 409
27. See Pearsall, op. cit., p. 469
28. Ibid., p. 470
29. Ibid., p. 472
30. Ibid., p. 475
31. Ibid., p. 470
32. Ibid., p. 458
33. Ibid.
34. See http://math.boisestate.edu/gas/patience/webop/pat18.html
35. See J. M. Cohen and M. J. Cohen, *The Penguin Dictionary of Quotations*, Penguin, London, 1962, p. 417
36. Ibid.
37. See Ellman, op. cit., p. 387
38. Ibid., p. 417
39. Ibid.
40. Ibid., p. 418
41. Ibid.
42. Ibid.
43. Ibid., p. 419
44. Ibid., p. 447
45. Ibid., p. 410
46. Ibid., p. 439
47. Ibid., p. 441
48. Ibid., p. 442
49. Ibid., p. 443
50. Ibid., p. 441
51. Ibid., p. 442
52. Ibid., p. 448
53. Ibid., p. 449
54. Ibid.
55. Ibid., p. 451
56. Ibid.

57. Ibid., p. 452
58. Ibid., p. 477
59. Ibid.
60. Ibid.

CHAPTER TWELVE

1. See Linnane, *London the Wicked City*, pp. 319–20
2. See Ziegler, *London at War*, p. 326
3. See Showalter, *Sexual Anarchy*, p. 24
4. See Nicolson, *Portrait of a Marriage*, p. 105
5. See Houlbrook, *Queer London, Perils and Pleasures in the Sexual Metropolis 1918–1957*, p. 45
6. Ibid., p. 147
7. Ibid., p. 158
8. Ibid., p. 152
9. Ibid., p. 97
10. See http://www.lgbthistorymonth.org.uk/history/LGBTpeople.htm
11. See Alan Travis, 'Cock-up and Cover-up', *Guardian*, 13 September 2000
12. See 'Lesbian novel was danger to nation', *Observer*, 2 January 2005
13. See http://www.nickelinthemachine.com/tag/ww2/
14. See Lehmann, *The Weather in the Streets*, pp. 286–300
15. See Smithies, *Crime in Wartime*, p. 132
16. See Roberts, *Whores in History*, p. 278
17. See Smithies, op. cit., p. 133
18. Ibid., p. 134
19. Ibid., p. 135
20. Ibid., pp.135–6
21. See Srebnick and Lévy, *Crime and Culture*, p. 96
22. See Smithies, op. cit., p. 136
23. See Ziegler, op. cit., p. 214
24. Ibid., p. 219
25. Ibid., p. 217
26. Ibid., p. 219
27. See Smithies, op. cit., p. 142
28. Ibid., p. 219
29. Ibid., p. 142
30. See Ziegler, op. cit., p. 220
31. Ibid.
32. Ibid., pp. 220–1
33. See Ziegler, op. cit. and http://www.nickelinthemachine.com/tag/ww2/
34. See Ziegler, op. cit., p. 220
35. See Smithies, op. cit., p. 142

36. See http://www.time.com/time/magazine/article/0,9171,811034,00.html
37. Ibid.
38. Ibid.
39. Ibid.

CHAPTER THIRTEEN

1. See Alan Travis, 'Cock-up and Cover-up', *Guardian*, 13 September 2000
2. Ibid.
3. Ibid.
4. Ibid.
5. Ibid.
6. Ibid.
7. See http://en.wikipedia.org/wiki/Stephen_Ward
8. See Wheen, *The Sixties*, p. 93
9. See http://www.nickelinthemachine.com/2008/10/mayfair-the-duchess-of-argyll-and-the-headless-man-polaroids/
10. See http://www.nickelinthemachine.com/2009/02/no1-eaton-square-lord-boothby-and-ronnie-kray/
11. Ibid.
12. See Roberts, *Whores in History*, p. 288
13. Ibid., p. 287
14. See http://www.nickelinthemachine.com/2009/02/no1-eaton-square-lord-boothby-and-ronnie-kray
15. See Jim White, 'A Mosque in Mayfair', *Independent*, 14 March 1996
16. See Aidan Jones, 'Prostitutes in legal victory to keep working', *London Informer*, 22 May 2009
17. Ibid.
18. Ibid.
19. Ibid.

CHAPTER FOURTEEN

1. See Nick Davies, 'Inquiry fails to find single trafficker who forced anybody into prostitution', *Guardian*, 20 October 2009

Illustration Credits

Eros sculpture at chapter headings © Jon Bower/ Loop Images/ Corbis

p. 11 *Lupanaria* © Wellcome Library, London

p. 51 Treatment of syphilitic couple © Bibliothèque nationale, Paris/ Giraudon/ The Bridgeman Art Library

p. 63 Mary Frith © Mary Evans Picture Library

p. 70 Elizabethan whorehouse © Private Collection/ The Bridgeman Art Library

p. 95 Nell Gwyn engraved by Valentine Green, 1777, Sir Peter Lely © British Museum, London/ The Bridgeman Art Library

p. 134 *The Harlot's Progress* Plate 3: Apprehended by a Magistrate, 1732, William Hogarth © The Trustees of the Weston Park Foundation/The Bridgeman Art Library

p. 142 Portrait of Richard Payne Knight, *c*. 1793, Sir Thomas Lawrence © Whitworth Art Gallery, University of Manchester/ The Bridgeman Art Library

p. 176 Catherine Walters © Mary Evans Picture Library

p. 180 Haymarket prostitutes © Mary Evans Picture Library

p. 245 Illustration from *Lysistrata* by Aristophanes by Aubrey Beardsley © Private Collection/ The Stapleton Collection/ The Bridgeman Art Library

p. 255 Nineteenth-century male brothel © Wellcome Library, London

p. 291 Lesbian couple in 1913 © Mary Evans Picture Library

p. 298 Marie Stopes © Illustrated London News/ Mary Evans Picture Library

p. 322 Cynthia Payne © Getty Images

p. 325 Focus Cinema © Ronald Grant Archive/ Mary Evans Picture Library

p. 328 *London Life* cover © Illustrated London News, Mary Evans Picture Library

Index

'Rape of the Lock' (Pope), 244
Raped on the Railway, 233
Razzle, 324
Redshawe, Anne, 147
Redshawe, Elanor, 147
Reed, Det. Insp. 'Nipper', 320
Reeves, John, 261
Reformation, 55
Remus, 12
Restoration, 4, 85, 90–110
    years preceding, examined, 85–90
Reynold's Newspaper, 223, 269
Reynolds, Sir Joshua, 116
Rice-Davies, Mandy, 2, 314–15, 317
Richard I, King, 35–6, 37
Richard II, King, 43
Richard III, King, 45, 46
Richard of Devizes, 1–2
Richmond, Duke of, 117
Ritchie, J. Ewing, 204–5
Robert the Bruce, 78
Roberts, George, 264
Roberts, Nickie, 7, 30–1, 189, 214
Robinson, Emma, 86
Robinson, Richard, 61
Roche, Mother, 57
Rochester, 2nd Earl of (John Wilmot), 2,
    90–1, 97–100, 102–3, 103–4, 151–2
Rochfort, William, 175
Romance of Chastisement, The, 233
Romance of Lust, The, 233
Romano, Giuliano, 230
Romans:
    attitude towards sex displayed by, 15–17
    cruel nature of, 15–16
    in Britain, 10–24
Romulus, 12
Ronsard, Pierre de, 62
Room with a View, A (Forster), 292
Rose Theatre, 75
Rosebery, Lord, 275, 277
Ross, Robbie, 273–4, 283, 285
Rossetti, Dante Gabriel, 164–5
Rothenstein, Sir John, 246
Royal Wedding Jester, The, 232
Rugby School, 256
'Ruined Maid, The' (Hardy), 166–7
Rupert, Prince, 88
Ryan, Dr Michael, 167

Sackville-West, Vita, 290

Sade, Marquis de, 239
Sadler, Tom, 226
sailors, 23, 105, 200, 206–7, 287
St Augustine, 26
St James's Gazette, 219
St Mary Overie, 3, 24
St Swithin, 24
St Thomas Aquinas, 26
Salisbury, Sally, 117–18
Salvation Army, 217
Sandwich, Earl of, 128, 161
Sandys, Sir Edwin Duncan, 316, 317
Sanger, William, 16, 27
Sapphic Epistle to Mrs D, A, 150
Sappho, 62–3
Sargent, John Singer, 244
Satan's Harvest Home, 149
Saul, John, 270
Savidge, Irene, 300–1
Savile, Henry, 69–70
Savoy, 244
Scarfe, Ernest, 280
Schneider, Hortense, 174
Schwabe, Maurice, 280
Secret History of Georgian London, The
    (Cruikshank), 7
Sedley, Sir Charles, 92
Selleto, Sarah, 131
Sellon, Edward, 234
Seneca, 16
Septimus Severus, Emperor, 22
Sewy, Joseph, 39
sex dolls, 152
Sex in Elizabethan England (Haynes), 65
sex trafficking, 213–14, 307, 327, 332
Sexual Offences Act, 1956, 321
Shadwell, Thomas, 153
Shakespeare, William, 59, 70, 75
Sharpe, Insp., 298–9
Shaw, George Bernard, 219, 278–9
Shelley, Edward, 280
Shepherd, Mrs, 237
Sheridan, Richard Brinsley, 125
Shore, Jane, 45–6
Shrovetide/Bawdy House riots, 106
Sickert, Walter, 226
Siddons, Sarah, 114
Sidney, Sir Philip, 65
Simon, Sir Jack, 312
Six Windmills, 108–9
slaves, 2, 3, 9–10, 13, 19, 23, 49, 113